Searching for t.. ...

From Poetry to Zen in the Sixties

A Memoir

Christopher Lennox

Note: this is a work of creative nonfiction. Some names and details have been changed or omitted to protect privacy. Translations are by the author, unless otherwise indicated.

Credits

Earlier versions of some of the poems included here previously appeared in my chapbook, *Faces of the Moon*, copyright 1971, and *CoEvolution Quarterly,* Summer 1982.

Shunryu Suzuki quote, page 188: October 16, 1965, archives at cuke.com.

Front cover image: *Heroic Roses* (in part) by Paul Klee. Public domain, Wikimedia Commons.

Back cover image: photo by Lynda Efros.

First edition. Independently published.

ISBN: 9798650670964

Contents

For Lynda, with love

and for my mother, father, sister, family, and friends
and all those whose stories remain untold

Part One: Turning Toward Poetry

Chapter 1: Not Quite Fitting In

> Sometimes a man stands up from his evening bread
> and walks outside and walks and walks and walks—
> because a church stands somewhere in the East.
> And his children bless him as if he were dead.
> And another, who dies inside his house,
> remains living indoors, remains in table and glass,
> so that his children are drawn out into the world
> toward the same church, which he forgot.
>
> —Rilke

Discovering Writing

At fifteen, I was searching but not often finding. Searching for knowledge of the universe through astronomy and science fiction—but my homemade rocket of gunpowder packed in a cardboard paper-towel tube burned its support stick without lifting off, turned upside down on its pile-of-sand launching pad, and blew a large plume of fire and billowing smoke high in the air—all because I didn't yet know how to mold the powder into a hollow interior cone. Searching for communication through invisible electrons in copper wires and mysterious electromagnetic waves in empty space—but my attempt to build a primitive telephone from scratch did not get far, and my ham radio hobby stalled with slow Morse code. Searching for a girlfriend, someone to be close to—but at Star Island summer camp my first crush ended in heartbreak, and soon after I had to start wearing glasses to read the blackboard in math.

Looking for an alternative, in tenth grade I turned to writing. Inspired by an article in *Life* magazine on the Beat Generation, and the rousing finale of *The Communist Manifesto*, discovered on my parents' Great

Books discussion group shelf, I posted a white paper scarred with typos on the high-school cafeteria wall. The gist of it went something like this:

The Beatnik Manifesto

We teenagers are prisoners of a frantic, shoving society that is slowly drowning us in a sea of conformity. We are the proletariat in an imperialistic world where parents, teachers, and other pseudo-adults chip at us with the chisel of authority until we fit in, like well-adjusted little white rats deprived of the basic freedoms of speech, self-expression, and gum chewing. We are hip pegs crammed into square holes. Hey cats, let's cut out! Already, fellow gone rebels are escaping from psychological straitjackets all over the country. You too can be wild and crazy! Want to be free to search for Nirvana, and like that? Lost souls, we crave but cannot touch. We must fight back. Be hip, be cool. Rebel! Like I said, beatniks of the world unite! You have nothing to lose but the chains of your mind!

Fifteen adventurous students signed on as backers of the glorious cause, and Mr. Pederson, my tall, good-natured homeroom teacher, added "plus Beatnik Teachers." All the kids liked him because during home room period, the first of the day, he put his feet up on his desk, told jokes, and claimed to keep a bottle of Jack Daniels in his bottom drawer. "Did you ever hear the one about the broken pencil? Never mind, it's pointless," I can picture him quip with a good-sport smile.

One day he showed up at school with his arm in a cast—from an auto accident, he said, and joked it off. The next week he did not show up at all. We heard that alone in his car he had crashed into the same concrete bridge abutment he hit the first time, only this time he died. "Why did he do it?" "I heard he had a terminal illness." That was the rumor. But the fact was our favorite teacher, without a word, had suddenly disappeared.

I began writing poems, and learned to recite "Lament" by Dylan Thomas by heart for its musical bravado. A movie that moved me was *The Fugitive Kind*, based on the Tennessee Williams play *Orpheus Descending*. Anna Magnani as Lady Torrance, unhappily married to a vicious man, falls in love with a sensitive guitar-playing stranger—the young Marlon Brando as Valentine "Snakeskin" Xavier. This image of artistic rather than brute masculinity appealed to me. Sometimes I wore a beret to school and carried around Allen Ginsberg's *Howl* and Jack Kerouac's *On the Road* with my schoolbooks to show to my friends. It was Kerouac's *The Dharma Bums* and Ginsberg's "Sunflower Sutra" that first sparked my interest in Zen, and the eventual realization I was searching for something that could not be grasped.

Later the party planners in our class came up with an extravaganza called EMOC ("come" spelled backwards) with a dance DJ, refreshment table, and upstairs an improvised Greenwich Village café, perfect for a beat poetry reading. Of course I had to read, wearing my beret in the dimly lit nightclub atmosphere while would-be creative types lounged in imagined beatitude, with no smoking allowed. When my turn came I stood and read with a haunted voice a free-form poem about my first long bus trip alone, concluding with the lines:

> in the darkness lingers a dreaming nation
> bewitched by the paleness of a summer moon
> roll on, night bus, roll on
> to your rendezvous with dawn

As a friend pointed out, it was influenced by the midwestern moods of Carl Sandburg. In high school most of my writing emerged in styles inspired by the writers I was reading, from e.e.cummings to Edgar Allan Poe to Allen Ginsberg. At least I was searching for my own way, whatever that might be. I wanted to write, but what would I say, and who would listen? To find my own voice, I needed to step out into the world and get more depth of experience.

*

Political Theater

When we lived in Melrose, Massachusetts, every weekday my father rode the commuter train to Boston, where he worked for Atlantic Mutual as a marine insurance underwriter. He hardly ever talked about his job. But on a late-autumn afternoon when I was fifteen, for once he came up to my attic room, looked at me earnestly through his brown-rimmed glasses and said, "I have a decision to make. About a month ago I had an argument with my boss."

My dad having an argument wasn't surprising. I had arguments with him myself. But an argument with his boss? "Oh... about what?"

My father went on in a serious tone, "He was bound and determined to do things his way. I got angry, and we yelled at each other. I felt like a cornered rat." That got my attention. It was unusual for him to talk about his feelings.

"But you stood up to him," I said.

"Maybe so, but the upshot is, I was passed over for promotion to manage the Boston office."

I paused to take it in. "So what's the decision you have to make?"

"I can move back to company headquarters in New York with the same kind of job I already have, or quit and take a job at a small company in Jacksonville, Florida. It would be lower pay, but more responsibility—and risk." He looked out the window at the almost-bare branches of a tree in the yard. "Whatever I do will affect you, so let me know what you think."

Mulling it over, I felt torn. Going to New York, the cautious choice for him, might mean a new life of adventure for me. Taking a risk in Jacksonville might give him more self-respect, but leave me lost in what seemed like an alien nowhere. I tried to be honest and noncommittal. "I'd rather live near New York, but I can see how you might want to switch to another company." I didn't realize that in 1958 the Jacksonville schools were still segregated, and poorly funded.

My father and mother discussed what to do, and that summer we moved to suburban New Jersey on the outer cultural orbit of New York City. At Ridgewood High I subscribed to *The New York Times,* and picked up my copy each morning from a stack in the hall to read between and sometimes during classes, excited to be actually getting an education.

Eventually, in the early autumn of 1960 Mr. Ahearn, my liberal American History teacher, gave me a pass to go see *Operation Abolition*, a right-wing propaganda film that was shown at a local club by a man in a light gray suit from the John Birch Society. It claimed to present graphic evidence of a communist conspiracy to abolish the House Un-American Activities Committee. I watched newsreel footage of students from Berkeley picketing the committee's supposedly public hearings at San Francisco City Hall, and a crowd of students on the steps chanting "Open the door!" in protest when they weren't allowed in as promised.

In grave tones the narrator went on about the imminent threat of the communist conspiracy to take over our nation, as the police brought out high-powered fire hoses and blasted the students with raging torrents of water. Then officers pushed and dragged the wet protesters down the many stone steps of City Hall and put them in paddy wagons. What the narrator called a "riot" had been subdued; order had been restored.

Just an impressionable high school student, I was strongly affected by this film—but not in the way the presenter intended. My heart and mind were all with the student protesters.

That October, as the leaves turned yellow and orange, my teacher excused me again to see John F. Kennedy at a campaign stop near a mall in a nearby town. While we waited for him to arrive, an advance man led the small crowd in singing:

> K-E-double N-E-D-Y,
> oh he's a wonderful guy!
> A fearless pioneer,
> he'll win the New Frontier…

When JFK came through the crowd in a navy blue suit, leaning from the back seat of a slow-moving, open, black Lincoln convertible to extend his hand, I managed to reach out and brush his fingers as he swept by.

Back then, Bergen County was Republican territory. As the leaves turned to red and brown, we heard that Nixon was giving a speech Friday night at our football field. Sixteen of us organized a Young Democrats club and marched down Main Street with hand-painted Kennedy signs held up with thin wooden sticks. As we approached the high school, suddenly from out of nowhere a flying egg smashed into one of our slogans. Pieces of cracked shell, gobs of yellow yolk, and streaks of clear liquid egg white oozed down the cardboard sign.

Undeterred, we raised our signs high and walked on. Arriving early, we marched defiantly onto the field and stood right in front of the stage where Nixon would speak. As a hostile Republican crowd gathered around us, some football players in maroon jackets, incited by Nixon's advance crew, began pushing and shoving us back. At first we resisted, but they grabbed and broke one of our Kennedy signs, and we made a strategic retreat to the rear of the crowd.

I don't remember what Nixon said, but after the speech a middle-aged man in shirtsleeves loudly chastised us for holding a sign that said "20 Million Americans Live in Poverty."

"How can you say that when you live in this prosperous town?" His brow was knotted, his mouth distorted with disgust. We looked back, dumbfounded. Standing alone on the littered field when most people had left, the man went on yelling at us, caught up in venting his outrage, overriding our attempts to debate with him.

"What's the matter with this guy?" I asked a friend.

"Someone said he's our Congressman."

*

The Karamazov Quartet

I never had a brother. Maybe that's why in high school I decided to do a book report on *The Brothers Karamazov*. Along with *Moby Dick* it was the heftiest book I'd ever read, and one that affected me profoundly. Though now I don't remember many details of the plot or setting, the contrasting characters of Dmitri, Ivan, and Alyosha stuck with me, reflecting parts of myself and suggesting possibilities of how and who I might want to be. And the fourth brother, the illegitimate epileptic Smerdyakov, was like a shadow haunting my psyche.

I don't know how Dostoevsky did it, but he seemed to look deep into my inner being and hold up a mirror of imagination to my soul. It's now been so many years since I plowed through those 776 vivid pages and wrote my youthful essay, I don't know if my fuzzy memory will do it justice. But I feel compelled to tell my story before it and I both fade into oblivion.

First there was Dmitri, the swashbuckling soldier, sensualist, and romantic suitor, so passionately impulsive that he was all too ready to seduce a woman or draw his sword and clash with anyone who dared to cross the raging river that possessed him. I too had a tendency to plunge enthusiastically into any adventure that caught my fancy. Once when my girlfriend suggested that maybe it would be better if we broke up, without a second thought I jumped from the path into the pond to prove my love— or was it just romantic foolishness? In any case, the wristwatch my father gave me never worked again after that.

Then there was Ivan, the pessimistic intellectual who argued quite convincingly that the suffering of children proved the injustice of God, and even wrote a story called "The Grand Inquisitor" claiming that if Christ had come back to earth he would have been imprisoned by the so-called Christians of the Spanish Inquisition. I too had pondered whether there was anyone actually listening to my bedtime prayers, and took a subtle pride in the power of my reason. After reading a paperback introduction to the wonders of relativity, I argued intensely with a friend, claiming that whether the earth went around the sun (as he maintained) or the sun went around the earth (as the ancients thought) was just a matter of one's frame of reference, and that from the point of view of the Milky Way, both the sun and earth revolved around the center of the galaxy.

At times I wondered if my passionate enthusiasm for wielding an intellectual sword might at times be a problem. Was life just endless competition? I began to read Ginsberg and Kerouac, listened to modern jazz with my friend John, and sometimes hung out with Daniel, who played the cello and didn't seem to care about grades. Late one night with two girls we went skinny dipping in the modest pond in a park near the center of town, while the moon above looked down.

The further I read in Dostoevsky's novel, the more I was drawn to Alyosha, the spiritual brother who became a Russian monk. His teacher Father Zosima sent him from the monastery out into the world to continue his spiritual education, and Alyosha withstood the onslaught of Ivan's existential atheism. Maybe the true hero was simply this young man of kindness. Before long I began my own spiritual journey and eventually aspired to follow the magic, shining footprints of the bodhisattva path.

It might be more comfortable to ignore the bastard Smerdyakov, the fourth brother and servant of his father, Fyodor Karamazov. Smerdyakov hid in the shadows of the story until he killed his hated father in a faked epileptic fit, a crime of which Dmitri was wrongly accused. But I too was angry at my father, who seemed cold, distant, and critical. "Why don't you get a haircut?" "Why don't you get a decent job?" seemed to be all he had to offer in the way of fatherly advice. So as soon as I could I left for the vast reach of the West Coast, where wave after wave of new ideas came rolling in.

It wasn't until years later that we hugged each other for the first time, and years even later, after my mother died, that in the middle of an argument about how he thought I ought to be, I blurted "Why not just accept me as I am?" and suddenly silent, he seemed to finally understand.

My identity may sound inconsistent, then and now, when sometimes I act like one brother and then another. But perhaps identity is not as fixed, straightforward, and singular as we often assume. Maybe it takes at least four characters to sketch each one of us, like musicians playing a string quartet. In the words of Walt Whitman, the great grandfather of American poetry, maybe we all "contain multitudes," and with a change of attitude one's heart and mind can be transformed into a spiritual work of art.

*

Staying in Character

Getting your inner string quartet to play together harmoniously is not always easy—sometimes it's more like a Marx Brothers movie. When I found myself warming the bench for the high school soccer team, I decided to try out for the senior play, *Ah, Wilderness!* by Eugene O'Neill, a comic drama about how Richard, a rebellious 17-year-old carried away with romantic poetry, falls in love with Muriel, a neighbor girl, and how his family tries to deal with him, in the social milieu of New London, Connecticut, in 1906.

I wound up in the role of drunk Uncle Sid (though I'd never actually been drunk) mainly because I was willing to make a fool of myself by marching around banging an invisible Salvation Army drum—"Boom! Boom! Boom!"—and singing the old Army hymn "In the Sweet Bye and Bye," totally out of tune.

It was fun, but less than a week before the Saturday night performance in front of parents, relatives, and friends, many in the cast still had not mastered their lines. Mr. Whitby, our stolid, rumpled drama-teacher director, lost all patience, threw the script up in the air and declared, as pages flew everywhere, "You're on your own!" Then he turned and walked out of the rehearsal. With mouths wide open we looked at each other, near panic, then held frantic sessions without him each day after school and even some evenings in the back room of a local club, going over the script again and again, determined to remember our lines.

On the big night all went well until a mix-up during the family dinner when somehow the diners got caught in a repeating dialogue loop, and waiting offstage, I feared my fellow cast members would never arrive at my cue. But my friend Joshua, who had acting experience, was playing Nat the genial father, and he came through. He looked to the wings and shouted, "I'm hungry! Bring in the food!" Though we skipped a page or two, that got the scene back on track, and Nora the Irish maid entered with a large tureen and began serving everyone. When I came onstage as Uncle Sid, supposedly trying to look sober, I peered into the pot as if it contained something strange, then drunkenly raised the ladle and shared in amazement my sudden discovery: "Soup?"

And the high jinks began. Soon I was marching around the dining room banging the air with invisible drumsticks—"Boom! Boom! Boom! In the sweet bye and bye, we will meet on that beautiful shore."

Earlier, when Sid was still supposedly sober, he arrived cracking jokes about drinking to Lily, his long-time sweetheart who refused to marry him due to the dissolute habits he'd sworn to reform but had not. A bit later, when Nat wondered whether Richard was showing sensuous Swinburne poems to Muriel with seductive intent, as Sid I said with my best attempt at sincere concern that it wouldn't be good for him to get a decent girl like her "in trouble." I paused for a moment, taking care to keep a straight face. Then involuntarily my eyes rolled upward and the audience erupted in laughter.

After the show I heard Mr. Whitby was pleased we had pulled it off, but not happy about me hamming it up at a moment when Sid was supposed to be serious. But it felt completely spontaneous. Somehow Uncle Sid had taken over, insisting that despite his sincere concern, he still had a sense of humor.

*

Bites of the Big Apple

According to New Jersey law, at age eighteen I could drive but not buy booze. That didn't keep me from other forms of intoxication. Soon after I got my license, caught up in talking and laughing with a car full of friends, I drove through a red light suspended above an intersection. The cop let me off easy—beginner's luck—but that was a lesson in paying attention.

Some of my senior classmates drove across the border to New York State, where the drinking age was eighteen, to buy beer. But John, whose older brother was a musician, invited me to join a group of friends driving over the George Washington Bridge into Harlem to listen to modern jazz. We parked on a side street, bought our tickets and walked in past a poster, as now I imagine, of a man leaning toward a piano with fingers poised on a keyboard and another holding and blowing a saxophone. The concert was in a large hall that was part of the Harlem Armory, with a low stage for the musicians up front and rows of folding seats packed with middle-aged African Americans in suits and dresses for an evening in early spring. Once the music started, many tapped their feet to the beat.

The headliners were Art Blakey's Jazz Messengers, who delivered their fluent stories with Wayne Shorter pensive and witty on tenor sax, Lee Morgan nimble and soaring on trumpet, Horace Silver sitting in with funky, rhythmic piano, Jymie Merritt faithfully thumping the bass, and Art Blakey himself, splashing and crackling on drums. Their combined hard-bop energy rippled through the crowd on songs like "Moanin'" and "A Night in Tunisia." And when the Messengers finished there was a bonus: Thelonious Monk, with an enigmatic turn on piano, his fingers exploring exotic chords on "Blue Monk" and "Round About Midnight."

The next expedition was to Greenwich Village for an off-Broadway play, *The Connection,* featuring a quartet with Jackie McLean on alto sax and Freddy Redd on piano. They and some actors played jazz-musician junkies lounging around a half-furnished apartment waiting for the dealer to come, every so often jamming on a new tune, until the quartet had laid down an album's worth of stirring improvisation (later I bought the LP and listened to it over and over). Wandering around the lobby during intermission, the down-and-out actors panhandled the middle-class audience, calling attention to the fact that for years musicians like Monk and McLean could not work at clubs in New York City because their cabaret cards were revoked due to drug convictions, even for possession of marijuana. What were the "city fathers" trying to accomplish? Being unable to work might have driven the musicians further into drug use.

On another trip to the Village, I stopped in a small bookshop and bought the City Lights chapbook of Allen Ginsberg's *Howl,* and for a while watched the chess players under the trees in Washington Square Park. I could see that some of those shaggy old chess devotees were pretty damn good, moving decisively to organize their pieces—leaping knights, sliding bishops, squat rooks, ranks of mere but vital pawns, plus the tall and powerful queen—to attack the opponent's or protect their own stolid king, who was big but could only move one square at a time, in constant danger of being in check. That seems like a key, in chess, in jazz, and in life: stay focused, and develop your pieces to work together.

*

Taken for a Ride

After high school, in the summer of 1961, I worked as a camp counselor. Returning to my job after a break between sessions, I was hitching with Bill, a quiet arts and crafts instructor I had met at the camp, through the woodlands of western New Jersey toward the hills of eastern Pennsylvania. In the gathering dusk a light gray Chevrolet pulled over and a guy in a ducktail haircut and black leather jacket leaned out the window and called, "Where you cats goin'?"

"Camp Pocono."

The front and back doors opened, revealing four young men, all of them about our age and dressed like teenage hoods. There was barely room for both of us. Jack, their leader, directed Bill, who was tall and thin, to squeeze in between two of them in the back, and me to sit between him and the driver, who seemed heavier than any two of us put together and hardly said a word. Jack, on the other hand, liked to hear himself talk, and sometimes even interrupted himself to pepper a few questions.

"You ever smoke pot?"

"Uh... sure. How about you?"

"Are you kidding? Whenever I get the stuff."

I turned to look at him. "The green stuff or the brown stuff?"

"What are you, some kinda wise guy?"

Maybe he sensed I was bluffing. I held on tight to my closed umbrella, gripped like a staff between my legs. "It depends on how it's processed. How much it's cooked."

"Who gives a shit as long as it gets you high?"

"Right on," said one of his pals in the back.

Encouraged, Jack leaned back, turned his head further to the left, and went on. "Hey boys, what do you say we pull over and take these wise guys for a picnic in a quiet place where we can work them over?" There was no answer. I glanced back at Bill, who sat pale and tense. If Jack had his way, our chances did not look good. Jack turned toward the heavy driver and pointed ahead to where the thick woods encroached on a small gravel space to the left. "Hey Freddy, there's a good place to stop. Pull over."

After a pause, Freddy replied in a low voice. "I'm just drivin'. No messin' around."

"Oh come on, Freddy. Let's have some fun," said Jack.

Freddy held onto the wheel and stared straight ahead as the road unrolled from the darkness into the beams of our headlights. "Like I said, I'm just drivin'."

As we cruised through the depths of the forest and into the hills, Jack tried again several times, but Freddy never budged. I couldn't help but admire his stubbornness.

When we got to the sign for Camp Pocono I pointed the way up the drive that I knew led to a building with a well-lit parking lot. Freddy

17

pulled up the Chevy under the floodlights and we all got out. Bill and I went back to the trunk to get our packs. As Freddy unlocked and lifted the trunk, we turned toward it, and I felt the shadows of the others surround us from behind. Trying to stay calm, Bill and I hoisted our packs and turned to face the gang.

I looked at Freddy, then Jack. "Thanks for the ride."

"Yeah," said Bill. "thanks for getting us here."

Freddy nodded and turned toward the driver's door. The others looked at him and then at Jack, who stepped toward me.

"You're a wise guy," said Jack. "But I'm OK with that." And he slapped me on the back, just hard enough to let me know we were getting off easy.

*

Roll On, Night Bus

During the second camp session I ran into Peter, the head counselor, on the terrace outside the office. Tall, slim, tanned and athletic, with short hair and dark-rimmed glasses, he wore a Camp Pocono T-shirt, olive drab Bermuda shorts, and an air of knowing what he was doing. Peter called me aside for a "routine midterm self-evaluation," which we did then and there, standing on the flagstones beneath the pines. He started with "How's it going so far?"

"Oh, pretty well. I enjoy doing crafts with the kids." That was my specialty.

"Any problems come up?"

"Well…" I looked down, then back up to meet his gaze. "There's one kid, Frankie, who refuses to participate, and when I talk to him about it, he stamps around and starts cussing."

"Yeah, that sounds like a problem. Camp policy is that no one is forced to do anything as long as they behave—but if they don't behave, there can

18

be a penalty. We can't hit the kids, but it's OK to assign them a certain number of push-ups or sit-ups," he added with a smile.

"Thanks. Maybe I'll give it a try."

"By the way," continued Peter, "I haven't seen you at Peggy and Whitey's on nights off. Why don't you join us? Are you a loner?"

"No, I've been there with friends a few times for a beer. Maybe we have different nights off." I felt uncomfortable with the suggestion that I was a social misfit. But when I thought about it, I did prefer reading *For Whom the Bell Tolls* at night in my bunk to going out to get drunk. After that summer as a camp counselor, I wrote the following story:

Journey into Light

Still half asleep on the wide seat at the back of the bus, feeling the rear wheels bumping under him, Richard sat up and looked out at the pale light of early dawn. He was eighteen, but he felt old. Turning his wrist slightly, he contemplated the still-luminous hands of his beat-up watch. Slowly, irresistibly, the thin second hand ticked around in its tiny circle, keeping some obscure rhythm with the rolling bus. He stared at the steadily moving metal sliver, trying to stop time, knowing that he couldn't and feeling helpless at the futility of trying. He looked up the aisle at the empty seats. No one. Outside, houses, stores, and streets were becoming visible, moving toward him, passing by, then fading away. But always more came forward in an endless procession of lights, lawns, signs, trees, and telephone poles—and there he was, aboard the groaning bus, feeling it creak as it braked and turned, then accelerated and rolled on, grinding inexorably toward the great metropolis.

The thought of a destination awakened his spirit. He began to feel a subdued excitement at the way the world streamed by, the way the bus plunged forward irresistibly. I've got to move, he thought. Do something, change something. He remembered his poem about a previous ride. "Roll on, night bus, roll on / to your rendezvous with dawn."

Earlier that summer Richard and some of his fellow camp counselors had a night off.

Oh it's beer, beer, beer
That makes you wanna cheer
In the Corps, in the Corps.
Oh it's beer, beer, beer
That makes you wanna cheer
In the Quar-ter-mas-ter Corps.
Mine eyes are dim, I cannot see
I have not brought my specs with me…

The beer pitcher made the rounds again, and the merry crowd in Peggy and Whitey's blasted out another verse, voices swelling in joyous volume, singing the praises of nothing in particular. There he was, among his comrades from Camp Pocono, singing loud and way off key, drinking bravely onward even though he didn't really like the taste of beer. When they ran out of verses the song dissolved into laughter and conversation.

Richard grasped his wet, empty glass, and tried to feel like he was having fun. He looked around at the ruddy faces and focused on Chang-ho, a counselor several years older than he was, a tough but sensitive guy who knew karate and had been in the South Korean army at the age of fourteen. Richard watched him lift the pitcher of beer. "Here you go boy, have some more." Chang-ho poured the amber liquid into Richard's empty glass, and white foam rose steadily to the top. "Come on, let's drink," Chang-ho said, lifting his own glass as if in a toast.

"Hey look what I see," said Al in his half-buttoned shirt from across the table. "A full glass! Fellas, you know what that means." Standing up with arms outstretched like a drunken choir director, Al led the others in his favorite song:

Here's to Richard, he's true blue.
He's a drunkard through and through,

So drink, chug-a-lug,
Drink, chug-a-lug,
DRINK, chug-a-lug!

Richard hesitated, staring down at the foamy glass. When the song ended he tilted his head back and began to drink in one long draft, gulping swallow after swallow. He knew he could do it, he had done it before. About halfway through the beer felt like it was coming back up again, but he swallowed harder and managed to finish it all. He sat back, proud and disgusted, feeling bloated and slippery inside. What a waste of time, he thought. Across the table, Al was telling one of his jokes. Beside him Chang-ho was tilting back in his chair, frowning. Suddenly he let his chair fall forward and reached for the pitcher of beer, pulled it toward them, and said, "C'mon boy, just you and me. We gonna drink. Here, let's go."

Richard watched as Chang-ho started to fill a glass and then said, "No."

"What? C'mon boy, this is part of your social life."

"I don't care."

"Hah? What's the matter? Don't you want some beer?"

"I have to admit, I don't really like it."

Chang-ho turned away, grimacing in disgust. "Hey fellas, Richard says he don't like beer. What do you say we give him some ketchup?" He picked up the ketchup bottle but quickly slammed it down again, turned away, ignoring his own remark, and tilted back in brooding silence. A few people glanced questioningly at Richard but quickly returned their attention to Al.

"What's the matter, Chang-ho?" said Richard, "Have some more beer." Just then he felt intense pressure in his bladder and went to the men's room. Chang-ho did not look up.

Later, outdoors, they took a walk. The road was black, winding, and lonely. On either side lay fields, hills, and forests. Above and around was the starry night sky. Chang-ho walked stiffly along in angry silence, smoking furiously and looking defiantly up at the distant stars, as if he were a human bomb with the fuse lit. Richard wanted to say something about the way he felt about life and everything, but his friend's mood made him wait. They walked on in silence, Richard resolving to let Chang-ho speak first.

"Richard…" Chang-ho kept on staring at the stars, then said "Never mind," mumbling something about Asian philosophy. Richard almost said he would like nothing better than to hear some Asian philosophy, but was afraid he might break the spell that seemed to hold his friend in its grip. He kept quiet and waited for Chang-ho to speak again. When the words finally tore the fabric of silence, they sounded as if they were chained to heavy weights.

"I am a slave," Chang-ho said.

For a long moment, Richard felt the sky pressing down on them. "A slave to what?"

Chang-ho looked up at the endless night. "To the universe." He took the cigarette from his mouth without looking at it and flipped it onto the road. Red sparks sprinkled from the burning butt like little shooting stars.

As the bus descended into the Holland Tunnel, Richard sat up. Darkness closed in, surrounded the droning bus and wrapped around everything, leaving a stream of passing lights. He felt the lonely, uncertain beat of his heart. Everything was so tenuous that he wondered how he managed to stay alive for more than a moment.

Then as the bus emerged into early morning, Richard looked out the window and saw the stone towers of the city. His fear of death subsided. Whatever he was looking for, he might find it there if anywhere. Millions of people, all alive, doing all the things people do, hearts beating, blood flowing through them, a great river of humanity. And I am part of that, he thought. I am alive and I am here. Then as bright rays of the morning sun broke through the jagged skyline to the east, the bus pulled to a halt, and Richard stepped down into the bustling crowd of the Port Authority Terminal in midtown Manhattan, aware that no matter what, the next moment would always be unknown.

Chapter 2: First Year Ups and Downs

Entrance

Whoever you are: in the evening step out
of your room, where you know everything;
the last before the distance is your house:
whoever you are.
With your eyes, so tired they can hardly
free themselves from the worn threshold,
very slowly lift a dark tree
and put it before the sky: slim, alone.
And you have made the world. And it is great
and like a word that still ripens in silence.
And as your will begins to grasp its meaning,
allow your eyes to gently let it go…

—Rilke

Fellowship of New Arrivals

In the fall of 1961 the housing form for incoming freshmen, after inquiring about prospective concentration, hobbies, and interests, posed a question that was straightforward yet somewhat surprising: "Do you want a roommate of a different race or nationality?" It never occurred to me there would be such a question. It implied that prejudice was still an ugly if often hidden problem, and to avoid uncomfortable situations the college was assigning roommates who actually *wanted* to room together.

So I answered Yes. And sure enough, when I arrived among the stately elms and ivy-clad red-brick buildings of Harvard Yard, as a white would-be poet from suburban New Jersey I was assigned to a suite with Rudy, a genial, red-haired folk music buff from Putney, Vermont; Carl, a sincere, even-tempered African American from Atlanta; and Julian, a tall, serious chemistry student from Chicago, also African American.

Rudy, with his well-worn and well-tuned Martin guitar, had been at summer music camp with Pete Seeger, and he soon became the center of folk and blues jam sessions that drew other students from upstairs and across the hall, singing songs like the civil rights anthem "We Shall Overcome" and a haunting ballad of the Spring Hill, Nova Scotia, mine disaster, written by Ewan McColl and Peggy Seeger.

Rudy's record collection included great tunes like "San Francisco Bay Blues" by Jesse Fuller, a one-man band who played, sang, and tap-danced on street-corners. An aging black man who had survived a hard childhood in the South and could not afford to hire musicians to accompany him, Jesse Fuller would simultaneously strum or pick his 12-string guitar with his hands, blow harmonica on a rack with his mouth, splash a high-hat cymbal with a pedal for his left foot, and with his right foot thud out a line on a six-pedal bass of his own invention. After singing several verses about walking by San Francisco Bay, alternating with harmonica choruses, he launched into a vigorous kazoo solo as he thumped out a bouncing, syncopated rhythm on high-hat and bass.

While I loved Jesse Fuller's creative versatility, the album that really grabbed me in the gut and made me move was one I found on my own called *Muddy Waters at Newport, 1960.* Muddy Waters, the man who moved rock with "Rolling Stone," played the Chicago blues, live in a vinyl groove, from the folk festival, standing tall onstage on the album cover in a charcoal gray suit beneath blue sky with his big electric guitar, its twang and sting piercing my stereo. Electric bass rocked my bones in the living room, Muddy's powerful voice wailed out music charged in the heart with emotional energy. One song gave new meaning to a gasoline ad of the time: "Put a tiger in your tank." Later I heard him in Boston. For me Chicago blues embodied a thundering force that was virile and positive, spiced with imagination and humor, a life-affirming celebration. Muddy Waters was the "Hootchie Koochie man"—everyone knew he was there.

My roommate Carl soon realized that the pipe and tweed jacket with elbow patches he brought with him for college did not quite fit with the folk-music scene, so he switched to a T-shirt and jeans and joined in.

24

Now and then he picked up a guitar, strummed some chords, and sang the country blues. Julian smiled and was tolerant of our regular hootenannies, but often left early to study in the library. Other friends and neighbors who gathered found common cause in discussing left-wing politics and going to local demonstrations in support of the civil rights movement.

But we studied too. I took anthropology, philosophy, and a seminar on the creative process, but probably my favorite course was freshman expository writing, with an interesting reading list and weekly 3-page papers. My section was taught by Mr. Huggins, a lively and scholarly African American graduate student in the final year of his history Ph.D., who later became a well-known professor at Harvard. Graciously at home in his brown jacket and vest, with a trim beard and almost bald head, he had a dignified air that commanded respect, yet he really cared for his students. We read William James' *The Varieties of Religious Experience*, which opened a path in my mind through the unexplored forest of mysticism, treated as psychological fact rather than mere delusion. Though my camp counselor friend Chang-ho was not exactly a mystic, I wrote his name on the paperback cover in the Korean characters he had shown me. To some extent I felt a bond with him as a fellow outsider, not quite at home in American culture.

I still wonder what Chang-ho meant when he said he felt like a slave to the universe. Was he talking about karma—or culture, or fate? As I learned later, karma means action in Sanskrit, and by extension the results of actions—you could say moral cause and effect—but is not to be confused with fate, since karma implies free will. Past actions have present consequences; present actions can change future results. Yet maybe Chang-ho felt in the grip of forces from the past, not sure what he could do.

I can imagine asking him now what he meant then, if in his eighties he sat in a rocking chair on the porch of an assisted living facility in Southern California. He might stroke his gray wisp of a beard and say, "I felt trapped by the culture of manhood: being tough, getting drunk, not showing kindness or love. In the war I was macho, I wanted the respect of other men. When I came to America I was macho, trying to fit in—like at that bar where we were drinking. I was pushing you to get drunk, to be like me—and now I regret it. Would you believe I became a nurse and spent 20 years caring for soldiers in a veteran's hospital?" I would tell him yes, even then I saw warmth and compassion in him. Like him, I didn't want to get trapped in a macho image. And I would respect him for taking constructive action to change his life.

Back in Mr. Huggins' class, intoxicated with poetry, I wrote short essays on Hart Crane's "The Bridge" and Dylan Thomas' "Fern Hill." We even had creative assignments to write a parable (mine was about conformity in a colony of ants) and an argument about whether the college had a moral obligation to admit more of the equally qualified students it was turning down (I thought it did). And then there was Henry George's *Progress and Poverty,* posing the question of whether land should be privately owned or belong to everyone in common, like air and water.

Another course I enjoyed was Humanities 5, on the history of Western philosophy. Working on the final paper, I was sitting in front of my Underwood typewriter at a small desk next to a first-floor window looking out at the path toward the Yard. My gaze drifted to the line of bicycles on the rack about fifty feet way, next to the gray stone wall of the library. Leaning over one of the bikes, a scrawny young man in drab pants and untucked T-shirt took something metal out of his pocket and methodically severed the cable that locked the bike to the rack. Then he pulled the bike back and began to walk it along the path toward the street.

I jumped up and ran out after him, catching up with the guy as he pushed the bike along the cobblestone sidewalk. I stepped in front and grabbed the handlebars. "Is this bike yours?" I said. He mumbled something. "What's that in your pocket?" I pointed at the protruding handle of the wire cutters. He looked down for a moment, then suddenly let go of the bike and ran down the street. I watched as he wove through the crowd, wondering if he didn't have a bike of his own, or might be a professional thief. Then I slowly walked the bike back into the courtyard and reported the attempted theft to the campus police. Later the bicycle's owner, a grad student, came to my window and thanked me. I told him the story of what happened, and went back to writing my paper on divine love, *agape*, concluding that the human love it might inspire was equally important.

*

Rubber Shoelaces

The Freshman Seminar Program offered incoming students a unique opportunity to work with a professor in a small group on a special topic. It sounded interesting, so I applied for several, hoping at least to get into one. When I met with the professor leading the Socratic seminar on philosophical questions, he asked for my thoughts. I mentioned a book I had read in high school, Camus' interpretation of the myth of Sisyphus, who was condemned to keep pushing a boulder to the top of a hill, only to have it roll back down again. He had to push that rock back up, again and again, without end. Despite the hopeless absurdity of his situation, Camus imagined Sisyphus happy. To me this was a leap of faith that could give life meaning.

I also interviewed for the seminar on fiction writing, submitting my story "Journey into Light" with its original ending: when the bus arrives in New York, everything is annihilated in an all-consuming burst of blinding light. I explained to the professor that this ultimate explosion was either a nuclear bomb or spiritual enlightenment, or both at once—the culmination of all fear and yearning in one great release. But without explanation, it was not really clear. The later version brought the ending down to earth, closer to my own experience.

The seminar I ended up taking was on the creative process. It sounded unconventional, an unusual adventure that might be fun. The instructor, William J. J. Gordon, a charismatic inventor with rigorous curiosity and a quick sense of humor, had led a group at Arthur D. Little that developed ways of applying metaphor to practical problems. He called the method Synectics, and trained engineers and designers in informal, small group sessions. In this seminar, playing with metaphor, we would "make the familiar strange" to find new ways of seeing—and might actually invent something. Once we met at his house, and as I was leaving I asked Bill Gordon for an example of making the familiar strange. He said, "Look down at your feet, move slowly, and watch every step you take." Then I walked a few steps with a new perspective, right out the door onto the path through the grassy front yard.

Usually we met in the Synectics conference room, which featured couches and big pads of paper on easels for drawing ideas with felt-tip markers. I noticed that in addition to books on the history of science, his library included unusual items like *Autobiography of a Yogi*. Bill Gordon was a slightly pudgy, dynamic teacher with a ruddy, expressive face— like a more energetic W. C. Fields—who stalked around the room in open-necked shirt and khakis, vividly gesticulating as he urged us to find "elegant" solutions—not overly complex ones, which he called "hooligans," that might cause trouble or open "a can of peas."

One problem he gave us was to invent a better shoelace, one that would not come untied at the wrong time. Using the method of personal metaphor, I imagined myself as a shoelace going through an eyelet in a shoe, like a rock climber lowered on a rope through a narrow crevasse by my comrades. What if the rope broke and I began to slip down, what would I do? Closing my eyes, I pushed out my arms toward both sides to hold myself between the imagined opposing walls. What kind of shoelace could do that? Finally we hit upon it: a rubber shoelace. When stretched out it would narrow and easily pull through the hole; when released it would instantly expand to full size and stay stuck. It would not even need to be tied.

Bill Gordon suggested we put the idea to a test, and a tough one at that. A few days later we gathered in our winter clothes on the ice of the frozen Charles River and pulled on our skates. With the pieces of rubber tubing he supplied, we laced our skates up, stretching the tubes through the lace-holes and releasing them so they held tight. We skated our various ways with varying levels of competence and then met around Bill Gordon, also on skates, to assess the results. He agreed it was quite possible to skate with rubber shoelaces, but their natural elasticity kept them stretching in ways that lacked the consistent tight fit a skillful skater would want. It was an enjoyable experiment but a patent application was not in the works. When inventing practical things, just being creative was not enough.

Later we came up with something that was not exactly an invention but a way to keep the bathroom mirror from fogging when you take a hot shower. If you make yourself very tiny and walk among the drops of water condensed on the mirror, you see the uneven surface reflects the light in all directions. If only there were a way to smooth the drops into a thin and level film, the mirror would stay clear even when covered with water. What if you took a touch of wet soap and smeared it with your fingertips over the foggy mirror, just enough to smooth the drops into a thin, transparent film. Presto! You could see your reflection clearly in the mirror right when you stepped out of the shower. Even if really new, this discovery also could not be patented, since it was not a mechanical device but a simple, natural way of seeing more clearly—like sitting quietly by the river and letting your mind settle into smooth, transparent awareness.

*

Without a Tie

In the freshman dining hall the rule was that each student had to wear a tie. For many of us that meant putting on a tie as we entered and taking it off as we left. Luckily it was easy to buy a cheap clip-on tie, already tied, for that purpose. So it was that I sat with Joshua, my high school friend and now college classmate, and some others in a far alcove out of sight of the entrance, talking about politics, eating our lunch. When Joshua finished he got up and left, disappearing around the corner into the main part of the hall. A few minutes later he returned with a grimace of disgust.

"What's the matter?" I said.

"Oh, I took off my tie before I got to the door, and the proctor sent me back to put it on and walk out again."

"That's ridiculous. Here, I'll walk beside you." I stood up and pulled off my tie and put it in my pocket. We walked out through the main hall together, Joshua with his tie on in compliance with the proctor's order, and I with no tie, in protest. As we approached the proctor, a heavy-set fellow with close-cropped hair, his eyes grew wide and his mouth dropped open. Stepping in front of me he shouted, "Why did you take off your tie?"

I tried to stay calm. "Because making my friend go back was ridiculous!"

"Oh yeah? Give me your student card!" the proctor demanded. I fished in my pocket and handed it over. He examined my card and held it up. "You'll have to get this back from the Dean!" he barked, and that was that. I was in trouble.

The next day in class Mr. Huggins announced, "Mr. Lennox, I hear you stood up to Wickerman in the dining hall yesterday. Good show! He is well known for banging two students' heads together during a demonstration."

I was surprised and a bit perplexed that my gesture was now public knowledge, but at the same time appreciated the support from Mr. Huggins. When I went to see the Dean, a tall and gangly, quite approachable man, he seemed serious but not angry. "Do you object to the tradition of wearing ties in the dining hall?" he inquired.

"No," I replied, "I object to the way the proctor treated my friend."

"I understand," said the Dean, and gave me my student card.

*

Lonesome College Blues

One spring afternoon I sat at my desk in the dorm and looked out the window at the branch of a tree beginning to bud. For the first two-thirds of freshman year I had been excited and engaged, taking a smorgasbord of courses, but then my academic motivation began to flag. In philosophy class I wanted to explore existentialism—we are thrown into life with no road map and must choose our own destiny—only to find that the one existentialist on the faculty had left the previous year, supposedly because among the analytic and historical professors he had no like-minded colleagues to talk to.

After years of studying to get into college, here I was—beginning to feel sick of just studying. I wanted to get out and live life. But dropping out of school was a scary thing to do—in the long run, what if I couldn't find a job that I liked? For the last month of spring semester I just did the minimum, figuring I could cram for exams and get through. I began to find more time for protest marches, French new wave films, and hanging out in the Hayes-Bickford cafeteria at night with "tea and English," spreading butter and raspberry jam on my muffins.

One evening a thin pale figure in a rumpled brown suit coat wandered in. His face was drawn, his hair unkempt, and a large patch of skin below his left ear was corroded and blistered with eczema. He looked like a refugee from Widener Library across the street, a graduate student who spent most of his time in the stacks, buried in books. Was that the price of getting a Ph.D.?

Underlying all this, I felt lonely. I had friends but something was missing—intimacy. In classes I'd often choose a seat beside a woman if one was available, but it was hard to find a girlfriend when only one fourth of my classmates were women (from Radcliffe) and freshmen had to compete for their attention with upperclassmen. I was reluctant to go to mixers at other women's colleges because I didn't like the competitive ritual of trying to charm someone on the spot. Yet one evening I got so desperate I had to do something. I learned there was a mixer that night at

Wellesley, in the town next to Natick, where I'd lived as a boy, so I knew it was near where I used to watch the Boston Marathon at a place where the runners had to climb a long hill. I figured it would take more than an hour to get there by public transportation, but what the heck, like those marathon runners, win or lose I could make the effort.

I started out taking the MTA, then sat on a bench and waited for a bus in the direction of Wellesley (unfortunately unaware of the Framingham/Worcester railroad line). When the bus finally came, it turned out I had to transfer to another bus, which stopped near the town of Wellesley but still a couple of miles from the college. It was dark, and by now about two hours past the start of the mixer, but I'd come this far, so I decided to walk the rest of the way—as it happened, I began to realize, along the route of the marathon. Trudging on through the night, here and there past an isolated streetlamp, I imagined those runners, way back in the pack, breathing hard, sweating, intent on completing the race, while all I had to do was keep walking, one step after another, through the cool night air.

When I finally got there the mixer was ending, with the large dance hall almost empty. Party decorations still hung from the walls. I could hear the voices of a few remaining women going back to their dorms and some guys heading back to their cars, as a janitor brought out his broom and began pushing bits of trash into piles. I felt desolate. After all that time and effort to get there, it was too late. Like the myth of Sisyphus repeatedly pushing a boulder up a steep hill, only to watch it roll back down again. Futility. But not without meaning. Like Sisyphus, I had not given up. I had taken action, and persevered. Then I walked outside and hitched a ride back to Cambridge with some students who had a car.

*

Our first year of college came to a close, and with it the course in expository writing. Mr. Huggins asked if we could guess the underlying theme of our readings. None of us could. When we ran out of guesses, we asked what it was. Like a magician revealing his secret, he paused, then said, "Progress." At the dawn of the twentieth century, as electric lights lit up our cities, automobiles drove on our roads, and telephones began to dissolve the physical distance between us, questions arose about all this amazing progress, questions still with us today. What effects does technology have on us socially, psychologically, and spiritually? How can we make progress in those realms as well? Could humanity tame its destructive urges and live in peace, or as we often feared, would we be swept into nuclear war?

At the beginning of the spring semester I debated whether to take a course with Reinhold Niebuhr, the political philosopher, or Paul Tillich, the existentialist theologian. I chose Niebuhr, thinking that political issues were the most pressing then. But while I learned something from reading Lenin's short book on imperialism, Professor Niebuhr's view of humanity as divided into "the children of light" and "the children of darkness" seemed too dualistic. Eventually I thought I should check out the course I didn't take, with Paul Tillich, and sat in on his final lecture. Tillich's spiritual existentialism inspired me—he believed in taking a leap of faith beyond the seeming absurdity of life—and the crowd that came to hear him responded with a standing ovation. I was left feeling that politics alone did not go deep enough.

After finals I decided to hang around for a few months and found a part-time job at the ticket desk for the Loeb summer theater. For minimum wage and free admission to the current production of Richard Wilbur's new verse translation of Moliere's *Tartuffe*, I was assigned to sit four hours a day in a round kiosk in the spacious lobby, near a large plate-glass window that spanned the whole wall facing the tree-lined street.

Sometimes people walked in the door to buy tickets or called to make reservations, but mostly I sat there reading a book. On my second day a middle-aged woman came in and met my eyes with a hopeful smile. We chatted a bit, and she asked for October tickets, four months in advance.

"Sorry, I don't have those tickets here at the desk," I said.

"Is there a way I can buy them today? I'm not in town often, and I'd really appreciate it."

"If you wait here a minute, I can get them for you." I swung open the half-door of the kiosk and walked to the closet at the side of the lobby, where future tickets were wrapped in stacks, then returned to the woman standing by the desk.

"Thank you very much," she said, putting the tickets into her purse.

The next morning I was summoned to the office of the clean-cut young man in sport coat and tie who had hired me. He seemed a little nervous as he stood up and asked me to sit down, then sat down himself. He looked away and then gradually focused. "I'm sorry to have to tell you this. Yesterday the Business Manager walked by and saw a woman standing at the box office desk, and you were not there. The first rule of your job is never to leave the desk, which has hundreds of tickets. I'm afraid you've been fired."

"But you never told me never to leave the desk. I was helping a customer."

"I'm sorry. The Business Manager insists. There's nothing I can do about it."

In a daze, I walked back out into the sunlight, shocked that my fine summer plans lay in shambles. I stood on the majestic stone steps of Widener Library and looked out over the spacious green of the Yard with its congregation of venerable red brick buildings. It was unfair. I had not been warned of the rule, and was taking good care of a customer. But what could I do?

I went to the Bick, the cafeteria in Harvard Square, and ordered tea and English. There at a small table near the door was my teacher Mr. Huggins,

34

looking a little bedraggled, blowing his nose into a handkerchief. I walked over and asked, "Mind if I join you?"

"Not at all, have a seat—but beware, I have a wicked cold." It turned out he had just finished his doctoral orals and was taking a break to recover. I told him the story of how I got fired. "Too bad," he commiserated, "That's a bum rap."

"Any ideas about what I should do?" I asked, in the hope he might suggest how to protest.

"Get another job," he replied. "Harvard Student Agencies has part-time work if you want to stay around for the summer."

So I wound up working with Jay, an energetic, fun-loving fellow student, providing refreshments during intermission from a cart on the patio at the same theater where I just got fired—but now I was working for the caterer, not the business manager. Jay and I enjoyed joking around with the patrons as we served them coffee, tea, brownies, and cookies. The clean-up was quick, and we got to watch the hypocrite Tartuffe get his comeuppance in rhyming couplets at every performance from our free seats at the back of the hall.

*

Flirtation with Modern Poetry

With an evening job serving refreshments at the theater, my days were free, so I looked into summer school classes. In a mood of misguided practicality I decided to fill a math requirement by taking Intermediate Calculus, but soon realized I'd rather be sitting under a tree daydreaming in the soft summer breeze than trying to digest the abstract patterns of differential equations. Before long I was auditing Modern American Poetry in a modern American lecture hall, sitting beside a lively young woman with long light-brown hair, white blouse, and short skirt, who for me embodied a vision of beauty. I was surprised that I found the audacity to sit down and chat with her, but glad that I did—she was an English major, smart and passionate about poetry. Maybe we could share our love of literature.

"What kind of poetry do you like?" I ventured, as the professor assembled his notes.

"I just took a course on the Romantics. Keats really got to me. Seeking truth in the beauty of art and nature. How about you?"

"Back in high school I was into the Beats like Ginsberg and Ferlinghetti, but now I'm curious about other poets—like Yeats, and Keats too."

During those warm summer days the clean-cut middle-aged professor calmly went on, with suit coat unbuttoned and wearing a tartan tie, reading poems aloud in a respectful monotone—followed by animated commentary that transformed his voice and face, like the time he analyzed "The Emperor of Ice Cream" by Wallace Stevens and walked around gesticulating as if building a castle in air.

Eva and I often sat together, then sometimes walked to a shady café after class. It turned out she went to a different college, and casually mentioned that she had a boyfriend there, so we were just poetry friends, discussing such things as whether Archibald MacLeish was right that poetry should not convey meaning, but simply be. For example, were some critics correct that William Carlos Williams' image of a red wheelbarrow in the rain would be more pure if he had left out the first line about everything that depends on it? Upon reflection, I found the pure-image argument unconvincing. Why couldn't poetry *both* mean and be, like MacLeish's poetry itself? Wasn't meaning inherent in language?

At the end of the summer Eva and I rode on the Greyhound together to New York City, and when the bus pulled into the Port Authority Terminal, we were the last to get off. Taking our time, we stretched in our seats, and I took off my glasses to wipe them clean on my shirt-tail. Then our eyes met. With a smile she said, "Some guys look more handsome without their glasses." Our faces were close. I felt tempted to kiss her, despite the problems that might ensue.

After a long moment we reached for our bags. Outside the bus we exchanged phone numbers, hugged goodbye, and walked toward our separate connections, as the afternoon rays of the sun split apart through the opaque prison of Manhattan's concrete buildings.

*

Evening

The evening slowly changes the clothes
that a ridge of ancient trees holds up for it;
you look: and the lands divide from you,
one ascending to heaven, and one that falls;

leaving you, not really belonging to either,
not quite so dark as the house that is silent,
not quite so surely calling the eternal
as what becomes star each night and climbs—

leaving you (inexpressibly to untangle)
your life, fearful and huge and ripening,
so that now bounded and now beyond measure,
it becomes alternately stone in you and star.

—Rilke

Chapter 3: The Need to Get Out

The Panther
In the Jardin des Plantes, Paris

His gaze has from the passing by of bars
become so weary it holds nothing more.
To him it seems there are a thousand bars
and behind the thousand bars no world.

The soft pace of powerful supple strides,
that in the smallest circles turn him,
is like a dance of strength around a center,
in which dazed a great will stands.

Only sometimes the pupil's curtain pushes
silently open—then an image will go inside,
go through the limbs' tense stillness—
and in the heart, cease to be.

— Rilke

No Time Like the Present

By the fall of 1962, getting drunk to the point of puking and lying on
my back on the floor with my head in the dark of the closet was no longer
fun. Instead, when I wanted to get high, I went down to the basement of
Dunster House and walked beyond the student storage area along the
underground passageway beneath a fat, white, insulated hot air duct, and
at a certain place, without breaking stride, suddenly reached up with one
hand above a pipe, grabbed a small package wrapped in foil, slipped it in
my jacket pocket, and kept on walking, past where Paul had shown me the
entrance to a labyrinth: a network of steam tunnels that carried warmth in
winter to far-flung radiators in all the major buildings on campus.

Upstairs in our room my friends and I pulled down the shades. We were, after all, the only students we knew in the dorm who were smoking marijuana, so it was like a secret society. The usual ritual was to sit in a circle, unwrap the stash, roll a few joints, light one up and pass it around among friends—like Dave, a lanky biochemistry major from St. Louis, and Carl, my roommate from Atlanta—each taking a toke and saying things like "Hey man, this weed is outa sight." I almost singed my fingers when I passed the roach to Paul, the Darien-bred explorer of exotic drugs who lived down the hall and had bought the pot from an unknown "friend" who was his connection.

As the evening wore on we often retreated into worlds of our own introspection. One night I turned on WGBH, the public radio station, and listened to a talk by Alan Watts on *The Way of Zen,* his introduction for Westerners. Stoned as I was, it grabbed my attention. Tuning in to the present moment… it made perfect sense. Yes, perfect sense… that was it. Everything was perfect, just as it was in this moment… the flickering candle… the barking dog in the distance… but the moment kept changing… I couldn't hold onto it… and what was enlightenment? I took another drag and kept on thinking.

Strict Zen training at a monastery in Japan was not that appealing: waking up at 4 a.m. and sitting motionless for hours trying to solve koans, spiritual riddles like "What is the sound of one hand clapping?" But maybe there were other ways. Supposedly far more potent than pot, psychedelics like psilocybin and LSD were rumored to be on the horizon, offering deep spiritual experiences at the drop of a tablet. The question was how to get them. According to Paul, "My connection says acid can't yet be bought on the street. But the word is that two psychology professors are doing psychedelic research on volunteer subjects."

"Hey man, let's look into it," I replied, and took one last drag.

Paul asked around and invited me to join him at an unpublicized talk with Richard Alpert and Timothy Leary, held in a well-upholstered college conference room. Nicely dressed in gray suit and tie, the balding Richard Alpert was the gregarious one, smiling and chatting with everyone.

He introduced a quiet man in a light brown suit, jacket unbuttoned, the crew-cut Timothy Leary, who nodded and sat down, mysteriously silent in a big leather chair at the front of the room, as if about to give a talk.

Leary stared into space and said nothing for several minutes. Then he made a series of calm pronouncements interspersed with portentous pauses, as if reporting from an unknown planet somewhere in the vast space beyond the solar system, each time trailing off afterwards, his words like spreading ripples in a pool of mystic silence. "We are free… to choose… the games we play… we are children… of the universe." No doubt he was high, most likely on acid or mushrooms.

I don't remember much of what Leary said; maybe his words didn't matter so much as his state of mind. Paul and I hung around afterwards, and Alpert, the future Ram Dass, who would write *Be Here Now,* introduced us to Leary, the future charismatic psychedelic guru, who would advise us to "Tune in, turn on, drop out." Leary shook my hand politely, briefly meeting my gaze without a word.

Unfortunately, from our point of view, Alpert and Leary were no longer accepting student volunteers to take part in their clinical research. The university was not happy about negative publicity and potential bad trips, and six months later they were both fired. For Paul and me the realization sank in: we would have to find other ways to satisfy our curiosity about psychedelics, which seemed to promise a transcendent high where the present moment opened like a door into magical realms.

*

The Cuban Missile Crisis

Since childhood my generation had crawled under our desks during air raid drills to huddle in fear of the atom bomb. Now the world was actually poised on the edge of nuclear destruction, and there was nothing we could do but wait as Russian warships steamed toward JFK's blockade of

Castro's Cuba, where U.S. spy planes had discovered new missile installations. So I went to an emergency meeting of The Warning Bell, a student anti-war group, and listened to young activists discuss the desperate situation. After a while I spoke up: "We've talked enough. Let's get out on the street and protest."

"Yes, but first we need to write a statement defining our position. Then print leaflets and make signs with slogans." Tad Brightman, future sociology professor and chair of the meeting, earnestly intense behind horn-rim glasses, knew how things should be done. "No way we can be ready to protest until Saturday."

"Saturday may be too late," I replied. "The crisis is now." As the debate over position and tactics dragged on, I walked out of the meeting and back to the dorm, where Paul was putting a knapsack into the back seat of his Volkswagon Beetle. "What's up?" I said.

"I'm getting out of the city. It may be a target."

"Wait for me." I went to my room, grabbed a few things, and soon we were on the road. The turnpike unspooled before us as the little beige car zipped along toward the forests of western Massachusetts.

"We can stay overnight in Stockbridge," said Paul, his eyes peering straight ahead, fixed on the road. "I know some people there."

It turned out "there" was Austen Riggs, a mental health center that looked like a woodsy retreat for the well-to-do, with warm carpeting, comfortable furniture, and landscaped gardens. Paul said James Taylor had stayed there. We slept on living room sofas in that comfortable, open asylum, where no one seemed much concerned about the prospect of nuclear war. Maybe they had other things to worry about.

The next morning our portable radio announced that the Russian ships had turned back, to our great relief, so we drove home the way we had come, this time with me behind the wheel. It was then that Paul, who had gone to Andover, an exclusive prep school, and liked to wear a rumpled sport coat, began to share some of his expert knowledge about dextromethorphan, an active ingredient in certain cough medicines that was supposed to have hallucinogenic effects. "A hipster goes into a drugstore and pretends to cough—eh, eh—(covering his mouth)—and says he needs some cough medicine. Then he takes it outside and drinks the whole bottle. He sees visions, man. It's crazy!"

"Did you ever try it?"

"Sure. It tastes sickeningly sweet, but it works."

For some reason I don't quite understand—maybe because the reprieve from imminent nuclear annihilation made me feel, for the moment, invulnerable—I abandoned my usual caution about unfamiliar drugs and said "OK, I'll try it." At the next strip mall with a drugstore I pulled over and purchased a glass bottle of pink cough syrup. On the label in tiny letters it listed dextromethorphan as the active ingredient. "Here goes!" I drank the whole bottle, almost puking from the thick, sticky, sweet medicinal liquid, viscous as molasses. Then I resumed driving. Before long I was gleefully weaving back and forth from lane to lane down the almost vacant highway.

"I think I better drive," said Paul.

"Maybe you're right," I replied.

Back at the dorm, I lay down and closed my eyes, watching the flimsy cartoons of my imagination, seeing right through them. It felt as if I'd been kicked in the head by a mule. Never again for this stuff, I mused.

Many years later, after the fall of the Berlin Wall revealed classified Russian records, I read that worldwide destruction was barely averted when, despite being shaken by warning depth charges from American Navy destroyers, a Russian submarine captain defied an order to launch his nuclear missiles.

*

Motorcycle Misadventure

Alan, a thin pre-med student with a slight goatee whom I knew from high school years, pulled up in front of Alcott Hall, where tendrils of ivy clung to age-old brick walls, and offered me a ride on the back of his motorcycle. We took a spin around town. It was refreshing to feel the brisk wind on my face and weave through traffic with ease. When we got back I said, "Wow. That was cool. I'd like to get me a motorcycle."

"I might be willing to sell you this one," said Alan, who always seemed to be in the know. "I've got my eye on a newer model."

"What kind of bike is it?" I asked, looking at the dark olive frame with its black rubber tires, leather saddle, and hefty metal engine.

"It's an NSU, a German brand with a great reputation. I don't remember what the letters stand for, but I read that in 1956 an NSU set the motorcycle speed record of 211 mph at Bonneville Flats in Utah."

"No kidding! I don't think I want to go that fast."

"Don't worry, that was a supercharged model."

"How much do you want for this one?"

"How much have you got?"

"I guess about… $250 in my savings account."

"It's worth more than that, but it might need some work. Sometimes it's a little hard to start. So it's yours for two-fifty cash."

"It's a deal," I said, and soon I was riding the NSU. At first it started after just a few tries, but it kept getting worse until in a few weeks it took many cranks with my boot on the starter for the engine to catch. Alan referred me to Speedo Repairs, a small shop in Boston, to get it fixed.

The place looked a bit sleazy, with dirty rags, overstuffed trash cans, an outdated pin-up calendar on the wall, the smell of oil on concrete, and old motorcycle parts everywhere. The grimy mechanic with the skull and crossbones tattoo on his bicep checked the bike out and said it needed a valve job for $120. More than I could afford, but I needed to get it fixed. I went back to Alan and suggested that since the engine had a bigger problem than he let on, he could help pay for the repairs. He didn't agree that he owed me anything. "I told you it needed some work," he said, turning his hand palm up.

"Not that much work."

He pulled on his small goatee. "I don't think I'm obliged to pay for it… but if you need some help, I can chip in." And he gave me a check for $60.

I liked riding the bike along Soldiers Field Road beside the Charles River and over the Western Avenue Bridge onto Memorial Drive, as below a scull slid swiftly forward with each stroke of its slender oars. I gripped the handlebars with the breeze in my face, alert to the feel and sound of the throbbing engine beneath me as trees and houses swept by under the distant clouds of the all-embracing sky.

But only a month later I went to get my motorcycle in the student parking lot and saw that some cables had been cut. Loose nuts and bolts were lying around on the ground. That's strange, I thought. Why would anyone do that? Thinking it must have been vandalism, I screwed the nuts back on, patched the cables, and thought no more of it—until a few weeks later when I went out to the parking lot again. Once more, the same cables had been cut, the same bolts unscrewed. But this time there was a gaping space in the frame. The whole engine was gone.

Gradually, it all fell into place. The first attempt had been called off half-way, maybe because a watchman or someone was coming. The second time the thieves took the engine, as they had planned, and not the frame. But wouldn't it be easier to take the whole thing? Who would steal just the engine of a rare German motorcycle, and why? My thoughts went back to the mechanic at the Speedo shop. He knew my address from the repair order, and could easily install the NSU engine on another frame, so where it came from couldn't be traced.

I took the empty frame back to the shop and told the grimy mechanic about the stolen engine. He gave no obvious sign of guilt, but looked down to the left and said with indifference, "Too bad. That can happen."

With only suspicion and no solid evidence, I knew it would be pointless to accuse him. "How much will you give me for the frame?"

"$25," he said. It was way too low—but what could I do? I refuse to get ripped off like this again, I thought. Without a word, I took it in cash and walked out the door to the end of the block and then down the hard stairs to the underground rattle and clank of the subway.

As I rode the train home, I might have imagined what the mechanic would say if I confronted him. He might rub his hand on his greasy

44

overalls, then pick up a wrench and point it vaguely in my direction. "I didn't steal that engine, but whoever did deserved it more than you. He must have known motorcycles. He knew what he was doing, while you're just a college kid, a know-it-all who knows nothing about the vintage bike he bought with his parents' money." And he would be partly right—except that I made that money selling Christmas wreaths door-to-door for three or four years.

*

Smarter Than We Thought

It was a brisk autumn day and a steady wind pushed a stream of clouds across the sky, carrying a blackbird forward in a straight line with no need to flap its wings. Then the bird did a wide U-turn and flew upwind, flapping with a strong effort to go back where it came from—whereupon it turned around again and rode the stream of air downwind. The blackbird was like a kid with a sled climbing a steep hill for the thrill of streaking back down. That bird is having fun, I mused, with the sport of riding the wind. Maybe birds are smarter than we thought.

Pursuing my interest in understanding the mind with a concentration in psychology, I decided my research project would undertake a novel experiment: teaching a pigeon to count. It didn't have to be spectacular— from one to five would be good enough to prove the point. In those days, the mid-sixties, academic psychology was trying very hard to be "scientific." B. F. Skinner and others had reduced the quest to understand the mind to the experimental study of behavior as reinforced by rewards or punishments, which in my college lab meant a pigeon in a cage pecking at a lever when a light flashed on, to be rewarded with birdseed. All I had to do was train the pigeon to peck in response to a certain number of flashes, but not to a different number.

I believed the pigeon could do it. For a week, each day at 10 a.m. I entered the sterile, florescent-lit lab, with its wooden tables and rows of pigeons in cages, to test the lively gray subject of my experiment, as it bobbed its head around, trapped in its solitary wire-mesh enclosure. Despite my setting the birdseed to spill into the tray only when the pigeon pecked the lever after the stimulus light flashed twice, there was no apparent pattern to its pecking. Now and then the pigeon would jab at the lever with its small pointed beak, seemingly whenever it felt like it, regardless of the blinking-light stimulus. So one day in the elevator I confided to Professor Hernnstein, my well-groomed advisor in his charcoal-gray suit and maroon tie, "My pigeon is not behaving as predicted. I'm wondering if it might be emotionally disturbed."

Professor Hernnstein paused and looked at me with no facial expression, but steady eyes. "The pigeon is always right," he replied.

I went back to the dorm, sat at my desk, and studied the data, but it remained meaningless. The big orange print on the wall looked down at me quizzically: Paul Klee's "Senecio, or Head of a Man Going Senile," his face a pale blank disk with two red-dot eyes, slightly askew. Then I reviewed my methodology, and eventually realized that the pigeon was not behaving for a very good reason. There was a lack of motivation. It wasn't hungry.

Research revealed that every morning the lab assistant fed all of the pigeons unless the experimenter put a sign on the cage saying DO NOT FEED—which I had not done. Starving the pigeon to make it behave did not occur to me. So I wrote up a report portraying the failed experiment as a learning experience, an investigation leading to the explanation of puzzling behavior, and managed to get a B.

But maybe experimental psychology was not for me. I just wasn't hungry enough for that kind of knowledge. Rather, I felt for the pigeons pecking for birdseed in cages, the mice running through mazes to avoid electric shocks and find a bit of cheese despite all obstacles, even with their sense of smell removed—innocent animal prisoners of academic masters, working tirelessly to avoid starvation. Yes, the pigeon was always right. I walked out the door of the lab and did not return.

Eventually, research would show that pigeons can count, as well as navigate, and some birds, like parrots and crows, can also use tools.

Meanwhile, that spring I went on long walks amid the green buds of reborn trees, and listened to joyful birds singing and flying from branch to branch, celebrating the outdoor freedom of countless possibilities.

The Alchemist

Strangely smiling the alchemist pushed
the flask away, which smoked half-pacified.
Now he knew what he still needed
for the very illustrious object

to arise within it. He needed time,
thousands of years for him and this glass pear
in which it bubbled, stars in his brain
and in his consciousness at least the sea.

The immensity that he wanted
he let loose into the night. It turned
back to God and in its original measure;

but he, mumbling like a drunkard,
lay over the secret drawer and coveted
the scrap of gold that he possessed.

—Rilke

*

Mind is the Key

To behaviorists the mind was a "black box," beyond our understanding. All science could do was correlate its output, behavior, with its input, stimuli. But could that approach really give us an explanation, or was it an over-simplification? I began to believe that mind was the key: we needed to unlock the black box. Neurophysiology (now neuroscience) and cybernetics (now artificial intelligence) might eventually provide some physical clues. Meanwhile, there was much-maligned subjective experience and introspection—which for me might include searching inside through poetry. And maybe becoming a therapist, going into clinical psychology?

I began volunteering at a mental hospital, visiting patients and talking to them. One was Grace, a slim and elegant middle-aged lady in a dark dress who welcomed me warmly and walked me around the ward, introducing me to the other patients like a gracious host giving a dinner party. What could possibly be wrong with her? She was so much easier to talk to than the others, who seemed preoccupied with their own inner worlds.

I also talked to Suzanne, a young woman about my age, with long light brown hair and a subdued, distracted manner. Wringing her hands she haltingly shared the story of her breakdown—something not quite describable had happened to her after getting off a plane without her family in New York. She said she felt lost and alone. I thought maybe if we talked further she might find more trust. I began to look forward to visiting these two women and saw them as friends, feeling they both had good hearts.

Then one day I walked into the ward and saw Grace sitting silent and alone, with a sad, drawn face. I sat down with her, but she could hardly speak—it was as if she had become another person. It took about 20 minutes to learn that she was now in the "down" phase of manic depression (drugs like lithium were not yet in wide use). For the next half hour I tried to help Grace focus on lifting her spirits, then wished her well and went to look for Suzanne, who seemed nowhere around. A nurse directed me to another part of the ward, and as I went down the hall I heard a woman screaming from a room with a small barred window. Inside was Suzanne, stalking around in a hospital gown, pounding the walls of her padded cell with her fists, her long tangled hair obscuring a grimace that made her face grotesque, screaming like a wild animal confined in the cage of her mad rage.

A heavy gray sadness welled up in me. My two friends were now lost in the bottomless black box, which had closed over their hearts. I began to feel I got too emotionally involved with people's problems to become a psychotherapist.

But if mind was the key, how to transform the mind? Earlier that year, in the room of a shaggy student, I had noticed the picture of a black and white Chinese brush painting above his desk. "What does that mean?" I asked.

"The Tao—the Way," he replied as if sharing a secret. "Both yin and yang entwined."

Some weeks later I decided to check out a Vedanta group on the third floor of an old building in Boston. The exotic talk of the bliss of the Brahma-world put me off a little, and the young man sitting in a trance with his eyes rolled back, deep in yogic meditation, seemed a bit much. But I felt a spiritual energy that seemed genuine.

Then one night a long-haired young man with scraggly beard, loose clothes, and colorful beads, the first real hippie I'd met, crashed on our couch after wandering all day by the river. He looked like a hobo Jesus. Intrigued, after chatting a bit, I asked "What's your philosophy of life?"

His answer was simple: "Say yes to everything!"

Skeptical, I stroked my chin, mulling it over. Taken literally that might be impractical—should one say yes to foolhardiness, or even evil?—but his radical attitude of embracing life in all its imperfection was sort of inspiring.

The pigeon is always right, I recalled, and went on taking long walks and looking at the world more closely. When spring finally came, I sat on the grass by a tree, and wrote a poem:

> The tree in the courtyard
> stood through the stiff season, desolate and strong.
> We crawled out of our holes and threw crumbs in the cold.
> No birds.
> Numb fingers with nothing to hold.

A stubborn wish in the emptiness—
or if you prefer,
an intricate engraving on the hard air.
We waited, and slowly
the sun woke the buried world.
But long after the river ran free,
and the breeze had eased our hearts,
the tree still held out against the season.
Then gently the rain
bent down to its root,
the wind
loosened its limbs,
and slow as sunrise,
soft as dusk,
the tree came forth,
seeped through itself,
and spring sweetly exploded
in a jungle of buds.

I began to see that meaning did not have to be like an iceberg, mostly underwater, as Hemingway supposedly said, but more like a tree, connecting earth and sky, half above and half below the ground, showing itself and reaching high, but with roots that go deep down.

*

The Wisdom of Experience

It wasn't Paul, who had turned me on to marijuana, but Joshua, my pre-med friend from high school, who called and said, "Want to come to a party with Allen Ginsberg after the reading at Eliot House?"

"Of course." The reading itself was bizarre. Ginsberg did not read from *Howl*, only some quirky new poems in his delightfully human semi-prophetic style—but then he turned the microphone over to his younger, rambunctious lover Peter Orlovsky, with a long, light-brown ponytail, who proceeded to read an interminable, unabashed, sexually explicit piece, as if a college dining room were the perfect place for such revelations. Ha! Maybe it was, for along with the crowd I stood up and cheered for his sheer outrageous bravado.

Later, at the party, about ten of us lay on the floor of a darkened off-campus attic room, smoking pot while a strobe light flickered. Eventually a loud student voice announced, "That light is freaking me out!" Someone hustled to turn off the strobe, but the voice still muttered in the darkness. Then lying on his back with his beard flowing over his chest, Allen Ginsberg, who once lamented that "the best minds" of his generation were "destroyed by madness," now calmly intoned, as if composing a poem on the spot, "Blinking light having gone, we are still ourselves."

*

Compassionate Listening

I learned a lot in my sophomore year, but my grades were not so good. The main problem was math. I persisted in taking calculus despite the fact that I had stopped studying the subject or even going to class. Cramming before the exam was not enough. I got a D in the first term of Advanced Calculus, then took the second term for an E (Harvard's version of an F). Throw in a D for physics and that was that.

Influenced by Bill Gordon's advice to study hard science first, I had the idea that to combine psychology with cybernetics I needed a background in science and math, but was not actually interested in solving differential equations.

Or maybe I was exploring how it felt to flunk.

Anyway, I'd already decided to take a year off.

Instead of studying, sometimes I went to a music practice room in the basement of Dunster House, where I'd close the door and improvise contemplative, wandering lines on the Steinway piano, without much musical cohesion. Once as I left, a graduate English tutor of medium build in jacket and tie, with tousled brown hair, passed by and asked if I was having a difficult time.

"Why did you think so? I was just meditating at the piano."

"Most people are more purposeful in their practice."

"Well, I have to admit I haven't been studying much. Maybe I'm still looking for my purpose in life."

"What do you most like doing?"

"Being creative. Writing poetry."

"There's a book you might like, Rilke's *Letters to a Young Poet*. I can loan you my copy."

That book, with its direction to go into yourself as a creative source, regardless of what others may say, gave meaning to my quandary. And it began my fascination with Rilke, leading me to his *New Poems*, with their careful observation and spiritual depth.

The tutor had listened, not just to the music, but to the inner search where it came from—and I was grateful.

When my parents learned I was on probation, my father wrote the college a letter that explained I was taking science and math to please him because he had gone to MIT, but my real interest was creative writing. Despite the overestimation of himself as a role model, his recognition of my writing was touching.

For once, I felt he understood.

*

Morning Glory Seeds

At the time of the solar eclipse on July 20, 1963, I was living for the summer in the third-floor Synectics office and workshop on River Street, reading about the creative process of scientists and inventors, such as the story of how the organic chemist August Kekule discovered the circular structure of the six-carbon-atom Benzene ring from a daydream of a snake biting its own tail—actually an age-old symbol of primordial unity, the *ouroboros*.

My interest in psychedelics was pretty much dormant, due to the lack of supply at the time, until I read an article about the hallucinogenic properties of morning glory seeds, which contain lysergic acid amide, a relative of LSD. The variety was Heavenly Blue, in seed packets from the gardening store. There was only one problem—they may be poisonous and coated with pesticide. So I followed the article's instructions and boiled the seeds first.

Fred, a future psychiatrist in khakis and button-down shirt, was keeping me company, but did not ingest. As I lay there waiting to see what would happen, a pipe joint jutting out from the ceiling began to dissolve. I had been hoping for visions, and that seemed like a step in the right direction. Then Fred winced and said he didn't like the Sonny Rollins saxophone solo blaring from the stereo. As I continued to listen, the sound of one of my favorite records gradually became ugly, and I began to feel sick to my stomach. I took off the record, and noticed that Fred's face looked pinched and frowning. Could he be trusted to be there for me?

Everything around, the walls, the floor, the furniture, looked drab and flat. I felt really bad and had to lie down. Then I looked up at the clock on the wall. The hands were no longer moving. The clock had stopped. Time was intolerable. This must be hell, I thought. To be stuck in a frozen moment of ugly existence in a body destined to die, feeling unbearably terrible. Then came the fear. What if I never got out of this? I'd be condemned to eternal nausea, committed to a mental institution. I recalled the novel by John-Paul Sartre where existence itself makes Roquentin feel sick.

But if this was all in my mind—why couldn't it change? I remembered the book I left in the other room, *The Psychedelic Experience*, by Leary, Alpert, and Metzner, a manual for LSD trips with instructions adapted from the *Tibetan Book of the Dead,* an age-old guide for those in the *bardo* between death and rebirth. I vaguely remembered a couple of lines saying to let go of attachment and aversion, your perception is all a projection of your own mind. So I decided to go with the flow. As I began to relax, my nausea gathered together and all my bad feelings rose up and exploded in a burst of vomit. I felt cleansed, relieved, purified. After cleaning up with a towel, I turned toward Fred, who now looked like a caring friend.

"Are you OK?" he said.

"Now I feel better. Man, this whole trip has changed."

My claustrophobic self had dissolved into a new, more expansive identity. The drab room now glowed with possibility. I was hip, alive, and open to everything. Bounding out into the street, I rode the subway on a wave of awareness, noticing how each passenger's eyes avoided everyone else's, each one lost in their own private suffering. It was sad for them, but I was glad to be free from the hell I'd been in. From then on the trip was good, but the first part was so bad that I never took morning glory seeds again. Why take poison to get high? Instead my path led further into poetry, and later, Zen.

*

Archaic Torso of Apollo

We cannot know his extraordinary head
where the eyes' apples ripened. But
his torso still glows like a gas-lamp candelabra,
in which his gaze, only turned down low,

holds firm and shines. Otherwise the curve
of the chest could not dazzle you, and in the gentle turn
of the loins a smile could not go toward
that center which bore procreation.

Otherwise this stone would stand defaced and short
below the shoulder's translucent fall
and not glisten so like a wild beast's fur;
and would not break out from all its borders
like a star: for there is no place
that does not see you. You must change your life.

—Rilke

Part Two: Going Beyond

Chapter 4: Time Off in New York

Memory

And you wait, looking for the one
that increased your life without end;
the powerful, the outrageous,
the awakening of the stones,
deep, facing you.

It dawns on the bookshelf,
the volumes in gold and brown,
and you think of the lands you traveled through,
the images and the dress
of women lost again.

And then you suddenly know: that was it.
You rise, and before you stands
one past year of
fear and form and prayer.

—Rilke

A Long Way to Go

In the gathering dusk I walked along Massachusetts Avenue talking with Carl, my roommate from Atlanta, when an old gray sedan came up from behind and passed by with a low-pitched chant, repeating the N-word as if it were a verbal automatic weapon. I was shocked. Being white from suburban New England, I had never heard anything like it.

Carl said, "Where I come from that stuff happens a lot."

As the car drove on the pitch of the chant faded down and away. Even in Cambridge, I thought.

Later that year in rural Maryland I was standing on the edge of the road holding a sign picketing a fast-food restaurant, supporting a sit-in, when from the distance a black Pontiac approached, speeding up as it came closer. Then it veered onto the shoulder of the road where I stood, heading right at me, and quickly grew larger, as its bright chrome grille burst forward toward me. I stepped back leaning away, and the right headlight just missed me. The car zoomed by with two young guys in black leather jackets and ducktail haircuts, laughing as they stepped on the gas and tore down the road to nowhere, leaving me breathing their dust.

*

March on Washington

"I hope you break a leg," the lady said.
Was that the showbiz good-luck wish
or just the opposite?
In August I rode the bus for hours
to where a hundred thousand people
were streaming in, filling the National Mall
around the long and placid pool
from the embrace of the Lincoln Memorial
to the towering Washington Monument.

Fresh from southern sit-ins,
a coterie of spirited young African Americans
marched as if dancing in, clapping and singing
"Ain't gonna let nobody turn me around,
turn me around, turn me around,

ain't gonna let nobody turn me around,
I'm gonna keep on a-walkin',
keep on a-talkin',
marchin' up to freedom land—"
and the whole crowd rose with applause.

When the Reverend Martin Luther King, Jr.
took the podium, all listened as one,
and his words soared high as mighty birds:
"I have a dream, I have a dream!"
Now in close-up black and white
his image fills glowing screens around the world,
and his powerful voice still calls us
beyond the chokehold of the past
here on Earth to breathe free at last.

*

Harlem Education Project

In September 1963, when I took a year off from college and moved to the Lower East Side, there was already a picture in my mind of the shoes that I wanted: a pair of black leather work boots with laces up the front, sturdy shoes that were ready for anything.

After walking up six flights to the rundown two-bedroom apartment my roommate and I had rented, I wandered through the kitchen into the small living room with its beat-up wood floor and window with a wrought iron fire escape. To my surprise, when I pulled open the door, there on the bare floor was a pair of black shoes like the ones I had seen in my mind. One at a time, I put them on and laced them up—and they fit, a bit big, but well enough.

From then on I wore those tough shoes with my denim jeans and jacket on the streets of New York, whether walking to the neighborhood bakery to supplement my oatmeal diet with an occasional bialy, or trudging back home after nursing a tall glass of beer (the one-drink minimum) through two sets of jazz at the Five Spot Café, entranced by the midnight sounds of Thelonious Monk. Those tough shoes took me down stairs into the subway and the Van Cortlandt Park train to my part-time job delivering mail to professors at Columbia University, and later all the way to 142nd Street in Harlem, where I tutored a ten-year-old boy in reading.

As Damien struggled to decipher the schoolbook descriptions of blonde suburban kids and their puppy, it became clear why reading was not engaging him. If only we could find something he was interested in.... Well, under his bed was a cardboard box full of mica-specked rocks from a vacant lot. He and his friend Booker liked to do "experiments" by smashing one dusty rock against another, breaking it open to reveal the tiny sparkling stars of quartz inside.

I went with them on their next expedition to the vacant lot, and after watching one of their experiments, suggested we go to the children's library and get some books about the hidden wonders of rocks. But tutoring reading was still slow going. One day after school I followed the program's recommendation and went to confer with Damien's teacher, a middle-aged woman in a maroon dress and matronly necklace, her dark brown hair carefully done, who took pride in her work. After we talked for a while and I told her about trying to find books Damien was interested in, she bristled and said, "I've been teaching for 20 years. I don't need a college student to give me advice."

In any case I was now spending more time doing things with the kids, rather than tutoring reading. To broaden their perspective I began taking them on field trips, to the Statue of Liberty, the Empire State Building, and once to an exhibit of Pop Art sculpture by Claes Oldenberg—an eight-foot-long giant toothpaste tube in the middle of the gallery floor, a soft plastic pay phone sagging from the wall, and other everyday objects transformed by giant size or unusual materials. It was like Alice in Wonderland with a touch of Salvador Dali. I'm not sure what Damien and Booker thought of the Pop Art. Curious yet a little bewildered, they didn't say much.

A month or so later, someone broke into the office of the Harlem Education Project, which ran the tutorial program, and painted the walls, the furniture, the typewriter, the globe of the world—all of it black. Was it a political statement inspired by the burgeoning Black Power movement— or could it be the anti-white gang of Blood Brothers I had heard about?

The tutorial program continued, and I went on visiting Damien and Booker. But sometimes walking alone through the streets of Harlem, I felt twinges of fear. And I wondered—despite my good intentions, was I inadvertently reinforcing the false stereotype of African Americans needing a white person to teach them? As the movement evolved from civil rights to Black Power, it was becoming less clear what place I might have in it, beyond general support. Each time I finished tutoring, I walked back down Lenox Avenue to the subway stop, placing my sturdy work boots on each step, one after the other, down the long stairs into the world underground, and took the train home, the Seventh Avenue Express toward Flatbush and New Lots Avenue.

*

Expect the Unexpected

It was a long subway ride from the Lower East Side, but I needed the money, just enough to get by, so in the fall of 1963 I took a part-time job at Columbia University. One sunny October day as I sat with my bag of campus mail near the top of the granite steps leading up to the majestic Roman columns at the front of Low Memorial Library, taking a break from delivering letters to English professors, I looked up and saw a balding figure in a well-tailored suit emerge from a door in the shadows between two columns. There was something familiar about him. Could it

60

be former President Eisenhower, now president of Columbia University? He walked part way down the high and broad stone steps, then paused and gazed out over the campus to survey the realm.

I looked again—it was really him, standing about twenty-five feet away from me. Dwight D. Eisenhower, the man whose smiling face had been on a campaign button in my childhood, with the homespun slogan "I Like Ike." Now I disagreed with him politically, but Eisenhower's presence commanded attention. His gaze seemed to reach far into the distance, over the wide courtyard of the campus on Morningside Heights and beyond to the gritty yet towering panorama of New York City, perhaps the de facto cultural and economic capital of the American nation he presided over during its rise to unprecedented world power—which some might call empire. In that pause for an overarching view, what was he thinking? Eisenhower lowered his gaze and continued down the steps, and I stood up to deliver the campus mail.

In the last five years my perception of America and the world had certainly changed. Later that day as I rode underground on the South Ferry train to 14th Street and transferred for the Lower East Side, refuge of immigrants, artists, and writers, it seemed clear that the Eisenhower era was over. For years beneath the placid suburban surface there had been signs of unease. In the South there were struggles over segregation, the Russians had put Sputnik in orbit, and as kids we hid under our desks in fear of the nuclear war that any moment might obliterate us all in a world-wide chorus of mushroom clouds. What could I do? Putting most of my stuff into storage, I took a year off from college to think things over.

We were now in the reign of the youthful, adventurous John F. Kennedy. With mistakes like trying to invade Cuba at the Bay of Pigs it was not exactly Camelot, but imaginative initiatives like the Peace Corps and the space program inspired our generation to move in new directions. While not quite ready to follow the path of the wandering hippie who advised me "Say yes to everything," the next autumn I found myself living on East 10th Street and Avenue B, in a sixth-floor walk-up with a bathtub on stilts in the kitchen and toilet in the closet. Layers of worn-through linoleum exposed the geologic history of the kitchen floor. Each room had a low dark hole in the baseboard, a gnawed-out entrance, as if rodents were the real tenants. Even the rent of $46 a month was paid through a hole in a plywood wall, in a nondescript building in a nameless neighborhood further downtown. Subsistence was on daily oatmeal and inexpensive meals of rice and beans at ethnic restaurants on Avenue C.

My roommate and I devoted our time to exploring whatever avenues opened, often under the influence of smoking marijuana. All the way through Andy Warhol's movie of a man sleeping, the entire six hours, we sat there eating bananas and gazed at the man on the bed peacefully breathing, even as the other four people in the audience gradually left.

The camera was motionless for an hour at a time. Staring at the black and white picture was hypnotic. At one point in my perception the white sleeping figure surrounded by shadows suddenly turned into a black abstract pattern on the flat white screen. It was a figure-ground reversal, like the white vase on a black background that can be seen as two black silhouettes facing each other. As I began to look around the room to see if the reversal might spread to the world beyond the screen, the pattern switched back to simply a white man sleeping.

Later, walking back home, I became painfully aware of my racing mind. I could only focus on this awareness for a few seconds, then fell back into the flow of my thoughts, to escape from being so intensely present. But watching that movie gave me a glimpse of how most of the time I was absorbed in figures of thought, ignoring the ground of basic awareness.

On another occasion, an anonymous notice on a bulletin board announced a Happening at a certain date, time, and address. Upon showing up I was led to a room with a couch, chairs, and a hodgepodge of artistic paraphernalia, including a battered cornet and parts of a manikin, sprawled on the floor. I sat down and waited, but nothing happened. After a while a man in a paint-stained T-shirt and jeans came in, sat on the couch, and began reading a magazine. Eventually he turned to me and said, "You're the only one who came for the Happening. Would you like to go to a party instead?"

This was New York City, where we danced to a jukebox on the sawdust floor of an East 2nd Street bar as the Beatles sang "I Saw Her Standing There,"

New York City, where we stayed up until 4 a.m. and slept until noon, and whatever happened was art and whatever you wrote might be poetry,

New York City, where you could hear the lonesome cry of a violin down the hall or bedsprings thumping in the apartment above, and during a lecture on Dada suddenly some artists in nifty suits stood up from their chairs, opened umbrellas, and chanted crazy slogans,

New York City, where Allen Ginsberg was expelled from Columbia University for writing "fuck" with his finger on a dusty dorm window, and where a subterranean network of steam tunnels connected most of Columbia's buildings, conducting heat and electricity through the campus on Morningside Heights, the previous site of the Bloomingdale Insane Asylum, and the oldest tunnels, small, hot, and unbearably humid, with exposed electrical wiring, led to the only remaining building from that era, red brick Buell Hall, originally a separate residential facility for the wealthy male mentally ill,

New York City, where in 1860 Walt Whitman with his abundant beard, wide-brim hat, and carpenter's clothes liked to hang out with roustabouts, then join a festive gang of bohemians, artists, and writers at Pfaff's, a basement café under the sidewalk in Soho, while overhead passed the countless footsteps of Broadway, an endless flow of humanity, and Whitman got there by walking two miles from his mother's house in Brooklyn to the East River, where he boarded the Fulton Ferry to ride the waves past tall-masted ships and hardworking tugboats, trading jokes with the deck hands under clouds sailing through the sky—and when Emerson came to visit, Whitman brought him to the Fireman's Hall for a glass of beer.

Later that autumn of 1963, I sat again on the steps of Low Memorial Library, taking my usual break, and noticed some people crowding around a portable radio. A woman cried out, "Kennedy's been shot!" It felt as if I'd been hit in the gut. I ran over to find out what happened, and heard the announcer barely contain his emotions. "The report from Dallas… our president is dead." As sadness welled up through my body I thought of Abraham Lincoln—whom Whitman had mourned at home with his mother in Brooklyn, writing "When Lilacs Last in the Dooryard Bloom'd," and later saw the president's body lying in state at New York City Hall, draped in black with flag at half staff beneath the "spires of Manhattan," before the funeral train rolled on across the country. Now President Kennedy joined Abraham Lincoln in our nation's sad history of violent assassination. Something had begun and was left undone. Though spring might come, nothing would ever be the same.

*

Jazz at the Five Spot

During my year off in the East Village I finally took the time to read *The Way of Zen* by Alan Watts. I liked the emphasis on being present in the moment—it might be the solution to my problem of getting swept away by the express train of my thoughts. The poetic and paradoxical koans and provocative actions of Zen masters were appealing and dramatic, but it seemed like the way of Zen would take ten years in a Japanese monastery to truly practice.

Jazz, on the other hand, was a way of improvising spontaneously in the present moment, and there I was in the Big Apple, where great musicians were playing almost every night. I could walk down to the Five Spot Café on St. Mark's Place and hear Charles Mingus, the creative, outrageous bassist, bandleader, and composer, wailing through "Better Get It in Your Soul" up close and live with his latest small group. Or Sonny Rollins, the great tenor saxophonist, back from his several-year sabbatical when he played alone day and night on the Williamsburg Bridge, now walking around the smoky room between the listeners at their tables, blowing exploratory solos that went on and on, digging down into the source within. Or the legendary mysterious pianist, Thelonious Monk, in a dark felt hat with small brim, idiosyncratic and self-possessed, entranced by the strangely harmonic notes his fingers found on the piano, playing "Blue Monk" or "Evidence," then standing up to do a cool little dance and spin around once, as Charley Rouse constructed a tenor solo, like building together a tower of blocks, both maintaining evocative balance, while I sat at the bar nursing my beer, taking it all in, present in the adventure of the vibrant moment. One night in the break between sets, a ringing came from the empty phone booth beside the bar. When no one responded, on impulse I got up and answered the call. It was Charley Rouse's wife. I walked over and told him matter-of-factly, "Mr. Rouse, your wife wants to talk to you," secretly pleased to be the messenger.

Another night I went over to the West Village to hear John Coltrane playing in an intimate setting at the Half Note. The tiny stage was perched in the middle of the oval bar, so I was looking directly up at Coltrane, a big man in a dark suit with his golden horn, drums on the right and bass on the left. He ripped through extended solo after extended solo, the cascade of notes pouring over me as if I were standing in the midst of a sonic waterfall that was searching for something indescribable, some musical-spiritual revelation that would reverberate right through me from head to toe. When it was over I stumbled out into the street. The concrete sidewalk seemed to echo in my ears with the buzz of sudden silence.

When Ornette Coleman came out with his double album *Free Jazz,* it seemed a door had been opened to play spontaneously, without the harmonic rules that were a problem for me as a student. When I stood and sang with the other kids in elementary-school music class, the teacher, dark hair tied back, came over, leaned toward my ear, and whispered, "Don't sing so loud. You're off-key." Chastised, I lost confidence that I could carry a tune. But I still enjoyed music, especially rhythm.

Now with "free jazz" I sensed the chance for a reprieve. At a Second

Avenue pawn shop I picked up an old brass C-melody saxophone, the size between alto and tenor. When my roommate was out I'd play it in our tiny sixth-floor apartment, improvising freely without regard for chord progressions, expressing my emotions, inspired by Coleman and Coltrane.

Then one night I walked over to a small nightclub on Bleecker Street— it might have been Cafe Wha? or the Bitter End. Upstairs on a small stage Don Cherry, from Ornette Coleman's original quartet, was playing his pocket trumpet. As he leaned into his horn in a loose white shirt with rolled up sleeves, Cherry's slender intensity cast a thoughtful spell on the room. Then a young white guy in a dark sport jacket sat down at the nearby piano and began an atonal, arhythmic accompaniment. This went on for a while, with Cherry patiently persevering on his trumpet as the piano wandered in various directions. Then Cherry suddenly stopped, and with pain in his face looked at the would-be pianist. "You don't know what you're doing," he said.

Later I heard that Ornette's music I liked best, with his early quartet on *The Shape of Jazz to Come* and *Change of the Century*, was mostly in B-flat. It was not atonal but what he called "harmolodic," with harmony that developed organically along with the improvised melody and rhythm, not confined to a predetermined pattern of chord changes. Rather than a new kind of theory, Ornette's approach was an invitation to more flexible improvisation. The musicians were free to follow their intuition while interacting, much as in group improv theater, without a set script. It took practice, intelligence, and awareness to play—and most importantly, listening to each other. To me it was like free verse in poetry, which left behind formal meters and rhyme schemes to explore new realms of creative possibility.

*

The Spirit of Art in New York

In the sixties Manhattan was brewing with offbeat artistic activity. A production of Samuel Beckett's recent play, *Happy Days,* began with Winnie, the main character, buried up to her waist in sand. In the second act she was buried up to her neck, all the while chattering along trying to maintain her spirits. In a later offering, simply entitled *Play*, Beckett's three characters, a man and two women, were three heads, each sticking up from an urn in the dark, speaking only when lit by a spotlight in turn, each telling one side of a triangular story from their previous lives. Off-Broadway, in its production of *Frankenstein* the Living Theater constructed onstage a huge head in profile, with a framework of scaffolding holding up platforms which lit up in turn to portray dramatic scenes in various parts of this giant brain. The climax came with more than a dozen actors in their underwear hanging from the frame and entwined with each other, transforming the construction into an enormous swaying human sculpture seemingly several stories high, a demented Frankenstein monster of twisted mind—a dramatized visual image of how people get so messed up.

In Upper East Side galleries the transition from Abstract Expressionism to Pop Art was gaining momentum. I was particularly taken by Robert Rauschenberg's style of combining abstract splashes and streaks of color with silkscreened images from magazines and newspapers and various found objects mashed together in vibrant collage. About that time I finally called up Ramona, a young woman from Sarah Lawrence College I'd met at a party the previous summer. Intrigued by the subtle sensuality in the way she moved her body when she danced, her hips swaying beneath her loose dress, I had asked for her number. I don't know whether she remembered me, but we agreed to meet, and that eventually led to a ritual kiss on New Year's Eve in Times Square, and before long an erotic adventure in her Bronxville room, where she showed me how standing up. We didn't have a lot in common otherwise, but made a date to meet there again the next weekend.

When I arrived, she was not home. Instead Marilyn, her beautiful dark-haired roommate, invited me in. Over the phone Ramona explained that an old boyfriend unexpectedly came to town and she had to see him. Would I mind spending the evening with her roommate, whose boyfriend was not around? That was OK with me, so Marilyn and I went to a concert and art exhibit by a group of guys in brown suits trying to pass as avant-garde for the college audience. But their attempt at free jazz devolved into "Roll Out the Barrel," and their paintings turned out to be drab geometry.

Back in the room we decided to make something more interesting. Using ordinary materials at hand, starting with a wooden board about one foot by three feet, we made a wild collage, pasting on pictures clipped from magazines and gobs of multicolored yarn hanging in tangles, interwoven with crayon scribblings in crazy patterns. The crowning touch was a cardboard toilet paper tube sticking out from a knot in the wood, labeled "Don't Look Here." If you peeked through the tube you saw a tiny lady posing for a lingerie ad.

Admittedly a Rauschenberg influence was at play. Marilyn liked this concoction so much that she hung it in the college art gallery (where she worked part-time) next to the drab geometry exhibit. On a neatly typed card was her title: "Quintessence of Antithesis." When I came back to look a week later, our spontaneous creation was still there.

One day Ramona came to meet me in a midtown café and gave me a white paper bag that contained a very big chocolate chip oatmeal cookie. She explained that she had a new boyfriend, a schizophrenic violinist who would get jealous if she continued to see me. Actually, I was touched by her kindness in breaking off with me this way. It was a really good chocolate chip cookie—very chewy—and if she wanted to get involved with a jealous schizophrenic, I was not going to contest it.

So I called Eva, my sometime companion at the summer school poetry class. She was home with her family at the start of spring break, and I told her about my current fascination with French New Wave film, especially Truffaut's *The 400 Blows, Shoot the Piano Player,* and *Jules and Jim*, plus Godard's *Breathless* with Jean-Paul Belmondo. And how I sat through

Last Year at Marienbad twice to study the film technique as the camera rolled through the luminous corridors of a claustrophobic old luxury hotel until the concrete balcony crumbled into light. A question in all these might be, should we accept our socially-imposed fate, or could we escape and create a new way of life?

It turned out Eva's father was an executive with a chain of New York theaters that often showed forcign films. She offered to loan me her pass for a week. I jumped at the chance and went to every movie I could, often two each day—up, down, and across the length and breadth of the city—hungry for the black and white montage of the cinema, the bold ray of flickering light dancing its pattern of shadows across the blank white screen of a darkened theater. It seemed like a new kind of poetry. I began to have fantasies of becoming a filmmaker, but was deterred by the prospect of fund-raising—production costs would be a lot more than for writing poetry with a pen on paper. So I went on filling up my notebook with moody introspections:

> Once a drop of rain hit my tongue
> when I was young enough to stick it out.
> Now, hands buried in my pockets
> I stand in a river of darkness,
> trying to remember who I am.
> Far off the still stars
> burn coldly through thin clouds.

I decided to go back to school in the fall and focus on poetry. But first, do something new: pursue my wanderlust and hitchhike through Mexico.

Chapter 5: Alone and Together in Mexico

Lament

Oh, how all is far away
and long gone by.
I believe that star,
which seems to me so bright,
has been dead a thousand years.
I believe, in the boat
that passed,
I heard something fearful said.
In the house a clock
has struck...
In which house?
I want to step out of my heart
under the great sky.
I want to pray.
And one of all the stars
must really still exist.
I believe I know
which one alone
has lasted,
which one like a white city
at the end of a light beam stands in the sky...

—Rilke

A Stranger at Home in Another Land

In the aging building on New York's Second Avenue the long winding stairway was lined with luminous arrows pointing up toward the doctor's office on the third floor, where a man in a white coat and sporting a shaggy mustache answered the knock and ushered me in. Before he could talk, I said, "I'm leaving for Mexico tomorrow morning, and I'm sick with the flu."

"No problem." He opened a cupboard and took out a large jar of white pills and placed it on the table. "Take one of these before you leave and you'll be fine."

I don't know what the pill was—antibiotic, amphetamine, placebo, or something from *Alice in Wonderland*—but it seemed to work. The next morning I felt well enough to go. After nine months of hanging out on the Lower East Side in a seedy sixth-floor walk-up, in the spring of 1964 I was ready for adventure on the road. My driver, a taciturn, wavy-haired student whom I found on an NYU ride board, picked me up in his MG convertible. We drove all day and night (except for a doze by the side of the road in southern Indiana) from New York to Oklahoma, where I took a bus to Dallas and waited three hours for the Greyhound to Mexico City.

In Dallas I walked out of the bus station and stared down the street where tall buildings gave way to a desert beyond the shimmering urban mirage. As the sun continued to rise in the heat of the day, I took refuge in the air-conditioned Dallas Public Library, in cool seclusion among the books, my old companions, and strolled down the aisles until a title caught my eye: *All and Everything* by G. I. Gurdjieff. I'd heard that the author taught a path of awakening from the "dream" of ordinary life through various practices including self-observation. Curious, I took the fat book from the shelf and opened it to a random page—maybe the one where the narrator Beelzebub expresses dismay that cosmic beings traveling through the solar system did not foresee and prevent the disastrous collision of the comet Kondoor with planet Earth, which caused the misfortunes that subsequently plagued humanity. It seemed like just a fantastic fable, until later I read about the scientific evidence for the impact of a comet or asteroid 66 million years ago near Chicxulub, Yucatán, which created a 93-mile wide crater, shrouded the earth in ash, and led to the extinction of most dinosaurs and many other species, leaving the meek to inherit the earth: insects, birds, and the little mouse-like mammals that became our ancestors. And left an unsettling question: when will the next one hit?

That day in the Dallas library I was intrigued enough to wander through Beelzebub's tale like a maze until my reliable watch showed it was time to depart. Feeling that a book this big, kooky, and complicated was not the answer, for me anyway, I slid the heavy tome back into its place on the shelf, resolving to turn away from books like that toward living, direct experience.

In the Greyhound bus we rode through the brush-country plains of southern Texas, and after a brief pause in line were waved over the border between Laredo, on the north side of the Rio Grande, and Nuevo Laredo, on the south. The south side streets were more crowded, lively, and colorful. A mariachi band serenaded the diners at a sidewalk café. Looking out the window, I began to chat with the crew-cut, middle-aged man who had been sitting beside me all the way from Dallas. "Ever been to Mexico before?"

"No," he replied.

"Me neither." I showed him my guidebook, *Mexico on $5 a Day,* and asked, "Where are you headed?"

"I'm going to the Basilica of our Lady of Guadalupe in Mexico City."

"Are you a Catholic?"

"Yes. I'm a priest."

"Oh... but you're not wearing a collar, just ordinary clothes."

"Like you," he said with a smile, then asked, "What brings you to Mexico?"

"Well, it's my first trip out of the country, you know, and I want to experience another culture. And I'd like to explore some pre-Columbian ruins. I read about the Mayans and Aztecs in my anthropology course."

"I'm sure you'll find plenty to explore," the priest said, looking out the window. I wondered whether he would be exploring too, perhaps in a spiritual sense. But not being Catholic, I felt too shy to ask him what might be a personal religious question.

The bus tires hummed on the road as we rolled on through the dry and mountainous regions of northeastern Mexico. Now over the border I felt a bit anxious but free, unattached, released from the weight of the past— or so I thought, gazing at a mesquite tree with my nose on the window, intoxicated with anticipation.

Where the country was open and desolate, I noticed the roads had no center line. With very little traffic, a car drove down the middle of the road until it encountered a car coming down the middle in the other direction— then they both swerved to their right just in time to avoid a head-on collision, and continued on their way.

After a 12-hour ride our Greyhound emerged from wide valleys peppered with yucca and cactus into the gathering mountains of southern Hidalgo, and climbed to the high plateau of historic Mexico City, where the huge metropolis spread like a Spanish colonial octopus in its mountain lair, a dense population of millions cradled by the Sierra Madre, with the great-grandaddy of volcanos, the massive Popocatépetl, the Smoking Mountain, rising in the distance, along with his dormant lost love, Mujer Dormida, the Sleeping Woman.

From the moment we stepped off the bus, what happened in Mexico was different from anything I might have expected. When the priest and I decided to share a ride downtown, I suggested we follow the advice in my guidebook, and not wanting to be taken advantage of, strode past the throng of men who lined the walkway calling out "Taxi!" "Taxi!" But soon there were only the two of us, me with my small pack and the priest with his suitcase, standing on a deserted street in a nondescript residential neighborhood on the outskirts of a vast, unknown city—without a taxi, official or otherwise, anywhere in sight.

It was warm, and the wind blew a crumpled poster past a pothole in the pavement. There were no sidewalks. We walked down the street in one direction but seemed to be going nowhere, so turned and walked back the other way. There was no one to ask for directions. Even a stray dog ignored us as he trotted on. We went back to the bus station and climbed into an unmarked car that the driver with a bushy mustache assured us was a cab. "The Alameda," I said, referring to the central park that I knew was near Juanita's Pensión, the boarding house recommended by my guidebook. After a hair-raising ride we arrived in the center of town, driving around a large rectangular plaza surrounding a peaceful park of lawns, trees, and paths. The driver slowed and looked toward me with eyebrows raised, and I realized my lack of Spanish was already a problem. Pulling out a pocket dictionary I looked up a word, and pointing outside and down said "Aquí!" And "here" was where the driver stopped.

The priest and I parted ways and I walked a couple of blocks to the pensión, where I had a bed in a room with some other students and two meals a day, prepared by Juanita, a motherly woman with gray hair in a bun, wearing a white apron over her house dress. Some of her boarders, like me, were Norteamericanos, just here for the summer, and despite our desire to experience Mexican culture, we tended to hang out together.

There I met "Pancho," a stocky and savvy Italian from Brooklyn; Richard, a pleasantly buttoned-down law student from Boston; plus two women from New York I wanted to get to know: Sally, a Spanish major at Barnard, and Evelyn, an artist from the Lower East Side. One night Pancho, who had been in Mexico for a while, took us out to a bar, where he showed me how to drink tequila with lime and a lick of salt between thumb and forefinger on the back of my hand, then went on to share his expertise by talking about and drinking tequila and other kinds of mescal, distilled from the brilliant agave. He held a bottle up to the light. "See, there's a worm inside. The larva of a moth that lives on the plant." Inspired by this insight, I drank some myself. The pungent liquid was pretty strong stuff. As we wobbled outside, Pancho spied a political poster up high on a lamppost, with three big red letters, PRI. "One-party politics!" he decried, and before long I was boosting him up, not an easy task, to pull down the souvenir. Apparently the Institutional Revolutionary Party (no irony intended) had been in power since 1929.

There was plenty of time each day for exploring the streets, the markets, Chapultepec Park, and the National Museum—especially pre-Columbian art, like a fantastic ceramic animal with a handle on the back of its neck to pour liquid out of its mouth, and the colossal stone heads of Olmec spirits or kings, larger than a man is tall, who had been silent and still for 3,000 years.

But in Mexico 1964, the poor seemed poorer than any I had seen in New York. The sad, worn face of a brown woman in a tattered shawl who looked at me pleadingly and held out her hand was heart-rending. And there were sometimes cultural conflicts. In a crowded market street a tourist snapped a picture of a beggar, and a nearby man in a light gray suit, offended, stood up and made a passionate speech with gestures of protest to the crowd. Another time at the edge of town a well-to-do middle-aged woman with American plates on her car stopped at a gas station and chastised the attendant for not speaking English, as if she were still in Texas. It reminded me of a book I'd read called *The Ugly American,* about clueless, arrogant tourists abroad. The woman sped off and I went back to hitchhiking beside the road.

But cultural friction was only part of the story. On the sidewalk near the park when I stopped two young Mexican women who looked like college students and asked for directions with a few Spanish words and pointing various ways, they were friendly and full of good humor. We chatted part English, part Spanish, exchanging dramatic gestures, and laughed together over our misunderstandings.

I decided I'd better learn some Spanish, at least enough to get by, and signed up for a two-week intensive course taught by Juan Carlos, a dapper dark-haired graduate student in an open-necked white shirt and tan sport jacket who addressed us in fluid Spanish and liked to write on the blackboard. Gradually I picked up a few more phrases to add to "Muchas gracias, señora," when Juanita served us a spicy dinner of rice, beans, and mixed vegetables.

One morning after a few weeks in Mexico I woke up with my bed slowly rocking, like a rowboat in a rough sea, creaking back and forth with the undulating floor. This must be an earthquake, I thought—I'd never been in one before. Cautiously I climbed out of bed and went step by unsteady step toward the door, raising my hands slightly for balance, riding the primordial waves, alert in the moment. How bad would it be?

Even when the rolling eased I was left wondering if and when it would happen again. What can you do when you can't depend on the ground you stand on?

Later that morning at Spanish class, Juan Carlos abandoned the usual grammatical exercises and, seeming a bit tipsy, took a piece of chalk and drew sketches of a house and yard and a map of Mexico on the blackboard. "This is where I live," he said slowly in English, pressing the last crumb of chalk onto the sketch of his house, "Aquí es donde vivo." Maybe he had downed a few drinks to celebrate surviving another earthquake in the shadow of the great volcano.

That day, walking the streets of Mexico City, 7,200 feet high, and looking toward the mountains, I realized that back home in the U.S., with my Levi jacket and wispy young beard, I felt out of place, kind of a beatnik nonconformist, whereas here, where people accepted me as different since I was a foreigner, I felt more at home.

That may be part of the reason I traveled to Mexico after a year off from school. If I could have found the money I might have gone to Europe, as many college students did. But to me Europe was the Western Tradition, and I wanted to get away from it. Or I might have gone to Mississippi to work for civil rights, and maybe even died a martyr, like Chaney, Schwerner, and Goodman, the three young men murdered by the Klan that summer. But in Mississippi I would be marked as a "carpetbagger," a Yankee intruder from out of state.

Having grown up in the chilly winters of New England with its heritage of pilgrims, puritans, and witch hunts, balanced by writers like Emerson, Thoreau, and Emily Dickinson, the prospect of laid-back sunshine south of the border appealed to me. And I was drawn to exploring the ancient mysteries of pre-Columbian ruins and the jungles of Chiapas. In an anthropology course I had learned about the great civilizations of the Mayans and Aztecs, yet was puzzled by their practice of human sacrifice. Was it sincerely religious, or a brutal way of maintaining ruling class power—or both? In any case, I was curious to learn more about indigenous American cultures and their tragic experience of European conquest. But ultimately, why I went to Mexico was something I would need to discover from the journey itself.

After a week or so I did my meager laundry by hand at a sink on the roof, and took off the watch my father had passed on from my grandfather after he died, with its stretchable silver wristband, and put it nearby. With my clothes hung out to dry, I went down to relax in the dorm. Later I noticed the watch was not on my wrist, and went back up on the roof to retrieve it. But it was gone. At first I felt sad to lose it, but after a while I realized things would be fine without it. A stranger at home in Mexico, now I was living on flexible time.

*

Yearning Among the Ruins

That summer I found myself falling for Evelyn, but wound up traveling with Sally. The three of us met at Juanita's, where our genial host presided over a brood of international students, greeting each of us with "Buenos días" at breakfast every morning.

Evelyn was an intense, dark-haired artist, a painter, from the Lower East Side of Manhattan, five years older than I was. As a would-be poet of sorts, I admired her devotion to living the life of an artist. The watercolor she painted at Chapultepec Park suggested the verdant landscape with spontaneous blues and greens that managed to keep their form on the verge of dissolving into abstraction. I liked the color and texture, but it wasn't just decoration—it expressed a feeling.

We were entranced by a folk song we heard a mariachi band play at a small café over green enchiladas and beer—Dos Equis, a dark amber brew with two red X's on the brown bottle.

> Todos me dicen el negro, Llorona,
> Negro pero cariñoso.
> Yo soy como el chile verde, Llorona,
> Picante pero sabroso.

Neither of us understood much Spanish, but we both felt the pull of the soulful song. "It sounds full of sorrow," said Evelyn. "I wonder what story it tells."

Later, using a dictionary, I translated that verse of "La Llorona," the weeping woman, trying to keep pace with the song's mournful rhythm. I could imagine Evelyn singing it, if she had a guitar.

> Everyone calls me the black one, Llorona,
> Black yet very caring.
> I am like the green chile, Llorona,
> Spicy yet full of flavor.

As the mariachis moved on to another song and drifted away, our conversation turned to pre-Columbian ruins. After a pause I heard myself say, "I'm thinking of taking the bus out to see the pyramids of Teotihuacán. It's about an hour northeast of the city."

"Would you like some company?"

"Just what I had in mind."

The next morning we left from Juanita's and rode a rumbling bus down wide avenues crowded with cars, bicycles, and pedestrians, and on through the outskirts of the city and beyond, into a valley spotted with brush and ringed by mountains. Pulling up at a dusty parking lot, we stepped off the bus and walked into an ancient complex of ruins, built by an earlier people but claimed as ancestral by the Aztecs—temples, pyramids, and sculptures of mythical beings—now what was left of Mexico's once greatest city. A massive stone pyramid rose in the background, but first we came to the Citadel, a large square courtyard around the temple of Quetzalcoatl, the Feathered Serpent, a smaller pyramid with a four-level carved stone facade of serpent heads bursting out toward us.

"Look at that!" said Evelyn. "The serpents are coiling around the pyramid with fierce faces and fangs bared, as if ready to strike."

"Every other head has a ring of petal-like feathers," I added, "That must be the Feathered Serpent. But what about the others? They look like they're wearing masks, hats, and goggles."

"Maybe two kinds of serpent gods," said Evelyn. Later I learned she may have been right. A legend from southern Mexico describes the dawn of creation with two opposed serpents, one of life and peace, the other of fire and war, circling each other in the vast, primordial ocean.

The great stone Pyramid of the Sun towered above us as gray clouds gathered around. It was said to be almost as large as the Great Pyramid of Giza in Egypt. One foot after the other, Evelyn and I climbed countless steps up the wide stone stairs of the giant pyramid in the midday heat. Gradually I worked up a sweat. At the top we stopped to rest and looked out over the broad paved Avenue of the Dead, lined by ruins on either side, some crumbling, some partly restored, beneath which were later found tombs. The Avenue led toward a similar pyramid—the Pyramid of the Moon, not quite as high as where we now stood. The shapes of the pyramids echoed the line of obsidian mountains etched in the distance. During Aztec times this was a place of pilgrimage, perhaps the site where the sun and moon were born, or even the universe. When we climbed back down, we were tired but exhilarated.

As we sat on hewn stones, a light but ominous rain began to fall. The drops spotted the dust faster and faster, and we had to decide whether to respond to the smiling man with black hair slicked back and an untucked shirt with hieroglyphic designs, who was waving us toward a dark doorway at the base of the pyramid's massive bulk. He shouted, "Come on, we go inside!"

I looked toward Evelyn. "OK," she said, and we joined a procession of Mexicans, a bunch of rambunctious 10 or 12-year-old boys and a couple of middle-aged men, stepping out of the rain and into the narrow darkness of a tunnel through the pyramid's core. Ahead the leader reached up and, one at a time, screwed in a series of bulbs on the ceiling to light the way. Behind us another man partly unscrewed them in turn, leaving our small party isolated in a gradually moving island of light beneath the invisible weight of darkness above and around. As we moved further in and the spot of light at the entrance behind us receded, I felt the increasing mass of the pyramid pressing down on my mind. Ahead was the unfathomable depth of the unseen. Then a small bright spot appeared, a faraway square that must be an opening on the other side. I wanted to get there soon.

Meanwhile right behind Evelyn the boys were chattering and giggling in Spanish. One reached out and pulled at the long flowing skirt she had bargained for in a Mexican market. Evelyn looked back and frowned. For a moment the boys quieted down, but then continued kidding around with growing excitement and kept trying to pull at her skirt. She kept brushing their hands away with annoyance, and thoughts flowed through my mind: if things got out of hand I would have to step in and help her. But what if I couldn't come up with the right words in Spanish? Maybe it was only a moment of claustrophobic paranoia, but we were buried under a pyramid.

At last we arrived at the small window set in a rough wooden door at the end of the tunnel. Fresh air blew in through the metal bars. But it turned out the door was locked, and apparently no one had the key. We were trapped in the darkness under the unknown weight of ancient stone. The men stood around for a while talking in the dim light of the slightly larger space near the door, but neither Evelyn nor I could understand much of their conversation. The boys were quieter now, under the eyes of their elders. Finally the men smiled and led us back through the tunnel the way we had come, screwing and unscrewing the light bulbs as before. Evelyn leaned toward me and whispered, "Please walk behind me so the kids won't keep pulling my skirt."

"Sure," I said, and it kept me busy. The boys were shadows behind me, now and then furtively reaching around toward Evelyn as I brushed their hands and arms away. They still seemed to be competing to see who could grab her skirt, though now with me there it was more of a challenge.

Gradually the distant light square of the entrance grew larger. Finally we stepped out from under the massive pyramid and looked up at the gray sky, breathing in the warm moist air. The rain had stopped. The dust had been rinsed from the ancient stone buildings around us.

Now another memory comes back to me: riding a burro with Evelyn. It may have been on a weekend trip of some kind, maybe near Taxco. We were both wearing jeans, squeezed together on the back of one animal, holding on tight as the burro trudged along a dirt trail with its extra load, up and down the rock-strewn path on a small green hill with a few gnarled trees in the open. The burro knew where to go without our direction. But where were we going? Was it all a mirage? I'm not sure, but remember it still.

About that time at Juanita's, Richard had appeared with his big black Cadillac Eldorado, a swept-back boat of an automobile with flaring fins. He was a law student at Harvard, and his father, a prominent lawyer, had loaned it to him for the summer. Richard offered to drive us, whoever wanted to come, on weekend excursions to picturesque places like the silver-work city of Taxco, the hill town of Guanajuato, and even the west coast beach resort of Acapulco.

When we went to Guanajuato, "the hilly place of frogs," we hiked up the narrow and twisting cobblestone alleyways between colorful houses and viewed the famous collection of mummies, disinterred from the nearby cemetery between 1865 and 1958 when their families could no longer pay the periodic burial tax then in effect. Some of the mummies had grasping hands, grotesque faces with wide-open mouths, and traces of clothes. They may have been buried hastily to avoid contagion during a cholera epidemic in the 1800's and were naturally mummified. I imagined we were surrounded by the ghosts of indigenous people who died from diseases for which they had no immunity, brought in by the early Spanish explorers and conquistadors.

When we stopped in a little plaza for tacos and beer, I noticed there was no sign of Evelyn. Someone said she was looking for a room to rent in the village to work on her art. If she did I would not see much more of her later that summer.

The next weekend our group, minus Evelyn, piled into the roomy Cadillac and rode to the white sandy beaches and dramatic cliffs of Acapulco, once called the "Pearl of the Pacific," where JFK and Jackie went on their honeymoon in the early fifties. We cruised on La Costera road along the bay, then parked and swam in the sun. Together we ate at a small café among shady trees in the plaza, walked around until dusk, and wound up sleeping on the beach. Just before dozing off to the sound of the surf, I remembered the advice in my guidebook and buried my wallet in the soft sand under my head—luckily, as it turned out, because the next morning several others who slept on the beach discovered they had been ripped off.

I went over to Sally, the lively Spanish major from Barnard, about my age with a light brown ponytail, who looked as if any moment she might start dancing. She had been sleeping nearby on the crystalline sand.
"Did you get ripped off?" I asked.

"No, I lucked out."

"Great. It would be good to get away from the crowd that will soon be here. The map shows a smaller beach called Playa Icarus over there," I said, gesturing with my head. "Want to explore?"

"Yeah, sounds like fun," she replied. Richard and the rest of the crew were heading home soon, so we decided to bid them goodbye, hitch a ride back later, and spend the morning together. The beach turned out to be Playa Icacos, not Icarus, who flew so close to the sun his wax wings melted and he fell down into the sea. With my mind on Greek myth, I had misread the map, much to Sally's amusement. We took off our shoes and followed the shorebirds as the sea drew back its watery breath, then scampered back to dry sand with them as the big waves came roaring in.

Later, we stood in the heat for an hour by the road toward Mexico City, and finally a light gray compact car pulled over. The back door opened, and out spilled several Mexican students in high spirits. Sally's Spanish came in handy. "They say they only have one seat left, so I'll have to sit on your lap."

"That's fine with me." And though I could hardly follow a word of the repartee in the rest of the car, there in the crowded back seat next to the half-open window, Sally and I chatted and laughed together. I felt the warmth of her body, comfortable on my lap, not too heavy, and she seemed at ease, leaning back into me.

On our return to Mexico City some of us visited Alberto, a writer and teacher at an international school in his late twenties who hung out with students and friends in his modest apartment after hours. As we drank herbal tea, I talked to Kevin, a long-haired exile from Oklahoma, who said he could not return to the States because the food supply was poisoned with pesticides. At the time it seemed like an overreaction, but perhaps showed the power of the book he brought with him: Rachel Carson's *Silent Spring*, published in 1962.

Then Alberto read us one of his own stories and talked about writers like Jorge Luis Borges and Gabriel García Márquez, pioneers of magical realism, neither of whom I had read yet. But I was intrigued by the magical aura of surreal "reality" that Alberto's story conjured.

When Evelyn reappeared at Juanita's, several of our friends were talking about going on a longer trip south to Oaxaca, with its markets and crafts, watched over by the ruins of Monte Albán. I wanted to go there too, then further south to San Cristóbal de las Casas, Palenque, and east into Yucatán and Chichén Itzá, to see more of indigenous Mexico. I wanted to travel with someone, and my first choice was Evelyn. She was an artist, living the life I yearned for, yet feared. So I sat down with her and told her my plan. "It should be an amazing trip. Would you like to come with me?"

"Well... I plan to go to Oaxaca and stay there awhile, then come back and work on my art at the place I rented in Guanajuato."

While I respected her decision, it was disappointing that beyond Oaxaca we would be heading in different directions. Evelyn left and I quietly reflected on karma. Then five minutes later there was a surprise. Sally came in, pulled up a chair, and sat down in front of me.

"I hear you want to travel around Mexico. I'd like to go with you."

It was not an offer I could refuse.

So a bunch of us climbed into a third-class bus painted with colorful graffiti, with luggage tied on top and several passengers clutching their chickens inside. It was a bumpy, dusty, winding ride that got hairy on a steep, narrow road through the mountains. On a turn, as the bus lurched uncomfortably close to the cliff edge, I looked fifty feet down and spotted a truck perched upside down in a tree. Whew, I thought. That could have been us.

In the mile-high city of Oaxaca, we crammed ourselves into a 15-peso room in a small hotel. The men sprawled out on the floor, while Sally and another woman slept in the bed, except for Evelyn—she wanted a room of her own.

The next day Pancho and I went up the hill to Monte Albán and wandered off in separate directions. I climbed the wide stairs of Plataforma Sur and looked out over the ruins surrounded by mountains. One building was shaped like an arrowhead pointing southwest, aligned with the bright star Capella in the northeast. The guidebook said it may have been an observatory.

Coming down I noticed Pancho off to the side poking around with a stick in the dirt and asked him what he was doing. "Here's what I found," he said, holding out a handful of gray, dusty ceramic fragments, most likely from cups or bowls, and part of a small broken figure. They were probably not worth much—though later I learned that taking them was illegal.

Excavation of one of the oldest buildings revealed carvings called Los Danzantes, the dancers, whose strange postures probably meant they were corpses of conquered enemies. They were accompanied by hieroglyphs from around 500-100 BCE, the earliest known examples of writing in Mexico. These mysterious messages from the ancient past were probably history, maybe even history written in poetry.

That night in our crowded hotel room we smoked pot and listened to an expat American writer with shoulder-length hair read a chapter from the novel he was working on. It seemed realistic, but featured an unusual character: Mr. Peanut, with black top hat and cane, one foot jauntily crossed over the other ankle, as if he had just walked into the story from a Planter's ad. In the discussion that followed, I ended up arguing with the writer about some trivia I've since forgotten—maybe the deeper meaning of Mr. Peanut?—and later asked Evelyn for her view of what happened. "Sometimes men get aggressive," she said. At first I thought she meant him, then realized she may have meant both of us.

Several days later, the night before she was set to leave for a better hotel, I couldn't stop obsessing about her. I went upstairs to her room around midnight and knocked.

"Who is it?"

"It's me."

"Come in."

I opened the door. Evelyn was lying in bed, with a sheet pulled up to her halter top, leaning back on a pillow, her hand wiping her black hair away from her eyes. A small lamp burned in a plain shade on the bedside table. I stepped into the rundown room with its dark woodwork and faded wallpaper. Then feeling like an intruder, I paused. There was a distance between us; I wasn't sure what to say. "Before you leave, I have something to tell you."

"What?"

"I really have… feelings for you." A silent moment.

"I just spent the afternoon with a new friend," she said. "Bad timing."

"Oh… Who is your friend?" I tried not to sound jealous.

"An artist, a painter. He lives here in Oaxaca."

As I left I quietly closed the door and tied the blue scarf I had brought around the knob.

Several months later, back home, I wrote a poem about the next day's goodbye.

Last Day in the Mountains

I carried her suitcase to another hotel.
It was a clear morning,
Strangers walked through the plaza
amid arrangements of green oranges.

As we made our way up the
crowded street on market day,
I told her what I really wanted
was to be with her, stay with her.
We wove through the rigging of
white canvas canopies filled with sun,
past mats on the ground where
acid limes were stacked in pyramids.
The old indigenous women
had wrinkled brown beautiful faces.

Maybe we could stop, turn back,
and find a hidden path
to another world.
But she smiled quietly
down at the cobblestones
in a fresh print dress with
thin clean air all around.
This was Oaxaca, Mexico,
and the next morning I left
for hot, heavy, humid Tehuantepec.

   More precisely, I left Oaxaca with Sally, and together we hitched down
to Tehuantepec, the city of the jaguar, 100 degrees in the shade, and then
up through the misty mountains of Chiapas to San Cristóbal de las Casas
and through the lush jungle to Yucatán. But it was not until a year later

that I really got over Evelyn. During a visit to New York when I sat with her in an almost-empty subway car, I realized that my crush on Evelyn was a projection of my own yearning to be an artist—in this case, with words.

Evelyn knew where she wanted to go; Sally was open to exploring. My desire for Evelyn got in the way of falling in love with Sally. Yet sometimes I wondered whether our traveling together could lead into something deeper.

Further along the road, maybe a few hours from Tuxtla, the capital of Chiapas, Sally and I were picked up by Roberto and Rita, a friendly middle-class couple in a compact tan Fiat. Rita opened the door and gestured for us to get in. Calm and clean-cut Roberto was at the wheel.

"Where are you going?" he asked, turning toward us in his blue polo shirt.

"San Cristóbal," I said, unshaven and shaggy-haired, in T-shirt and jeans.

"Where are you from?" asked dark-haired Rita in her flowery white cotton dress.

"New York," said Sally, looking surprisingly fresh in her ponytail and beige sleeveless blouse. So our conversation began. Rita and Roberto were upwardly mobile and wanted to practice their English. After talking of life in the U.S. and Mexico, we eventually received a kind invitation: "Would you like to stay overnight at our house?"

"Yes, that would be great!" Maybe by then a middle-class break was just what we needed.

They drove to their modest home of modern design, with a small swimming pool, in the suburbs, and offered us their guest room—treating us, like themselves, as a couple. The next day, after bacon and eggs for breakfast, we were back on the road again, hitchhiking.

San Cristóbal, or Jovel, "the place in the clouds," was indeed tucked away among cloud-shrouded mountains and teemed with indigenous people in colorful dress, with wide-brimmed hats and wool ponchos or shawls to keep warm at high altitude morning and night—but their feet were bare or clad in sandals. Brilliant blue and red textiles were piled in market stalls in front of Santo Domingo church. Here and there we met a tourist or an anthropologist. In the distance, above cobblestone streets, red tile roofs, and balconies with flowers, the green, irregular contours of Huitepec Peak reached toward the sky.

By the time we arrived in Chiapas I'd abandoned my knapsack and switched to a flexible Mexican shoulder bag, woven like a basket from maguey fibers, with wide orange stripes, to carry my one change of clothes. I washed my laundry in the creek and laid it out on the rocks to dry, as I saw the indigenous women do.

Sally and I sat outside our hotel as a few young men walked by in white shirts, short below-the-knee pants, and brightly-dyed neckerchiefs, ponchos, and hats. One stopped, pointed down at my legs, and spoke in a native language, which might have been Tzotzil or Tzeltal, the Mayan tongues of local tribes. When he saw I didn't understand, he switched to Spanish, and Sally translated.

"He wants to trade his pants for your pants." I looked down at my worn green jeans, which I didn't think I could spare. Besides, wearing his clothes might make me feel inauthentic.

"Thank him for his offer, but I need my jeans." Whatever Sally said in translation left them both laughing, and the young man smiled goodbye and walked on with his friends.

If we had stayed longer in San Cristóbal, we might have climbed up and seen the views from the hilltop churches of Guadalupe in the east and San Cristóbal in the west, visited a village of skillful weavers, and maybe discovered Casa Na Bolom, the Jaguar House, a museum and research center for the study and support of indigenous cultures, full of photos, relics, and books, founded by a pair of husband and wife anthropologists. And I had no idea that amber was mined to the north around Simojovel. We might have been awed by clear, golden brown, fossilized pine-resin gems, some with petrified insects embedded inside, buried deep underground for 30 million years, much older than the pyramids.

But all this I read about later, when I realized my yearning to move on to the ruins of Palenque and Yucatán meant we missed out on some hidden treasures that were right there at hand. Yet that urge to go further was what brought me to San Cristóbal in the first place. After all, though I no longer considered myself a Christian, I was named for Saint Christopher, the patron saint of travelers, who according to legend carried the Christ child across a river on his shoulder.

The next morning, eating quesadillas in a nearby café, I looked over at Sally and said, "Are you ready for the jungle?"

"As ready as you are," she replied, and I knew that whatever lay on the path ahead, we would find our way through it together.

*

Do you still know: falling stars, that
leaped like horses crosswise through the sky
over the suddenly held-out hurdles
of our desires—had we so many?—
then countless stars were leaping;
almost each look upward was wed
with the swift risk of their play,
and the heart itself felt whole
under this disintegration of their splendor
and was healed, as if it would survive them.

—Rilke, June 1924

Chapter 6: Stranded in the Jungle

Black Cat

A phantom is more like a spot
your sight hits with a sound;
but here, in this thick black fur
your strongest gaze is absorbed:

as a madman, when in full
rage he stomps off into the dark,
suddenly in a calm padded cell
stops, it evaporates.

All the glances that ever struck her
she seems to conceal in herself,
in order, menacing and sullen,
to watch over and sleep with them.

Yet all at once she turns, so awake,
her face right at you:
and there you meet your gaze in the golden
amber of her round eye-stones
unexpectedly again: enclosed
like a prehistoric insect.

—Rilke

Palenque to Yucatán

Our adventure led us next into eastern Chiapas, part of a jungle without
borders that merged northern Guatemala and southern Mexico into one
green ecosystem, teeming with plant and animal species, including the
howler monkey, the quetzal bird, and the almost invisible lord of the night,
the jaguar. It was here the ruins of Palenque rose from a rainforest of

cedar, mahogany, and sapodilla, in a clearing carpeted with green in the midst of a forest of leaves. A gray stone pyramid, the Temple of the Inscriptions, and its nearby Palace dominated the landscape, ancient yet very alive. At the edge of the clearing, dense vegetation encroached on the ruins. Thick exposed roots branched from a tree above ground and wound down between crumbling stones, like boa constrictors reaching for their prey, and as they slowly grew, split the stone porch apart.

Sally and I climbed the pyramid staircase and looked out over the roof of the rainforest from the entrance of the temple on top. In 1952 a Mexican archeologist discovered and opened a hidden stone passage with steps leading down through the core of the pyramid to a sealed chamber at ground level, where the body of K'inich Janaab Pakal, Great Sun Shield, the Mayan king who rebuilt Palenque and sparked a creative renaissance in the seventh century, lay entombed for more than a millennium. The dead king wore a mask of green jade with flaring pole earrings, an open mouth, and white shell eyes with black obsidian pupils, slightly crossed (a Mayan sign of beauty), staring out blankly into eternity.

"I saw the jade mask of Pakal at the National Museum in Mexico City," said Sally. "This must be where it came from."

We were only allowed to climb part way down the winding steps of the narrow passageway. Like a railing, a stone tube called a "psychoduct" continued down to connect the tomb below to a hole at the entrance above. Through this thin exit the king's spirit could communicate with the world of the living, or depart from the prison of bodily death into the sky, where the "white breath" enters the heavenly road.

"I can see why an anthropologist who lived here awhile said that Palenque becomes an obsession," I said.

"Maybe you're getting obsessed too," Sally observed with a smile.

"Well, I still want to see Chichén Itzá."

To get from Chiapas to Yucatán we hitched under cloudy skies on what soon became a muddy dirt road through the mountainous jungle, with us in the back of a dump truck with several others, including a few men with shovels. We found out what the shovels were for when the truck crawled along the side of a hill through the trees and stopped where an avalanche of heavy mud had buried the road. As the workers patiently dug with their shovels, we followed the other passengers in trekking up a small path across the body of the landslide and down to where the road emerged on the other side. There we waited about an hour until another truck was ready to leave, then climbed in the back and continued on our way.

We bumped along the mountain dirt road in and out of the forest for a half hour or so, when a peasant woman with dark skin and black hair, sitting with legs crossed in her long loose skirt on the bed of the truck, reached into her brown bag and pulled out a stack of tortillas and a bowl of black beans. She rolled each tortilla with a load of beans and graciously passed them to the passengers one at a time, including the workers in their muddy overalls, a few other Mexican travelers, and Sally and me. I was moved by her generosity. She may have been the poorest person there, yet she shared her food with all of us, quietly smiling. After Sally thanked her profusely, I made my best effort in Spanish: "Muchas gracias, señora. Me gusta frijoles."

At dusk in the rainforest we pulled up to a thatched hut built on a frame of wooden poles with a hard dirt floor. The interior was unfinished, with walls of damp brown planks stretched between slim tree-trunk poles that seemed to grow from the ground. A few men in work clothes sat on stools at a makeshift bar, eating and drinking, while women worked in an open kitchen behind them. After a brief supper of corn tacos and black beans we joined the others from the truck curled up on the floor in the alcove where they had spread out some blankets. Sally and I were hoping to sleep there as well, but the business-like woman in charge insisted we could not. Instead we must go to Don Pedro's hacienda.

A boy led us there, a ten-minute walk on a misty path to a modest house of gray concrete blocks with an open veranda in a small, overgrown clearing. The boy looked around until he found Don Pedro, an aged aristocrat with a gray beard and wrinkled face, wearing rumpled tan slacks and white open-necked shirt, who squinted at us quizzically.

Sally addressed him politely in Spanish.

"Uh?" he grunted. It soon became clear he was almost deaf, apparently living alone in this simple home, which at least was a house, in the midst of the jungle. He gave us two hammocks to hang in what looked like the laundry room, for 15 pesos, the same as we'd paid for a room at the hotel in Oaxaca. But he probably needed it. After we strung up our hammocks, I thought about our elderly host. "I wonder what Don Pedro does with his time, out here alone in the wild?"

"Maybe he sits in a chair, smoking his pipe."

"He probably can't hear the songs of the birds."

"Maybe he reads. As we came in, I saw a few books on the shelf."

"I'll bet one was *Don Quixote*."

"Could be, but he should also read *One Hundred Years of Solitude*."

"I'd like to read that myself. Rudy, my roommate, said it was good."

"Yeah, the English translation is not bad." Sally paused and scrunched up her face. "I'm feeling kind of woozy, I need to get some sleep." She climbed into her hammock.

"OK. Hope you feel better in the morning. Sleep well."

"I'll try. Good night."

I eased into my cocoon of suspended fibers and listened to the texture of night in the jungle, thoughts drifting toward dreams. Was that sound the crack of a twig and something brushing through the bushes at the edge of the forest? It might be a jaguar, or the jaguar of my imagination, out there stalking its prey. The darkness was mysterious and deep as a Rilke poem.

Pont du Carrousel

The blind man who stands on the bridge,
gray like a stone marker of nameless kingdoms,
he is perhaps the thing that is always the same,
around which from afar goes the starry hour,
and the stars' silent center.
For all around him stray and run and point.

93

He is the immoveable upright one,
placed among many confusing paths;
the dark entrance to the underworld
amid people who live on the surface.

The next morning I went over to Sally, still asleep in her hammock, and touched her arm. "Good morning, time to wake up."

"Oh... I feel really sick."

"Is it your stomach, or what?"

"Yes, my stomach and all over."

"Can you get up and walk?"

"I don't know."

I helped her up but she had to lie down again. It was clear she needed a doctor. I found Don Pedro, and brought him in. Leaning toward his ear, I said firmly,"Está enferma. Necesario un medico, por favor."

"Uh," he grunted, then nodded, and before long a boy was standing outside with two burros. I helped Sally up and onto one burro, then paid the boy and climbed with our bags onto the other. Luckily a burro is not as tall or as fast as a horse. We plodded along a meandering trail through the thick rainforest, with Sally slumping forward and to the side, holding onto her saddle, while the boy led her burro by a rope in front or walked in back tossing pebbles at its legs, and I followed on my burro behind.

All around us, awareness of intertwined life came into focus: wide green leaves and long fans of ferns grew dense beneath a canopy of shade, while a yellow butterfly fluttered unpredictably through misty shafts of light. Stalwart trunks of trees dug roots in dank soil and Spanish moss clung to branches that reached for the sun. With inexplicable rhythms, the calls of unseen birds seemed to urge us on, and slowly but surely the burros carried us, patiently plodding on the path that wove through the lush green jungle.

Eventually the trail led into the clearing of a little village near a small river, where we waited in the shade to ride in the back of a truck to a town in the Tabasco lowlands, where we climbed into a 1940s bus to Villahermosa, the "beautiful village," which was the nearest large city. It was early afternoon, and the bus was not air-conditioned. Sally was leaning against me on the seat. I asked her, "How are you doing?"

"Not so good. But I'll be OK," she said softly.

Villahermosa was flat, humid, modern and sprawling. We took a cab down a city street with signs, cafés, laundromats, and even paved sidewalks, and got out at a medical office. Antonio Mendoza, the doctor, was a poised and serious man with light, stylish glasses who met us immediately and began to talk with Sally in English. I noticed his diploma framed on the wall said Yale Medical School, and felt my tension relax. He asked her to lie down on the bed, prepared a hypodermic needle, gave her a shot—an antibiotic, he said— and told me to come back in a few hours to give her some time to rest.

It was still only mid-afternoon, so I walked a few blocks, managed to eat an empanada, and got a room for two in the nearby Hotel La Venta. Then I went out and happened upon a movie theater with LOLITA on the marquee. Directed by Stanley Kubrick from the novel by Vladimir Nabokov, it was, for me most importantly, a movie in English with Spanish subtitles. The book, which I hadn't read, is about a middle-aged man's obsession with a 12-year-old girl. The movie began with the story's dramatic ending: Peter Sellers as Clare Quilty, the human chameleon, was shot again and again as he tried to escape from his decrepit mansion. The rest of the film, a flashback, seemed anticlimactic. Later I heard they had to cut some scenes because of the Hollywood censors. Anyway, the movie helped get my mind off Sally's illness.

It was amazing how quickly we went from the jungle to a modern city with a Yale-trained doctor, and on top of that, a recent American movie. After the show, I returned to the doctor's office, took a deep breath, and went in to see Sally, who sat up on the bed and said, "I feel better already!"

"Ah, that's great!" I sighed with relief. Sally and I thanked and paid the doctor, chatted with him about his time in the U.S., then walked back to the hotel together.

The next day we hitched along the coast to Campeche, a port city founded by the Spanish in 1540 atop the Mayan town of Can Pech, of which little trace remains. We stood by the road near the beach looking out at the Gulf of Mexico where dark thunderclouds brewed in a row along the horizon. Flashes of lightning danced on the sea in a rhythm like distant fireworks, their thunder a muffled rumble. Where we stood the sky was gray but not yet raining. We could watch the rage of the primitive gods safely from the shore, at least for a while.

We were now in Yucatán, that wide, flat peninsula protruding around the Gulf into the Caribbean, and by evening we arrived in Mérida, a charmingly peaceful colonial city, provincial yet cosmopolitan. Near the Plaza Grande, the central park with benches and walkways under the shade of laurel trees, we found a room with a patio at the Hotel Estrella, and settled in to relax by the pool. I pulled out a thin book and showed it to Sally. "This was in the hotel library. *Exploring Chichén Itzá*. Want to go there tomorrow? We can get there and back on the bus in one day."

"First let's go shopping," she said.

"For what?"

"I want to buy a hammock."

"A hammock?" I looked up from the book.

"You could get one too."

"Too much to carry," I said. "I'm traveling light."

"But you might enjoy exploring the plaza. I saw lots of shops, and open-air cafés where we can hang out. You could read your book before we go to the ruins."

"OK... I guess I can wait another day." So we stayed in quiet Mérida, near where the giant asteroid crashed into the Gulf millions of years ago, cloaking the planet in ash and suddenly changing the climate, like an exclamation point at the end of the story of the dinosaurs.

Chichén Itzá looked quite well-restored. The stone carvings and hieroglyphs were clear, not crumbling. The most impressive pyramid,

El Castillo (The Castle) of the Feathered Serpent God, stood nine levels high with broad stairways on all four sides. According to the guide, once each stairway had 91 steps, and with one more step to the temple at the top, added up to 365, the number of days in a year. At the spring and autumn equinox the sun illuminated a zigzag strip down the side of the north staircase with the sculpted head of a snake at the bottom, as if a giant serpent of light were flashing down the stairs. And inside the pyramid a narrow stairway led steeply down to a chamber with a red jaguar throne, where the lords of the underworld took the form of jaguars in the darkness.

From the top of the pyramid we had a broad view of the flat expanse of Yucatán, not open prairie but a wide forest carpet of not-too-tall trees without a mountain to be seen, all the way to the horizon. Several hundred yards to the southwest we could see El Caracol (The Snail), a round, domed building on a rectangular platform. With window slits aligned to track the moon, planets, and stars, it was clearly an observatory. The Maya could accurately predict solar and lunar eclipses, and were quite concerned with keeping an accurate calendar recording their history, including the reigns of their kings, going back over 3,000 years to what for them was the beginning of time.

We went back down the steps of the Castle and sat in the sun for a while, then walked to the Great Ball Court, as big as a football field, between parallel walls over eight yards high, with stone scoring rings beyond easy reach in the center. The players had to hit a heavy rubber ball through the ring without using their hands or feet, and the games went on for hours. The losing team or its captain may have been sacrificed—or some say the winners, as that may have been an honor. Nearby was the Tzompantli (the Wall of Skulls), a platform decorated on all sides with carved skulls, skeletons entwined with serpents, and eagles consuming human hearts, where ceremonial sacrifices may have been held. The imagery shows the influence of the Toltecs from central Mexico, who took over this site a thousand years ago, after the fall of the great Mayan cities.

"I didn't realize all this about human sacrifice," said Sally. "Why did they do it?"

"From what I've read, part of it may have been to show power by publicly executing enemy captives. And it was a religious ritual, sacrificing the most valuable thing, human life, in hopes that the gods would make the crops grow. Aztec sacrifices may have been meant to keep the sun alive. Other ancient cultures had human sacrifice too. There are theories about why they did it, but no one knows for sure."

"What about the ball game? Sacrificing the losers is shocking enough, but sacrificing the winners is weird."

"Well, Roman gladiators fought to the death for a cheering crowd. But at least the winners survived and some even got rich and famous. So I tend to believe the ball game losers got sacrificed. Otherwise, who would play hard?"

"You don't think honor would motivate them?"

"Maybe some individuals, but two whole teams? Survival is a powerful instinct."

"But if the warriors fought for glory, then dying was an honor."

"I guess. One thing I remember from the *Iliad* was the Greek general Agamemnon sacrificed his own daughter, Iphigenia, to get favorable winds from the gods for the Trojan expedition. Do you think she felt that was an honor?"

"It was unfair! She had no choice!"

"Maybe the Mayan ballplayers had no choice either."

The next evening when walking along a pier back in Mérida, we heard an argument erupt in French between a man and a woman, a young couple gesticulating on a dock in the distance, their voices angrily rising. Suddenly the man slapped the woman on the face. There was silence. I was shocked. The way I was raised, a man should not hit a woman. I hesitated, and any impulse I had to intervene faded as the argument subsided with no further blows.

Later that night Sally and I sat by large stones at the hotel pool in the moonlight. After a long silence she said, "Day after tomorrow, I have to take the bus to Mexico City, to catch my flight back to New York."

"Oh…already?" A pause. "Too bad you have to go… I'll be thinking of you at Isla Mujeres," was all I could say.

"Will I see you again?" She looked directly at me.

"I hope so."

"No commitment, you mean?"

"Well, I still have a thing about Evelyn. We'll have to wait and see."

Sally tightened her lips and looked straight ahead, holding her feelings in check.

We spent the next morning relaxing at the hotel, taking turns on Sally's new hammock with its light brown zigzag design, then walked around the plaza. While Sally was shopping for Yucatán crafts I wandered into a small used bookstore, Librería Única, and bought an old book in English about travels in Chiapas and Yucatán by Stephens and Catherwood, explorers who found, described, and sketched overgrown Mayan ruins in the mid-1800s. Stephens' detailed narration seemed to include almost everything they encountered, from porters to mules to mosquitoes, matching the precision of Catherwood's drawings of imposing temples and palaces adorned by bas-relief figures with elaborate headdresses, ancient royal abodes choked by the growth of the jungle. Maybe I'd find time to peruse more of this book on the beach at Isla Mujeres.

When I saw Sally off at the bus station, we hugged each other and kissed goodbye. "I'll miss you," she said.

"I'll miss you too," I replied. "But we'll always have Mexico."

She allowed a small smile at the echo of Bergman and Bogart parting in *Casablanca,* then turned and stepped into the bus.

*

"Bistec tortuga," said the menu. A Mexican family at a nearby table had been talking about "corn flakkies," which I finally realized were Corn Flakes. Back in those days I still ate meat, so I tried the bistec tortuga, and it tasted OK, somewhere between beef and chicken. That was the only time I ate sea turtle, for reasons that will soon be clear.

Just off the northeast tip of the Yucatán peninsula, where it juts into the blue Caribbean, a thin strip of land about five miles long seems to sail through the sea going nowhere, bypassed by time, like a long graceful ship run aground. The southeast end forms the prow, a point crowned by the crumbling ruin of a small Mayan temple, and the northwest end, the square stern, receives a mild sea in its wake with an exquisite beach of white crushed coral. The Spanish called this Isla Mujeres, the Isle of Women, perhaps because they found stone images here of Ixchel, the Mayan goddess of fertility.

At Playa Norte I slept suspended above the sand in a hammock strung between palms for more than a week in mid-August, joining a small group of international backpackers gathered near a thatched enclosure opening onto the beach—Rodrigo's Restaurante, where a few pesos would buy you a plate of tasty rice and beans. If you ran out of pesos, you added a mark to your tally of meals on the wall and paid when you could. Some tallies reached more than ten or twenty, but Rodrigo was cheerful and patient. He had faith in Western Union.

At the far end of the beach was the one new hotel on the island, which otherwise had only a small quiet town with a few guesthouses and cafés. Most of the tourists visited Cozumel, a bigger, more developed island further south. So Isla Mujeres was the beautiful place I was looking for, to relax and explore before returning to college that fall.

But not all was so peaceful. One night at dusk on the beach a pale young man wandered, silent in shock. Someone told me his wife had been raped on their honeymoon by the guide who took her out in his boat.

Later, on one of my walks along a sandy lagoon I discovered a large circular wooden fence in the water near the shore.

Turtle Corral

The island excludes the shifting sea
like a thin hand
cupped around a match in the wind

slowly the huge shells
slide over each other
in the shallow water
pushed together

flippers pawing uselessly
hood-eye tired
over hook beak open

miraculously buoyant
in thick armor

the somnolent green sea turtles
confined in clear water

their hulls press against
the poles
hammered so closely together

The next day I rode in a cabin cruiser out to a coral reef in the Caribbean. The waves were rough on the open ocean, and I sat in the bow the better to feel the rise and fall, the surge and plunge of the sea, so close to the deep I could feel the ocean's indifference, profound and beyond our small concerns. When life evolved in the sea, we were born of a powerful mother, one who would support us if we learned how to swim, and if not, just as soon let us drown.

It may have been at Ixlache Reef near Isla Contoy that I donned rubber flippers, mask, and snorkel, eased down into the pale blue translucent water, and soon swam over an orange colony of coral, a sprawling jumble of intricate castles of tiny living beings. In and out of this fairyland structure a blue fish darted one way, a red fish the other, and a school of striped yellows cruised along swimming in synchrony.

That was only the prelude: before long I was surrounded by hundreds of small silver fish, flowing around me in a swirling vortex. However they moved, the fish adjusted spontaneously, as if all of one mind, to keep their silver sphere spinning intact. If I poked my hand into the flow, they flowed above and below. Whichever way I turned I saw the brilliant rays of the sun reflected in a multitude of silver fish streaming effortlessly all around me.

Several days later I was invited to a shark hunt. We rode in a pickup truck to a deserted beach on the rugged eastern shore of the island, where the surf from the open ocean was strong. We walked on the beach as the waves came tumbling in. After a while Benito, a wiry man in a T-shirt, lifted a large sea turtle from the back of the truck and placed it on the sand. He called us around and explained, "The sharks will come when they smell blood." The turtle moved its flippers in the waves of sand and lifted its beak, seeming to look for a route toward the sea. Then Benito turned over the turtle. He took a sharp knife from his shorts, cut around the large flat breast plate, and removed it like a lid from the turtle's flesh in the shell underneath. Benito worked like a surgeon, and a minute later he cradled the still-beating heart in his hands and held it out toward us.

I recoiled inside at the sight. Reminded of the sacrificial rituals of ancient times, I climbed on some sandy rocks to watch from a distance. Benito placed the turtle's shell, now a bowl of flesh and blood, in the crashing surf. The red stain spread in the waves. A fisherman put a chunk of the turtle's flesh on a hook and readied the line. When the black dorsal fin of a shark cut through the crest of a wave beginning to curl into foam, the fisherman cast his line out into the surf. He repeated the ritual several times, but the shark never took the bait. The afternoon wore on, and at last we drove back through the town, where the rest of the meat of the turtle would soon be served as bistec tortuga.

Many years later, sea turtles were declared an endangered species. In the peaceful lagoon on the other side of the island, their breeding ground was a wildlife refuge, where their eggs were protected from predators. For a small fee, people could visit the Isla Mujeres Turtle Farm.

Meanwhile, I ran out of money. My tally of unpaid-for meals on Rodrigo's wall kept growing each day. Finally I walked to the small Western Union office in town and sent a telegram to my father in New Jersey: SLEEPING ON BEACH IN MEXICO STOP NEED $50 TO GET BACK HOME. That would be enough, because I planned to hitch to Mexico City in time to catch a ride with my friends in Richard's Cadillac back to New York.

Somewhere outside of Mérida, where the road turned toward Campeche, workmen were loading big heavy coils of thick rope into two flatbed trucks with high wooden sides covered with canvas, open in back. The rope resembled manila hemp but was made of agave fiber. Several hitchhikers were climbing into a niche among the coils in the back of one truck, and I went over to join them. But it was crowded, and a few of us got off and climbed among the coils in the back of the other truck. The first truck took off down the road and a few minutes later ours followed after.

Speeding along through the hot afternoon, after a while I climbed up over the jumble of coiled rope and wormed my way under the canvas on top until I reached the front edge of the load. Lying flat with my chest, belly, and legs pressed against the hard, uneven fibers, I lifted up part of the canvas in front of my head and peered out over the cab, feeling the wind in my face as we raced down the road. To the left lay the broad reach of Yucatán, to the right curved the rim of the Gulf of Mexico, straight ahead stretched the narrow paved road without a dividing line. My senses were alert, awake and alive.

Then we slowed and pulled over. Ahead off the road on the left was the other truck, upside down, wheels in the air, rope spilled out in a chaotic pile. Some people stood behind, and I hoped all the riders got off alive. Whew, if I had been riding under the canvas on top of that truck I would now be crushed under a pile of tightly coiled rope. So I wormed my way down to the niche in the back of our truck, where I could jump off if need be, and stayed there the rest of the way, as we rode on to Campeche.

Later, outside Veracruz, I was hitching at a gas station when a vintage dusty brown Chrysler convertible pulled in. In the front seat were two easygoing students in loose short-sleeved shirts, Carlos in white and his brother Pablo in tan. I asked for a ride, and Carlos nodded "Sí." Then he motioned me back toward the trunk, and opened it wide. Inside was a giant green turtle with a dark red leash on its neck. The two of them lifted it out and set it down on the ground. Carlos held the leash and took the turtle for a walk, while Pablo used the pay phone on the station wall. As you might expect, the big turtle's walk was quite slow, as it lifted its limbs one at a time for each step. Carlos and Pablo seemed to exist in a timeless realm, where filling the tank, making a couple of calls to discuss an issue that needed to be resolved, walking the turtle, and filling its water bowl were all part of a normal routine that could go on indefinitely. I asked when they were likely to leave. Carlos shrugged and said something in Spanish I couldn't follow. Though I enjoyed the interlude with Carlos and Pablo and their pet turtle, I decided to find another ride.

*

Ordeal at the Border

I returned from my journey through Oaxaca, Chiapas, and Yucatán just in time to get a ride back to New York in the big black Cadillac Eldorado with dual headlamps on each side of its gaping chrome grille and dashing fins sweeping back like a giant shark—the car that Richard had borrowed from his father for his summer job at a law firm in Mexico City.

Fellow passengers included Pancho, the tequila aficionado from Brooklyn, now sporting a Mexican cowboy hat; Evelyn, my artist friend from the Lower East Side, after her retreat in the hillside village of Guanajuato; and Stephanie, a loose-limbed young woman with straight brown hair I had not met before, visiting Mexico after her first year of college.

We thanked our boarding-house host Juanita, who was now caring for Esteban, a student who had come down with hepatitis. After a final chorus of "Adiós, adiós," we headed northeast past the city limits onto the open road toward the Rio Grande border of Texas. As Richard stepped on the gas, the Hydra-Matic transmission smoothly lurched into fourth, and we settled in cruising mode. "Should we cross at Laredo?" he said.

I looked at the road map. "It might be pretty congested. How about Brownsville instead?"

Mile after mile, our mechanical monster ate up the road. Heat waves shimmered in the distance, and my body was moist with warm sweat. Richard eased up the windows and turned on the air conditioning. "Ah, that's better," sighed Evelyn. For a moment, we looked at each other, and I felt the distance between us.

"What a cool car," ventured Stephanie, breaking the silence. "No pun intended."

A half hour later the luxurious Cadillac coughed, sputtered, and rolled to a stop.

"What?" said Richard.

"Oh no," muttered Evelyn. We all got out and Richard opened the hood. The radiator hissed with a cloud of steam.

"The engine's too hot," declared Pancho, stating the obvious.

"We need water," said Richard. Surveying the dry, deserted, gradual up-and-down slopes of the landscape, we saw no one, not a house nor a car nor a stray dog anywhere.

Pancho softly said, "Shit."

Richard lowered the hood. "Evelyn, you take the driver's seat. When I give the signal, release the emergency brake, put the gearshift in neutral, and steer." Pancho, Stephanie, and I followed him to the back of the big black Eldorado and each placed both palms on its warm metal body. Together all four of us leaned into its huge inertia and pushed.

At the top of the rise we jumped back in the car and coasted gently awhile, then got out and pushed again. Eventually Richard called out, "There's a house, across the field on the right!"

Yes, there it was, a small wooden house in need of repairs, alone in the bleak landscape, with paint worn away by the wind. "Do you think they can spare some water?" Evelyn wondered.

"Well, I'm willing to pay for it," Richard said, and took a plastic one-gallon jug from the trunk. Accompanied by Pancho, he walked across the barren field toward the house in the heat of the sun. Evelyn, Stephanie, and I watched from the car, not saying much. Evelyn took out her notepad and began to sketch.

Stephanie looked at the scene taking shape on the pad. "That's really good. I like how you drew the broken-down shack and one scrawny tree. It has a desolate feeling." Evelyn nodded slightly and kept on sketching.

In the distance, as Richard and Pancho approached the small house, the tiny figure of an old woman appeared on the broken porch and spoke words that we couldn't hear. Then the woman took the jug inside and filled it with water. Richard took out his wallet and gave her some bills along with his thanks. Pancho turned to us, held up the jug, and smiled.

When we finally reached the Texas border at Brownsville and pulled into U.S. Customs, it was pitch-dark at 2 a.m. Our big black Cadillac was the only car there, and the idle agents looked up and took notice, as if a very big fish just swam into their waiting net. In a white short-sleeved shirt with a silver badge, the crew-cut agent in charge walked up to the driver's side as Richard lowered the window. The agent slowly looked us over, front seat and back, and in a gruff voice said, "Leave the keys in the ignition. Everybody out of the car."

106

We stood around uneasily while Customs agents searched every inch of the Eldorado. The head agent stood beside us. What bad timing, I thought —2 a.m. and Customs had nothing to do except put us through this rigamarole. One agent opened the trunk, reached in, and began to examine our luggage. What had I put in my bag? The agent felt with his hand in an open cardboard box, then pulled out a dark green folded piece of clothing and held it up. "Whose raincoat is this?"

There was an uncomfortable silence. "It's mine," at last Evelyn said.

"Come with me." The head agent stepped over and led her away.

"The rest of you go in there," said another agent, leading us to a glass-walled room nearby, with a row of wooden chairs. He locked the door and disappeared outside. We sat and watched as the agents put the car on a hydraulic lift and raised it up, exposing the Cadillac's underbelly, and searched every nook and cranny with the beams of bright moving flashlights. After a while the head agent returned without Evelyn and motioned to Stephanie. She followed him out and he locked the door again, leaving us there to mull over the situation.

"They'll question us one by one," warned Pancho, "and won't let us come back here, so no one will know what the others have said."

"In any case, we have nothing to hide. Or do we?" said Richard, looking over at Pancho and me. After awhile the agent came in and motioned again. It was my turn.

He took me upstairs, where a stocky, crew-cut Customs agent in a tan short-sleeve shirt sat behind a desk at one end of the room, twirling his pen. I was left standing alone in the middle. There was no other chair. After shuffling through some papers, the agent looked up and fixed his eyes on me. He spoke with a south Texas drawl, taking his time with each word. "You ever smoke any mary-juana?"

I saw no reason to lie. With my shaggy hair and wispy beard, we both knew I looked like a beatnik, and I had nothing to hide.

"Yes," I replied.

Ever so slightly, he tensed as if ready to pounce. Then he spoke slowly. "Did you smoke that there mary-juana in the U.S…. or in Mexico?"

I paused, realizing my next answer could be crucial. The truth was both, but it was an either/or question. If I said the U.S., I was admitting to a crime in this jurisdiction, though he had no specific evidence. If I said Mexico, he could accuse me of smuggling.

"The U.S.," I said.

"Did you ever smoke mary-juana in Mexico?" Now his intention was clear, and my fate could hang in the balance. To evade a false accusation, I had to lie after all.

"No," I said.

"Did you ever smoke mary-juana with Evelyn?" He was closing in.

"No," I said again, hoping she'd said the same.

"Do you know anything about a car-touche?"

"What's a cartouche?"

"A little package of mary-juana."

"No," I replied, wondering why he used a French term. Was he testing to see if I knew the lingo of smuggling?

Then the agent seemed to lose interest in further questioning. Instead he ordered, "Turn around and drop your pants down." Slowly I turned, unbuckled my belt and did as he said.

"Underwear, too." This must be what they call a strip search, I thought, pushing my jockey shorts down to my knees on top of my crumpled jeans. I stood up again.

"Now bend over." He inspected my rear end from a distance. As I looked down at the bare wood floor, I couldn't help feeling this ritual was getting ridiculous.

"OK, get out of here." As I pulled up my pants, he looked down at his papers, picked up his pen, and appeared to attend to whatever he meant to write.

Several hours later we were all together again in the U.S. Customs waiting area—all except Evelyn. Richard had been in a phone booth on the other side of the room for almost an hour, frantically calling his father about the car, which had been impounded by the State of Texas. A large, portly man in a dark blue uniform with a badge walked up and introduced himself. "I'm John McDonald, U.S. Marshal," he said. His tone was business-like and respectful. "Your friend Evelyn has been arrested for smuggling. There was a small packet of marijuana in the pocket of her raincoat. She'll be held in the Brownsville jail until she makes bail. Visiting hours are this afternoon from two to four."

"Thanks for letting us know," I replied. "When will we get the car?"

"According to state law any vehicle used in smuggling is impounded and held until trial. If Evelyn is found guilty, the car becomes property of the State of Texas."

"Even if it's not her car?"

"Any car used for smuggling," the marshal said.

Things did not look good for Richard. But when he returned from the phone booth, he appeared relieved. "My father called the head of Customs on the Texas-Mexico border. Since I didn't know about the marijuana, he finally agreed to give back the car."

When we picked up the Cadillac from the garage, the attendant, in a black cowboy hat and vest, was amazed. "This is the first time in seven years that anyone got their car back!" We piled into our big black metal boat and drove in search of the nearest cheap motel. Brownsville was nothing special, but different from Mexico. Even the plainest houses had well-defined yards with fences around them. After tacos and beer for brunch, we found a motel and all took a nap until we could visit Evelyn— Richard and Stephanie on the twin beds, me on a cot, and Pancho with a blanket on the floor.

From outside, the Brownsville jail was gray and drab. We went up the steps. Visiting hours were posted on a card on the wooden door. I tried the knob. It was locked. Richard knocked loudly. After a while the latch turned and the door pulled back with some force. A short wiry man in jeans wearing a large cowboy hat and a badge, with a big cigar in his mouth, stepped forward and glared at us. "What do *you* want?" he growled. He needed a shave.

"We came to see our friend Evelyn. It says here that these are your visiting hours," I said, pointing to the sign on the door.

He grabbed the cigar from his mouth. "Hell, I'm the sheriff here! I make the rules!" he barked, then shut the door hard. There was nothing we could do except go back to the car.

That summer night, stretched out on my cot in our room without air-conditioning, I felt an intense pain in my belly that grew until it consumed me, then after a few minutes faded. It may have been a prelude to what, a year later, was a full-fledged attack of appendicitis. But in Brownsville, Texas in 1964, I was glad it was gone, and drifted off down the peaceful river of sleep.

The next morning we learned that Evelyn was out on bail, wired from a friend in New York. She seemed subdued as we rode in our comfortable air-conditioned Eldorado across the baking plains of east Texas and the dry hills of southern Arkansas. "What happened?" I asked.

"I completely forgot that packet of grass was still in the pocket of my raincoat."

"How did the questioning go?"

"They tried to get me to implicate you, but I took responsibility. None of you knew."

"Thanks. Will you have to come back for the trial?"

"I hope not. I need to get a change of venue nearer to where I live. It seems that even for a small amount, smuggling in Texas is very serious. Hopefully in New York possession of a few ounces will not be such a big deal, and I have no previous record."

As we continued cruising along, Pancho took off his cowboy hat, turned it upside down in his lap, and with a fingernail lifted up part of the thin felt sweatband lining the inside rim of the crown. With thumb and forefinger he pulled out a roach, the squished inch-long remnant of a hand-rolled joint. "Anyone for a smoke?" He smiled as he held up the roach in one hand, then reached in his pocket with the other for his lighter.

"You got that through Customs?" said Evelyn.

"Some things are so small they don't get noticed," Pancho said on the sly, as he lit up the roach, inhaled, and passed it around. I took a drag, and so did Evelyn. Stephanie hesitated, then followed suit.

"Ever smoke pot before?" Pancho asked.

"No, it's my first time." She handed the roach back to Pancho. There wasn't much left, but he held it out again.

"No thanks," said Richard. "I'm driving."

The sun settled down into dusk as we crossed into Indiana, and a great cloud of fog engulfed us riding through Indianapolis. As if in a dream we drove on in our Eldorado, stopping at stoplight after stoplight, through the thick fog of night, so dense we could only see a few feet ahead in the glare of our headlights.

But Richard drove carefully. As we emerged from the grid of the city, the gray veil dissolved and the beams of our headlights reached out into darkness. Before long the aura of dawn appeared in the east, and then a bright edge of sun broke over the slow-motion turn of the earth's horizon.

I remembered diving off Isla Mujeres, submerged in a rich school of small silver fish, flowing around me in synchrony. However they moved, they moved with spontaneous harmony. If I poked my hand into the flow, they detoured above and below in an ever continuous stream.

Wherever I turned the brilliant rays of the sun were reflected in one living sphere, a silver multitude flowing together effortlessly, without illusory boundaries, and I was part of the fleeting magical pattern that coalesced here for a while.

Part Three: Both Trapped and Free

Chapter 7: Ghost Riders

From a Childhood

The darkness was like richness in the room,
in which the boy, quite hidden, sat.
And when his mother entered as in a dream,
a glass trembled in the silent cupboard.
She felt like the room gave her away,
and kissed her boy: Oh, are you here?
Then both looked uneasily toward the piano,
for many an evening she played a song,
in which the child was strangely deeply caught.
He sat very still. His wide gaze fixed
upon her hand, which fully weighed down with rings,
as if walking heavily through snowdrifts,
moved slowly across the white keys.

—Rilke

The Bright Red Fish

Meeting the bright red fish one summer when I had learned to walk but not yet swim is fresh in my mind as if it happened this morning. Aunt Nan took us kids out to the end of a long wooden dock that seemed to reach far into Lake Winnipesaukee, the largest lake in New Hampshire, with water so clear I could see the red fish swimming around at what must have been ten feet down. I stood at the edge of the dock, fascinated by the vivid redness of its fluid movements, and leaned even closer, curious to know the red fish deeply, until it seemed to grow bigger in my field of vision.

The next moment the red fish swam right before my eyes, as I plunged down into a world of swirling bubbles, mouth wide open in fearless amazement, gasping for breath underwater. Three times I sank down and rose up again, splashing and floundering in the water, nothing but water, the red fish now forgotten, with nowhere to stand and nothing to grab onto. Though my body was blindly thrashing, I had no idea of death, nor fear from the thought of it—only a primal instinct to survive.

Then the strong grip of a hand on my arm pulled me up out of the water and deposited me, bent over coughing, on the wooden planks of the dock. Aunt Nan slapped me on the back until I coughed up all I could of the water of life and stood there dripping in my bathing suit, unexpectedly initiated into a bright new awareness.

*

Exploring New Worlds

Early on, curiosity got me in trouble. During the war, when I was about two, my father was sailing on ships out of Newport News, Virginia, where my parents rented a cottage. In the large grassy yard was a chicken coop enclosed by a fence. I used to put my face up close to the wire mesh and stare in at the world of the chickens, wandering around in their feathered coats, pecking at specks on the ground. What was it like in their cozy little house inside the enclosure? Once I went to the gate and reached up and fiddled with the latch until it opened. Soon I was walking through Chicken Village. The chickens took note but did not approach me. I went to the small open door of their shed, got down on my hands and knees, and crawled in. What I saw there was strange and amazing: a long row of straw nests, some with plump, dark brown feathered chickens sitting in peaceful seclusion, others with perfectly shaped light brown eggs exposed, full of unknown potential. Then from outside I heard the voice of my father: "Hey, come out of there! You left the gate unlatched—the chickens will escape!"

I crawled out again in the dirt on my hands and knees. None of the chickens had gone out of the gate. I got yelled at but felt good that I'd seen how chickens live.

Another time I played in the mud with a little black girl, her braids tied with yellow bows, sailing a tiny blue and white wooden boat that bobbed about in a little rainwater lake in an old cast-iron frying pan. We laughed as we sat in the mud and spun out together the tale of an imaginary journey. That's my first memory of playing with another child.

From the start, I always liked to make things. An early memory was of making a book as a kindergarten project. The friendly teacher asked us to tell her our stories, and wrote each one down faithfully. We illustrated our tales with colorful crayon pictures, put the pages together with a primitive binding—and guess what, we had each made a book. When I showed it to my mother, she read me the teacher's encouraging comment.

Some early memories are hazy at a crucial moment. Once we were in Norwood, visiting Nana and Grandpa, my father's parents. While the adults were sitting around talking I went to explore a back room. There among chests and trunks and piles of cloth, perched on a stand was a big metal Singer sewing machine, inky black with curling green lines, that I had seen Nana use to make clothes. I wondered how it worked, and decided to try it out with a scrap of cloth held under the shiny metal guide for the needle. When I stretched down with my toes to press the pedal, suddenly the machine began rumbling, the needle rapidly jabbing.

Nana rushed in, very upset, and grabbed my arm with both hands: "You must never touch this! You'll get hurt!"

Then my mind goes blank. I'm not sure, but maybe Nana hit my fingers with a ruler—a shock that may have erased the memory.

Mrs. McGillery, my strict sixth-grade teacher, reminded me of Nana—but bigger and stronger. She once pulled a misbehaving kid by the earlobe down the hall to the principal's office. In high school, under the spell of e. e. cummings, I wrote a fantasy poem combining the two women:

Mrs. McGillery had a sewing machine
a black and green, metallic sheen sewing machine
and even Mrs. McGillery didn't really know
just how much her sewing machine could sew
until one day her finger got caught in the thread
and the machine sewed her fingers together
and on up her arm to her head
and sewed her ears into potholders
and sewed her all up in a ball
and the ball into the rug and the rug into the house
and the house into the town and the town into the sky
and continued sewing everything into everything else
until the whole universe was sewed up
and Mrs. McGillery's sewing machine saw
it could sew just so much and no more
then a little boy said so what
sew buttons on ice-cream cones
and laughing hysterically it sewed itself into itself
until it collapsed in stitches

The only other thing I recall from the day I got caught with the sewing machine was the vague, shadowy presence of Beverly, my father's younger sister. I never saw her again, and she was rarely mentioned later by anyone in the family. Eventually I got curious, and asked my mother about her. She told me that Beverly had a baby without being married, which upset her mother and father, and they made her give up her child for adoption. Then one day after a bath Beverly forgot to dry her hair, went out in the winter cold, and got sick and died of pneumonia. This story made an impression on me, and to this day, after a bath or a shower, I'm careful to dry my hair. Though he hardly ever spoke of her, his younger sister haunted my father, until sixty-five years later her baby girl, adopted and grown up, searched him out on the internet and visited him, her lost uncle, in a nursing home.

Struck by Lightning

My parents seemed like nice people, but could they be trusted? In 1947, after the war, when I was four and before my sister was born, we lived in a yellow clapboard house in Wakefield, Massachusetts, across from Lake Quannapowitt. Every morning I liked to eat my favorite food, a bowl of milky cereal sprinkled with a thick blanket of powdered sugar. I loved the soft powdery texture that covered my jumbled pile of crunchy flakes like new-fallen snow, and savored the sugary powder melting on my tongue.

One spring morning with green buds on the tree branch outside the kitchen window, I spooned the white powder from the sugar bowl, poured it on my cereal, dipped in the spoon, and took my first mouthful—but the powdered sugar tasted bitter. I spit it out and scowled. "Eck! Why does it taste so bad?"

My mother explained, "Today is April Fools' Day, and your father put corn starch, which looks the same, in the powdered sugar bowl."

Then like a stranger he came down the stairs, with his mouth smugly closed.

"Daddy, why did you do that?"

He broke into a smirk. "It was a practical joke. April Fools!"

I'd never heard of anything like that. All I knew was the bitter taste on my tongue. I didn't laugh. I felt hurt, betrayed. Perplexed, my father turned away and left my mother to console me. He didn't even apologize.

If he were alive today, he might say, "You were too sensitive, like your mother. You gotta be tough, learn to be a man." But I think it was more than that. A practical joke can express hostility, and this one, when I was too young to understand, surely did. The first two years of my life, when he was away in the war, my mother and I became close in a way that he was not part of. My father and I never had a chance to bond together. When he came back he was jealous of our closeness, and at best, just didn't understand kids. I lived in a child's world he had long ago left behind.

Alone in the middle of the backyard stood a gnarled gray apple tree, small enough for me to climb up and sit on the bottom branch. One night a big storm came. In a flash the tree was struck by lightning. The next day I saw the big branch broken off and bent to the ground, split open, revealing the light, splintered heartwood inside, releasing a fresh smell of sap in the air.

Soon after, my baby sister was born and my mother was busy with her. Younger than the neighbor kids, I had no one to play with, and one day sat alone on the small front lawn, desolate. Every once in a while I rolled in the cut green grass. Two young nuns, hair pulled back, all in black down to their ankles, walked by smiling and said hello. One reached inside her habit, pulled out a shiny red apple, and gave it to me. Shy and touched by her kindness, I softly mumbled "Thank you." As the two nuns walked away, she turned and glanced briefly back, with a smile and a twinkling eye. I held the apple in both hands and stared at its speckled crimson skin.

*

Digging Up Clams

I was just a kid when my parents took me to dig for clams. The Cape Cod beach was wide and flat, with no dunes, but big puddles where the tide had gone out. The sand was white where still dry, and moist brown where the water had been. The sun was bright, the sky a deep blue. I watched my father and others digging with shovels, far from the distant breaking waves, searching for clams that had burrowed down under the sand. When he saw a small breathing hole, he dug around it, making a trench a few inches down. Soon water seeped in. He kept digging until his shovel hit a clam with a thud.

117

Seagulls squawked above, flying by, looking down on us, as if to say "Why are you digging up clams? Seafood is for birds, not humans." My father reached down with two hands and pulled out the clam from the moist, dank sand. The breeze smelled of salt as he pried open the clamshell. It opened like a book, exposing the shapeless, peach-colored flesh to the air and human eyes. Did the clam sense that its life would soon come to an end? His shell had served him well. But now it was wide open, ready to become a serving dish for giant humans. I felt the clamshell's outer surface, with its rough corrugated ridges and streaks of color. "Sometimes oysters, which are like clams, have pearls inside them," said my mother. This clam had no pearl, only a hard shell and soft, moist flesh.

Eventually I became a vegetarian. As a kid, I liked fishing—it was always a thrill when the pond was smooth in the morning and the perch were jumping—but I did not like killing the fish, or for that matter, other living things. Anything alive is like me, feeling the sunlight and pain of existence, and if I have a choice of what's on the menu, I prefer not to chew on another sentient being, even if it's a dumb clam who can't tell its own story. If it can't tell its story, why should we care? Because inside our psychological shells we are all dumb clams, hiding from the world in fear —sometimes, anyway.

If we could learn to love the clam inside us, we would be happy in our soft flesh, braced by strong bones, walking along the Cape Cod beach in the sun.

*

"If You Don't Like It, Lump It."

Later, in Natick, we had a coal bin down in the cellar, where chunks of coal were heaped everywhere, and a long-handled shovel leaned on the wall. The coal came down the chute from a big delivery truck, kicking up dust. My father would open the door on the belly of the mighty furnace and shovel coal into the dancing red-orange flames, burning fiercely, hotly confined in cast iron, warming the house through the New England winter.

One Christmas morning I jumped out of bed early and rushed to the big red stocking with my name on it hanging from the mantelpiece. I took it down, stretched with mysterious bulges in various places, and excavated its contents with expectation. A shiny red apple, a firm round orange, and what—a potato. I knew Santa (actually my parents) sometimes threw in a potato to keep me humble. Then I dug down to the biggest bulge, a sharp lump swelling the stocking, and extracted a rough black object, hard in my hand. It was a lump of coal. Solid, inert.

Why did my parents put it there? I must have done something wrong, but didn't know what. When I asked them, my father said, "Nothing specific. At times you've been difficult." What was he talking about? Was this advised by the book I had seen on his shelf, *The Job of Being a Dad*?

"Sometimes New England families put potatoes or coal in stockings," added my mother with a strained smile, as if it were a Christmas custom.

Looking back, maybe I can see that lump of coal in my stocking as a metaphor of inevitable suffering, then find a way to burn it in the stove of my heart to keep warm from the simmering heat of its psychic energy.

*

Skidding on Gravel

Halfway up my right shin, there's a two-inch pale scar like a crescent moon. When I was seven I stood up and pedaled hard to ride my red bike over the hump of the hill to school in the mornings, the chill March wind biting my knuckles, no leaves yet on the skeleton trees. Riding back home one afternoon I cruised down the steep hill at high speed, coasting freely, my face full of wind, until the wide curve bent down toward our small clapboard house. There I hit a patch of loose gravel on the edge of the road, pressed back on the footbrake, steered into the turn—and my bike skidded out from under me. With a hooking foot-first swoop I sprawled with the bike in the gravel, like sliding into home plate, and looked up in a cloud of settling dust, my lower right leg painfully caught between the frame and the front wheel at an odd angle.

Pulling my leg free, I saw that the curved red fender had cut a crimson gash in my shin. I got up and limped, pushing my bike, to our small gray frame house and met my mother, who ran out the front door toward me with a look of concern. "What happened, Chris?" Pushing up my torn pant leg, she looked at the wound. "My gosh, you'll need stitches for this!" Then she helped me into the car and drove to the hospital as I gripped the painful leg with my hand.

Twenty minutes later four nurses, one grasping each arm and leg, tried to pin me down on the padded operating table. I struggled, rolling from side to side with all my strength. They could not manage to hold me still and apply the anesthetic. My mother stood watching nearby, and I called out, "Mommy, tell them I'll stop if they let go."

"Please listen to him," she said to the nurses, "he'll stop if you let go." The four nurses at the corners of the operating table cautiously loosened their hold on my limbs but continued to hover, alert in their clean white uniforms, each with both hands raised over my arms and legs, tensely poised as if ready to pounce at the slightest move.

My mother had stood up for me—now I had to prove I could follow through. I kept my word and held still as a white gauze mask appeared from behind my head and was placed by two hands gently and firmly upon my face. Then I breathed in the strange, pungent odor of ether, and faded off into a great wave of darkness, flecked with pinpoint stars.

*

Creative Vision

For most of my life I stepped outside the box—with one foot, that is. The other foot I kept firmly inside the box out of cautious concern for survival. But I could never be happy with both feet in the box of convention—the urge to explore and create was too strong.

Yet my forays into new realms were sometimes misunderstood. In third grade an art teacher, a serious woman in a white smock who came in sometimes to give us instruction, announced we were having an Art Test. We dipped our brushes in water and waited, alert at our desks, with our trays of watercolors. The test, she told us, was to paint a river. "Are you ready? Begin."

In my mind I pictured a river, streaming with gathering force down from the mountains, flowing through a small valley, and splashing over a cliff. It would be fun to paint the most exciting part of a river— a waterfall!

My painting came back with a C, deflating my balloon of enthusiasm. The teacher had written, "This doesn't look like a river. It looks more like a waterfall."

I felt completely misunderstood. If I told her I meant to paint a waterfall, she might say I had not followed the assignment. I was hurt. I tried to write it off as just another example of an adult who didn't get it —but I never forgot.

If she were still alive today I might tell her how I felt and ask her why she misunderstood my painting—and why the hell did she give us an Art Test? I imagine her sitting, gray-haired now, in a cozy chair in her modest apartment, looking at a reproduction of the Mona Lisa. After a thoughtful pause, she might reply: "I don't remember what happened that day, but I'm truly sorry. I didn't realize you meant that a river could be a waterfall. As for the Art Test, I was under pressure from administrators to give grades to measure students' progress. But how to evaluate a third-grader's art? All I could think of was a test to see how well you could paint something from memory. That was art to me, not so-called 'creativity.' It's easy enough for kids to be creative in a sloppy kind of way, but to paint something that looks real—*that* takes training and talent." And she might gesture toward the Mona Lisa. "Let Leonardo da Vinci be my witness."

At that point, I imagine, since I can see some truth in what she said,

I would let the matter rest—despite my enduring desire to show her a Jackson Pollock.

My luck was better in fifth grade, when the teacher told us to write a story about whatever we wanted. Feverishly scribbled, a fantastic adventure flowed from my pen and plunged into a mysterious underground chamber with a shimmering circular pool. Beside it stood a carved wooden idol, like a totem pole, with a single diamond eye.

Years later, when I discovered Buddhist meditation, I wondered where that dream-like image could have come from. Was it a spiritual symbol from some Far Eastern region of the unconscious? From then on, without yet quite realizing it, I began to search for the meaning of my vision.

*

A White-Bread Life?

Dinner at my house was often pretty much the same: a piece of meat, instant mashed potatoes, and Bird's Eye frozen peas, which unlike drab canned peas were actually a bright and sprightly green. Oh yes, and Wonder Bread: white, light, and 90% air. Even then as a kid in the suburbs, I had a yearning for bread that was more substantial—something that could be chewed. So I would take a slice of Wonder Bread, roll it up, then press and knead it together into a solid little ball. It became darker, dense, compressed, and satisfying. I slowly chewed and chewed it, savoring the texture, while I used my fork to mold a lifeboat from mashed potatoes and filled it up with bright green peas.

"What are you doing?" my father said sternly. He was a cautious, responsible man, an insurance underwriter for Atlantic Mutual, the company that paid up big whenever an ocean liner or cargo ship sank to the sea bottom.

"Making a place for peas," I replied, with creative satisfaction. Even then, I didn't want a white-bread life—I wanted something to chew on.

*

Hitting the Ground

As kids of about eight or nine we liked to play cowboys. Afternoons after school we huddled around the first TV in the neighborhood and watched Wild West shows (they were called serials, I later learned, because the story continued week after week, not because they were sponsored by breakfast cereals). After a half hour of Gene Autry or The Lone Ranger, we boys would go outside, run for cover behind a rock or a shed, and shoot at each other with imaginary guns, each sketched for a moment by an outstretched arm with a raised thumb and pointed index finger. When you got "shot" you grabbed some part of your body with your hand, yelled "Ah!," fell down and rolled on the ground. But no one stayed dead for long—we immediately recovered and rejoined the fight, an ongoing improvised drama that we called "playing guns."

Alone in my room I lay on the bed listening to a record called "Ghost Riders in the Sky," looking up at the ceiling imagining phantom cowboys riding through wind and clouds, swept along by haunting minor chords: "Yippie-aye-ay… yippie-aye-oh… ghost riders in-n-n the sky-y-y."

One day my parents took me to visit their friends on Nantucket island and I wound up playing with their son Bob, who was about my age, in a rustic barn full of antique furniture. This time we had real plastic squirt guns, so we knew when we scored a perceptible hit. Running around, hiding behind worn wooden desks, chairs, and chests, imagining ourselves valiant, invincible warriors of the Old West, we tried to outdo each other with fancy dramatic and risky moves.

Then, dodging the wet arc of Bob's squirt gun, I leaped behind a big trunk while aiming a shot back at him, not looking down at where I was going. As I came down, I never touched the wood floor, but dropped through an open trap door with no stairway below, nothing to break my fall, tumbling headfirst down toward the hard dirt floor of the dark cellar.

In the midst of the somersault dive my left arm flung itself out beyond my head in a primal instinctive attempt to stop the approaching blow.

But when hand and head hit the ground, it felt like hell exploding.

The next thing I knew I was stretched out flat on my back and wailing, with my parents kneeling beside me. For a moment I looked at the back of my bloody left hand, which thrown between my head and the ground had absorbed the first impact and probably saved my life. Strangely my hand felt nothing. All I could feel was the overwhelming pain in the crown of my head. That was the price I paid for getting carried away with fantasies.

*

Learning to Play on the Field

Once I got a chance to be quarterback in gym-class touch football, and called for a punt on first down. The idea was to take the other side by surprise, kick the ball over their defense, and recover it near the goal line. But all it achieved was we gave up the ball.

I had better luck in sports when we played informal pickup games on the playground where a bunch of us often got together after school. In the spring it was baseball, without uniforms, managers, or umpires. We chose up fairly even teams by making the two best players captains and giving them alternating picks. Then came a little ritual, more fun than just flipping a coin. One captain tossed the bat in the air and the other caught it with one hand in the middle and held it with the handle upward, while the first clasped his fist around the bat just above where the other held it, and they took turns grabbing the bat hand over hand, fist above fist climbing upward until they reached the rim of the handle. Whoever came out on top put his palm on the crown of the bat and got first pick of the rag-tag assortment of players who stood around watching expectantly. Then we played our own way, and settled disputes by yelling "He was out!" "No, he was safe!" until someone said "Oh, let 'em have it" and we all got on with the game.

Likewise in the fall we played tackle football, unsupervised, without helmets or shoulder pads. Sometimes there was a big guy named Rocco, who had stayed back a grade, so tough that no one could bring him down. When he showed up and got hold of the ball, he always bulled his way to a touchdown, often dragging several would-be tacklers with him.

Was there a way to stop Rocco? In the school library I found a book about how to play football—a hardback with no signs of wear—and looked up the chapter on tackling. It said not above the waist, because the runner could keep on running, and not below the knees, because it was hard to grab moving feet. As shown in the illustration, the trick was to push your shoulder into his legs above the knees and wrap both your arms around them.

The next time Rocco showed up, we tried an experiment: I stood waiting in a crouch while he, with the ball, came running across the field, full speed right at me. Following the book's instructions, on impact I lunged forward, thrusting my shoulder into his churning thighs above the knees, then flung my arms around him and hung on like a sprung trap. Amazingly, he came tumbling down. I had learned to tackle with the help of a book.

Before long the other kids learned how to do it too, and Rocco began to respect us. While still a powerful runner, he no longer ran away with the game. In fact Rocco stepped in to protect us when an older bully tried to push us around.

*

Snowball Fights

In winter we walked to school beside snowbanks the plows had piled up to clear the streets. Each intersection had lofty, mountain-like mounds of snow stacked on all four corners, perfect for building impregnable snow forts as we slowly made our way home in wool coats and mittens. Boys walking down each side of the street could toss snowballs at each other, quickly duck into a fort to take cover, and pack another double handful of sticky white snow into a fat solid ball and pop up, take aim, and let it fly— then duck behind the thick fortress walls again when someone threw a reply. These snowball fights were great fun. But I tried to avoid the more serious fights I'd seen where punches were thrown and somebody might get hurt.

One time my younger sister Wendy asked me to get back at a kid who was bullying her. So I went out in the snow and told him to leave her alone. Even though he was younger and smaller than I was, he talked tough and refused to give in. Finally to make the point I pushed him down in the cold snow. I didn't feel good about doing it, but felt I had to protect my sister.

Another time, in the fall, a guy my own size challenged me to a fight— I can't remember why—in the driveway beside his house. I tried to talk him out of it, but he came at me, and we wrestled onto the ground. I managed to get on top with one knee on either side of his torso and held him down with both hands clamped on his upper arms. "You're pinned," I said. "In wrestling that means the match is over. Give up and I'll let you go."

"I don't care. I'm not giving up." He scowled, tried to rock back and forth, and refused to concede no matter how long I held him down. For ten minutes I kept him pinned as he continued to struggle off and on.

Finally I said, "Let's make peace. I'm getting up, I need to go home." I let go, stood up, and started walking away, without looking back. But when I heard his quick steps approaching behind me I turned to see. He came at me with a flurry of hard blows to my chest with his fists. I stood there taking his punches without hitting back, in sad despair that he wouldn't accept my offer of peace. Then his mother opened the front door. "Come back here, Eddy!" she commanded. She sent him to his room, and listened as, breathing hard, I told her my story. Unlike the snowball fights, that fight was not fun, and I tried to avoid fights from then on.

*

Swimming Toward an Island

After his parents immigrated from Hamilton, Ontario, my mother's father Redge grew up riding horses on a ranch in Iowa. He became a dentist and settled into a big white house in Reading, a suburb of Boston, with his wife Millie, who as a young woman had been his patient. Tall, laconic, and solidly built, he had a natural dignity that earned him the nickname Redge. When I was growing up he had retired and devoted his time to investing in stocks and playing golf and poker with the mayor and the small group of politicians and businessmen who ran the town. On the mantel in his living room stood the shiny bronze trophy he was awarded for scoring a hole-in-one at age 76.

He gave me tips on how to swing a golf club, but I was more interested in learning to play poker, with its combination of luck, skill, and psychology. That combination also served him well in playing the market. When my seventh-grade math teacher assigned us to pick a stock and make a graph of its progress up or down for a month, I called Redge to ask for advice.

"Texas Instruments," he said.

"What business are they in?"

"They make transistors." His tip was spot-on. Portable transistor radios were a growing fad in the mid-fifties, as young people wanted to listen to rock and roll away from their parents, and during that month the stock went steadily upward. I thought of buying some shares with the money I'd earned selling Christmas wreaths door-to-door, but instead saved it and bought a used motorcycle when I got to college. Thirty years later Texas Instruments was worth many times that much—and the motorcycle's engine had long since been stolen.

What I remember best about Redge was his ritual of shaking hands with me at the end of each visit. When I was a kid he would look me in the eye and slowly tighten his grip until he overcame my best effort to match his strength. As I grew stronger it became more of a contest, but he would always win and then smile. As he grew older and weaker, eventually I was able to meet his grip, and could even have overcome it, but out of respect for him never went that far. For years he continued the handshaking ritual, but no longer smiled, probably aware I was holding back.

In that time of his aging, I remember going with Redge to a movie. As we walked down the aisle of the theater, his eyes were slow to adjust to the darkness, and I had to guide him by the elbow to a seat. Not long after he was driving his Oldsmobile with my mother as a passenger and didn't see a warning sign. Cars had no seatbelts in those days, and the accident threw her out into the street. She had to wear back and neck braces for months. My adventurous mother suffered a year feeling like an invalid, and it seemed like I might be losing the mother I knew. Gradually she recovered through daily swimming and went on to win races in her age group. From her I learned the sidestroke and backstroke, both of which I liked better than the crawl because with my eyes above water I could see the sky, the trees, and the mountains. Her ribbons and medals for swimming hung on the wall.

Redge's wife Millie had a jolly spirit, brightening social gatherings as she busily took care of everyone. She went to bridge club, traced her ancestry, and sailed across the Atlantic without her husband to see the coronation of Queen Elizabeth in 1953.

Millie maintained her good humor even when she began to have problems keeping track of things. On a small wooden table beside her favorite padded mahogany chair was a stack of form letters from charities requesting donations. She would go through the pile, writing a check for each one, though sometimes the same worthy cause received several donations. She remained happy and generous, even when unable to remember the names of her children and grandchildren, living in a small nursing home with Alzheimer's until dying at 97.

The decline and death of my grandparents affected me. No longer was Redge the indomitable strong man, nor Millie the welcoming, generous host. I knew my youth, too, would not last forever. Generations rise and fall like waves crashing on the beach.

My mother was left-handed and too dyslexic to attend college (writing appeared to her as a mirror image) but she went to art school and painted a beautiful copy of a Japanese print: an elegant woman in a black kimono, kneeling beside a hanging red flowering plant. She married my father, a marine insurance underwriter who she claimed looked like Cary Grant, and we lived in the suburbs of Boston and New York. When I was a kid she entertained me with limericks, such as one mocking how people from out of town might mispronounce the name of the city of Worcester:

> There was a young lady from Woos-es-ter
> who yoos-es-ta crow like a roos-es-ter.
> She yoos-es-ta climb
> two trees at a time
> and her sis-es-ter yoos-es-ta boos-es-ter.

She recited these lines with fun-loving *joie de vivre*. Looking back, I see it as a celebration of the athletic prowess of women like my mother and her sister. But another limerick she recited with fervor was a warning for the reckless adventurer:

> There was a young lady from Niger
> who smilingly rode on a tiger.
> They returned from the ride
> with the lady inside
> and the smile on the face of the tiger.

Many years later Aunt Nan told me that when they were young women, she and my mother were swimming in a lake toward an island, followed by Redge in a rowboat, when dark clouds and wind came in and the waves got rough. Redge told his daughters to turn back and he would pick them up in the boat. Nan did, but my mother kept on swimming toward the island, ignoring her father's commands. She was determined to prove herself. She knew she could make it, and she did. Every summer at our cottage in Maine on Lovewell Pond, my mother swam the mile across the lake to the beach on the other shore, with my father, me, or my sister Wendy rowing the boat. And unlike my skeptical father, my mother encouraged my creative adventures.

For the most part she was understanding, but one time she let me down was when I had my tonsils out. During hospital visiting hours after the operation, I waited in a big room full of kids in beds, as parents came to visit their children. But my parents did not come. Anger and hurt weighed down my heart. Was that man over there my Uncle Dan? No. Among all the visitors, there was no one I knew. The next day as we drove home I asked my mother why she had left me alone. She explained that the doctor advised her not to visit because it only made children want to go home, and then cry when visiting hours were over and their parents left. She had followed the doctor's advice instead of her heart.

*

A Surprising Prophecy

At my grandmother's house one Christmas we all sat together on the dark red oriental carpet around the warm, crackling fire in the brick fireplace and opened our presents one by one. I could feel the rich rug beneath me, the flickering glare of light on my face, smell the smoke of grandfather Redge's cigar and my father's pipe, taste the butter cookies and the hot cider I was drinking, and hear the chatter of voices in the air, as someone handed my mother a large, strangely shaped package.

Everyone stopped and watched as she undid the ribbons and pulled the paper away from a rather unusual object. It was a big ceramic bat, with a wingspread of a foot and a half, thick and heavy, its pouch-like belly evidently meant to be a vase for flowers when the bat was hung on the wall. The bat's cream-colored glaze reflected the gleam of the dancing fire as everyone stared at this monstrosity with pointy wings and beady eyes.

"Who gave you that?" asked Aunt Nan.

My mother looked at the tag. "Walter," she said. She glared at her older brother, who sat in an easy chair, sport coat unbuttoned, his mouth in a slight smirk. Walter revealed he discovered the bat in an antique shop and thought it was so ugly that it would make a perfect present to be passed from one family member to another each Christmas as a surprise, an annual prank that we all could enjoy—except the unfortunate recipient (adults only, of course) who would have to keep the bat for a year, whether hanging on a seldom-seen wall or stowed in a closet, while plotting whom to award it to next. Of course, on the following Christmas my mother gave it back to Walter. But he was glad to receive it and pass it on again, this time to his sister Nan, rejoicing in the new family tradition he had established.

The oldest child, Walter was tall and handsome, dashing in a way. According to my mother, as a young man his distinguished appearance and air of confidence helped him to crash coming-out parties for debutantes. Walter was a great salesman. He also had some talent as an artist. The copy he made of Franz Marc's painting of two red deer that hung in our den fascinated me with its graceful, curving forms and unexpected colors. It was my first up-close taste of modern art.

Walter could be intense, as well as a little eccentric—you never quite knew what to expect. At Millie and Redge's house one Christmas, Walter sat in a gray suit with his tie loosened as I leaned forward beside him in the big living room, intent on our conversation. The rich red rug spread out under everyone, talking in various groups, all lit by the tall floor lamp in the corner, but at that moment they did not exist for us. We were arguing politics, Left versus Right.

When Walter found out that for Christmas I had asked Millie for a subscription to *The New Republic*, at that time a liberal journal, soon he was yelling at her in the kitchen, "That's a communist magazine!"

"Well, I never..." answered Millie, flustered by his reaction. Of course, he had no way to cancel my subscription.

When after my first year of college I stayed for the summer in Reading with Millie, she asked me to escort her to a local presentation on Florida real estate, where, she was happy to know, they served free drinks. We sat together at a café table with a red tablecloth as she sipped her Martini, looking up at a slide show of sunny Florida landscapes. The salesman explained that for only a few hundred dollars one could buy a prime lot near a golf course, with electric, water, and sewage lines, as well as an access road, soon to be developed. This was our chance to get in early with an investment that could only increase in value with the Florida real estate boom.

Millie, evidently feeling a bit tipsy, decided to consult with me first. "Do you think I should do it?"

My philosophy at the time was to encourage my grandmother to be adventurous, not cowed by old age—and besides, I had visions of hitching to Florida and camping out on that plot of undeveloped land. "Well, Millie, it's up to you. If you want to, why not?"

"Yes, I think I will!" Her face was alive with enthusiasm.

The next day when she called Walter to tell him about her new investment, he reacted strongly. I could hear his raised voice coming through the phone. "What? You fell for that? You've got to get out of it!"

"But it seemed like a good investment…" It turned out that Massachusetts law allowed three days to cancel the deal, and Walter insisted she do so, since development plans in such cases were rather uncertain. Ever since Redge's death Millie tended to follow her son's advice, so that was that.

But not quite. Apparently Walter looked further into the prospects for Florida real estate, because some years later he asked my mother to buy a similar plot—from him! He was now selling undeveloped land in Florida, and was determined to win the company's salesmanship contest by buying a lot in the name of each of his relatives and reimbursing them with his own money. He won the contest, and for more than twenty years my mother owned a small plot of land in central Florida, which for all we knew could have been in a swamp. I never did go there to find out, and neither did she.

Walter had come of age during the Great Depression, and as time went on he became convinced that another one was on the way. He believed that the globalist liberal foreign policy elite would drive the economy off the road and into a ditch. So to guard against the coming depression, he invested in precious metals.

Years later, when Uncle Walter died of cancer, he left my mother a thin three-foot water pipe packed with silver dimes, relics of the days when dimes were actually made of almost 90% silver. As we sat on the floor extracting the coins and stacking them in paper wrappers, my father explained that Walter's basement held a number of such pipes, precious metals disguised as plumbing supplies. What's more, they were protected from burglars by home-made booby traps he had contrived. Banks might fail and the stock market crash, but Walter had his own Fort Knox, secured from home invasion down in the basement.

Despite our differences, I enjoyed our debates. In the year before he died I received a hand-written letter from Walter that may have revealed another side of him. He wished me well in my poetic endeavors, and quoted from his favorite poem, "Locksley Hall," written in 1842 by Alfred Lord Tennyson. After descriptions of future battles in the sky, there's a prophecy of peace:

Till the war-drum throbb'd no longer, and the battle-flags were furl'd
In the Parliament of man, the Federation of the world.

At that moment at least, poetry was able to bridge the gap between us.

*

While my mother's family could be described as upper-middle-class, of English and Scottish ancestry, my father's family was of working-class German, English, and French Huguenot immigrant stock. My father showed me letters in the attic between cousins who fought on opposite sides in World War I. His father, my Grandpa Bill, worked in a book factory, Colonial Press in Worcester. Grandpa's years on the assembly line were marked by three missing fingers on his left hand, long ago stamped off by the mechanical printing press. Grandpa Bill retired as a foreman, and took pride in making quality books. Once he showed me how to break in a new hardcover book without damaging the spine, by opening a few pages at a time starting from the front and the back, smoothing them gently down until the book could be opened to any page with no stress on the binding.

Grandpa Bill was sociable and liked to talk, as my father, his eldest son, could be at times. Nana, his wife, was quiet, proper, even a bit straight-laced. Maybe she was part of the reason my father sought security. Dad was very responsible and stayed at the same job as a marine underwriter with Atlantic Mutual for his entire career, even in his older years when they promoted younger men over him and he had to train them. Insurance was a good field for him. He carefully kept track of expenses, and was always early to everything. Whenever we went anywhere, especially to church on Sunday, he got impatient with my mother, who was always late. "Hurry up, people are waiting!"

"I'm coming, I'm coming, as soon as I find my earring."

When my father was younger he had some adventures at sea, sailing on merchant ships to far-off ports like Tokyo, Naples, and Singapore. He was the first in his family to go to college, and studied nautical engineering and ship design at MIT. In World War II he tried to get into Navy officer training, but failed to pass the security check because another man with the same name from a neighboring town had a criminal record. My father wrote a letter to the local sheriff, and eventually the mistake was cleared up. But that was too late for the Navy, so he became an Army cargo officer, escorting supplies on Liberty Ships through the Strait of Gibraltar, where German U-boats lay in wait, in waters of unseen danger.

What made him so cautious after the war was over? It may have been that he grew up in the Great Depression, when jobs were scarce, and now faced the responsibilities of becoming a father. Or maybe it was the war itself, and what it did to his brother Dan.

Uncle Dan was gentle and friendly, good at skiing and golf, with an artistic gift. He painted peaceful portraits of dogs in the unfinished attic, carved bird and animal sculptures in his workshop in the garage, and liked to sit in the living room smoking his pipe. As a young man Dan attended the Rhode Island School of Design until his mental and emotional state made it hard for him to continue. He returned home in time to be drafted into the Army in WWII, where he served in the 10th Mountain Division in Italy because of his skill on skis. He was one of three American infantry men manning a machine-gun nest dug into a hill above snow-covered woods—until German soldiers overran them in a shower of bullets. Dan saw his two buddies killed before his eyes. For the wound in his leg he received a medal, the Purple Heart. That wound eventually healed, but his heart and mind did not. Keeping those terrible moments to himself, for the rest of his life Dan suffered from "shell shock," now called Post-Traumatic Stress Disorder.

When I was a kid he lived at home with his parents, and I didn't realize there was anything wrong. He was friendly and liked to show me his tools and his art. One time I was happy to hear he had a girlfriend. Uncle Dan proudly showed me the engagement ring he planned to give her. But the courtship fell through; I never learned why. A year later we came to visit and Nana and Grandpa said Dan was having a hard time. I went up to the attic to see for myself. He was staring intently at a strange painting he was working on, an abstract pattern of black and white. "What's that?" I asked.

"The seven sides of the moon," he said gravely, and explained that alien beings were hiding there to avoid the wars on earth.

After his parents died Dan spent the rest of his life in the mental ward of a veterans' hospital in rural Massachusetts. Once in early summer I went to visit him, and took him out to lunch. As we drove back to the hospital, he invited me to go with him on a tour of Europe. "I haven't been back since the war, and my savings would pay for us both."

For a moment I pictured Uncle Dan and myself riding a gondola in Venice and standing in line at the Louvre to see the Mona Lisa. But what if he had a nervous breakdown or disappeared in a train station in Paris? I might enjoy the adventure, but feared to take on the responsibility.

"I'm sorry, Uncle Dan, but I need to work this summer."

After we said goodbye at the hospital, I drove home on a winding country road. Under the brick arch of a small bridge, a nail punctured my right front tire. As I looked at the flat a foreboding crept up my spine.

Some years later in the veteran's hospital, Uncle Dan hung himself in his room. I felt regret that I didn't go with him to Europe. And for a long time my father felt guilt that he hadn't done more to save his brother, who had said he felt like a burden on the family.

My father's younger sister Beverly was almost never mentioned, probably because she had an illegitimate child and died of pneumonia after wandering off in the winter cold when her parents made her give up her baby for adoption. My memory of her is vague, but she and Uncle Dan haunted my father. He worried that since both his brother and sister were unstable, there might be a genetic defect in the family. That made him careful to be normal. And he worried about me taking a year off from school and not pursuing a more secure career. Every so often he said with annoyance, "Why don't you cut your hair and get a decent job? Do you want to be a bum?" My father did not take chances, and I guess that worked for him—but not for me. Yet from him I learned not to go off the deep end.

Chapter 8: Back to Cambridge

The Sundial

Rarely a shiver of damp decay
reaches from the garden shade, where drops
hear one another fall and a migrating
bird is calling, to the column,
which in marjoram and coriander
stands and shows the summer hours;

Only as soon as the lady (whom a servant
follows after) in the bright Florentine hat
leans forward over the rim,
it becomes shady and secret—

Or when a summer rain
comes from the swaying motion
of the high treetops, it has to rest;
for it doesn't know how to express the time
that then in the paintings of fruit and flowers
suddenly glows in the white garden house.

—Rilke

Quarantine

After living around people of various ages and backgrounds on the Lower East Side of Manhattan and traveling in Mexico during my year off, living in student housing seemed less than exciting. So I found an apartment off campus with Paul, the second floor plus attic of an old gray clapboard house on Flagg Street. I took the room in the attic, with slanted ceilings on both sides and a double window looking out over the driveway and yard, where I could sit at my desk and write. We celebrated the move by drinking a six-pack of beer as we relaxed in the attic. It left me with a terrible headache, so much so I went to get checked at the clinic. The doctor, a middle-aged balding man wearing a tie and white coat, closely examined my eyes and said in a serious voice, "Jaundice. You may have hepatitis. Were you exposed to anyone who had it?"

"In Mexico City I stayed at a boarding house where someone came down with it."

"Were you eating together?"

"We may have used the same plates, but they were washed."

"You could get it from plates or utensils if they weren't sterilized." He let the diagnosis sink in. "Until you're no longer contagious, you'll need to stay in quarantine."

So for three weeks in September, I was confined in a room on the fourth or fifth floor of the newly constructed Student Health Center, a concrete high-rise overlooking Harvard Square with its antique news kiosk. It was not my idea of how I wanted to start off my junior year.

The room was quiet, in a shade of pale green, with a bed, sink, and private bathroom. One wall of the room was mostly glass, a big picture window with a sliding curtain of darker green that pulled back in ripples to reveal a broad view of the outside world, with its concrete sidewalks and red brick buildings, a pizza-joint sign, and, in the middle of the intersection, the subway entrance with stairs disappearing down in the ground, under the newsstand racks with headlines too far away to read.

At first I just lay in bed with my thoughts, too sick to do much. All day fatigue pervaded my body. In the bathroom mirror the whites of my eyes were tinged with yellow. When I looked down, my stools were gray clay. I was not very hungry, but simple meals like hot cereal were brought in by the smiling nurse in her hospital smock. No visitors were allowed. My roommate Paul could stand at the door, keeping his distance, but only came once. A couple of times I talked on the phone with my parents, but otherwise I was left to make the best of being alone.

At least I could study in peace with no drinking or drugs or adventures to distract me. The neurophysiology textbook was dense but fascinating, perhaps a step toward unlocking the mysteries of the human mind.

For diversion I read a book on chess, where I could explore tactics like the fork, the pin, and discovered check, then go over games by the masters who put moves together in unforeseen combinations.

Most intriguing were two new novels I read: *Herzog* by Saul Bellow, and *An American Dream* by Norman Mailer. The writing in *Herzog* was brilliant and polished. It was a pleasure to read each sentence. But Herzog the protagonist was stuck, unable to do anything about his failing marriage except wander aimlessly and write letters to friends, family, and famous people—without sending them. The letters were well-written, but when was he going to *do* something? In contrast Mailer's writing lacked that kind of style, but had guts. His fiction confronted sex and violence head on. Yet for me it showed the futility of his character's violent machismo, and Mailer himself was convicted of assault for stabbing his wife. The two books explored psychological crises, but both led nowhere.

Later when Mailer visited the campus in a dark brown suit with white shirt open at the neck, I squirmed through the crowd around him until, a few feet to one side, I leaned toward his right ear and asked about two character types he'd described in *Advertisements for Myself*: "What's the difference between a hipster and a hero?"

Pinned in place by the mob, he stared ahead without turning to face me and said, "The hipster is treading water."

For me, Herzog was like the hipster treading water. Mailer, on the other hand, aspired to be a hero by cultivating courage—but he seemed to lack an important quality: selflessness. His ego got in the way.

As I read these books in my peaceful hospital room, gradually I began to feel better. My stools were no longer gray, the whites of my eyes less yellow. One afternoon I was bouncing around on the bed, playing catch with myself by tossing a crumpled piece of paper up in the air, when I looked through the picture window and saw a small familiar figure talking to someone on the corner four stories below. It was W. J. J. Gordon, my creative process teacher, in work clothes, gabbing with someone, his crinkly face full of animation. I stood in the window waving my arms until finally I caught his eye. He looked up, smiled broadly, and waved back.

When I saw the doctor for my exit exam, after listening to his clinical explanations I asked him a question that had been on my mind. "What would you say—is it safe for me to keep drinking?"

"Well, it's up to you," he said. "But I would not recommend that anyone drink alcohol." From then on I tried to limit my intake to no more than one drink on any particular day. And to add to the obvious scar on my shin from a childhood bicycle accident, I now carried unseen scars inside on my liver from the trip to Mexico. But the solitary time spent healing motivated me to go back to my classes and follow my interests with gusto.

*

Getting into Poetry

After being on probation for low grades my sophomore year, I now found a way to somewhat relieve the academic pressure of final exams and papers by taking creative writing every semester. In my junior year it was poetry with Dr. Sandy. Early on he showed us "Mid-August at Sourdough Mountain Lookout," a short poem Gary Snyder had written while working as a fire lookout in the Cascades. With vivid details like drinking from a tin cup of cold water while gazing "through high still air," the poem conveys a sense of expanded awareness, a spiritual oneness with nature. Simple yet profound, it was a vision I began to tune into. I took long walks on paths among trees, carefully watching their branches drift and bend in the wind, as the autumn leaves turned yellow, orange, red, and fell light brown, scattering on the ground, except for the evergreens, which held their verdant hue. What was the nature of this world we live in— matter, mind, spirit, or what? Was "reality" just a vivid yet transient dream?

During the holiday break I went to a New York performance of Edward Albee's *Tiny Alice*, where the characters watch tiny replicas of themselves in a doll house onstage, and are watched by giant replicas somewhere above. Afterwards, when I walked outside the theater, the concrete buildings and sidewalks seemed to be made of *papier-mâché*.

140

Later, reading Thoreau in the college library, I looked across the silent room with students engrossed in their books and imagined, growing through wooden tables, the ghosts of trees. In poetry, dreams could seep into reality.

> Alone in bed
> with a headful of sex,
> reeling with dreams
> until reeling one in:
> skin on skin
> comes the feel of a woman
> into the realm of the real.

Poetry was becoming a vital part of my life. In American Literature I began reading Ezra Pound, and noticed his ways with word-music. Sometimes rather than rhyming words he was rhyming rhythms. In "Homage to Sextus Propertius VI," a poem not overall in regular meter, the rhythm ending the first line, "death closes our eyelids," is similar to the rhythm ending the fifth, "one tangle of shadows," and several others. Echoes like these pervade the elegy, moving it hypnotically toward its somber conclusion. Sadly, that pioneer of modern poetry suffered from mental illness, was anti-Semitic, and became a supporter of Mussolini.

*

Quadraphonic Talk

Instead of studying, I was reading a wide black book called *Silence*, by John Cage, the avant-garde composer famous for his piece *4'33,"* where a pianist comes in, sits at the keyboard, and plays nothing for four minutes and thirty-three seconds. It was not a joke but an invitation to listen to whatever ambient sounds arose in the silence. For Cage, music was everywhere, pervading our experience, if only we would listen. "…humanity and nature, not separate, are in this world together."

141

When I saw on a poster that Cage was giving a talk, I wondered what it would be, and decided to go, along with my abstract-artist friend Andy, who had gone to New York and met painters like Robert Rauschenberg.

In a staid Harvard lounge with oriental rugs beneath the falling vertical waves of beige curtains, a heavy sofa with leather upholstery giving the room a nineteenth-century air, rows of folding chairs were surrounded by four large plywood boxes housing big speakers, planted on the floor facing the modest audience of curious students, professors, and fans of avant-garde music. John Cage came in with a crew cut, a tweed sport jacket, and a matter-of-fact expression. He didn't look like the long-haired radical one might expect, but at least he was silent, in accord with the title of his book. Reaching down toward an amplifier on a small table, he flicked a switch, adjusted a knob, then stood up. Opening a manila folder, he began to read a lecture aloud in a poised and deliberate monotone.

After a few minutes, as Cage continued reading, in one of the speakers his voice began the same lecture again, so two stages of the talk were superimposed. Then one by one, the other speakers spoke up as well, until we had five phases of the same talk serenading our ears in counterpoint. The speakers paused and started up again by turns, so at times there were spoken quintet, quartet, trio, duet, or solo versions of Cage's voice, changing in a seemingly random pattern, punctuated by periods of silence. Some in the audience slightly opened their mouths and looked puzzled, others were smiling and nodding. The lecture was arcane and impossible to follow, but that was probably the point—to listen to the words as music. The concert finally lapsed into a longer silence, and when none of the electric speakers spoke up again, Cage asked, "Are there any questions?"

My friend Andy raised his hand and began what sounded like it might become an extended inquiry about music and abstract art. Inspired by the audacity of the moment, I stood up and started talking at the same time, phrasing a counterpoint question from whatever came into my head.

As Andy and I performed a spontaneous spoken duet, Cage looked our way with a quiet smile.

*

In Transit

I was riding in the back of a flatbed truck, hitchhiking to somewhere I don't remember. Down near the river the truck went past a vacant lot with a large, overgrown yard and a high wooden fence in the back, where a young black man in jeans and no shirt was climbing, reaching for the top, desperately trying to pull himself up, while below on the other side of the yard a blue-clad policeman crouched, intently aiming his pistol at the young man's back.

I stood up in the truck rolling by, possessed by a wave of indignation, and shouted as loud as I could at the cop, "DON'T YOU SHOOT HIM, MAN!" The officer did not move and kept his aim, without yet pulling the trigger. The young black man froze near the top of the fence, as if weighing his fate, then with a grimace turned and began to come down.

The truck I was in rolled on, and soon they were both out of sight. I did not hear a shot, and it looked like the young man would live, but be caught.

*

Victims of Fate?

I restricted my drinking, but Paul did not. And alcohol affected him differently than marijuana. Smoking dope had been an adventure, where we sat by the river or walked through the elegant trees of Mount Auburn Cemetery, transported by the yellow, red, orange, and violet shifting shades of the setting sun. He had turned me on to avant-garde art and music, like a fellow pioneer. But now he would get drunk on beer, lie on the floor in his rumpled suit and messed-up hair with the lights out, and mumble on about what was wrong with his life. Despite money, a good education, and stylish clothes, he had no idea for a career and no girlfriend. Eventually it came down to his parents didn't really care about him. "They sent me to prep school to get me away from them... I don't know why. They're too involved in their own lives. Or maybe they don't like kids."

I had problems with my parents too, but not like Paul did. "I can see how that would be hard for you. Have you been to a therapist?"

"Yeah, but it doesn't help. They're not going to change."

"Is there some way or other you could let go and move on?"

"I don't know. I just feel like shit. I guess that's my fate."

This kind of talk went on for hours, and happened so often it became Paul's typical trip. I urged him to get more help. I was his roommate, not his therapist.

It reminded me of how my mother confided in me, complaining at length about my father every time I went home. Then I would go to my father and try to mediate between them. This went on through my college years without much discernible progress. My parents would not consider the embarrassment of counseling, and divorce was out of the question, because, I supposed, they needed each other. I sympathized with my mother. But if she and my father were not willing to do something to help themselves, how could I help them?

When I came back to visit and they picked me up, they would start arguing on the way home, maybe something like this: my mother might say to my father, "Did you make a reservation for dinner?"

"No, I thought you were cooking."

"You expect me to do all the work. It's a special occasion, we ought to go out."

"You think I'm loaded with money?"

"You make enough to take us to dinner, if you were willing to spend it."

"Oh, all right. But don't order *filet mignon*."

Later I told them, "Your constant arguing makes it depressing for me to visit."

"We don't argue so much when you're not here," said my mother. I was a bit shocked at the irony that their opposing attempts to win me over might actually be driving me away. Eventually they did attend counseling weekends for couples, and their marriage improved.

In any case, I did not enjoy being put in the role of therapist, by my parents or by Paul. I began to spend less time with him, and at the end of the term moved to another apartment with different roommates.

Once around midnight on a Saturday night when my roommates were gone, Paul appeared at the door. He looked disheveled, his tangled hair spilling over the side of his face, which was pasty and void of expression. He mumbled something in monotone.

"What?" I responded.

"I need… somewhere to stay… can I crash here… tonight?" His words were slurred, and he belched.

"You can sleep on the couch." I led Paul into the living room. He didn't say much, and flopped down on the couch as if going to sleep. I gave him a blanket, said "Good night," and went back to my bedroom to go over a poem I was working on. But I couldn't find a strong conclusion, and set it aside for later. With my clothes still on I lay back on the bed and dozed off amid wandering thoughts.

After awhile, who knows how long, I felt something happening at the foot of the bed. Opening my eyes, I looked up. There was the tall, hulking figure of Paul, his feet planted on the end of the bed, standing straight up with arms pressed to his sides, his mouth half-open and eyes half-closed as if in a stupor, expressionless. Before I could speak or move, Paul announced in a booming voice, "TIM—BER!" And then he fell, stiff as the trunk of a lumber-jacked tree, his arms still glued to his sides, directly on top of me. The impact of being suddenly hit by this falling human log felt like a physical attack, and jolted me into an instinctive reaction. Possessed by adrenaline, immediately I grabbed him and threw him out of the bed. From his hands and knees on the floor he blinked his eyes and looked back at me in drunken surprise.

"Get out!" I said. He slowly picked himself up, looked at the floor, then trudged down the stairs and went out without closing the door behind him. I sat on the couch feeling angry and violated. I didn't question the force of my reaction. For me, our friendship was over.

145

About that time I began working on an English translation of a Hölderlin poem I had discovered in a German Literature course.

Hyperion's Song of Fate

You wander high in the light
on a carpet of clouds, blessed spirits!
Shimmering heavenly breezes
touch you lightly
like a maiden's fingers on
holy strings.

Beyond fate, like a sleeping baby,
breathe the unworldly ones.
Preserved unharmed
in its modest bud
their spirit blooms forever
and their soulful eyes
gaze in still
eternal clearness.

Yet for us it is given
there's no place to rest.
They dwindle, they fall,
suffering humanity,
blindly from one
hour to another,
like water from cliff
to cliff being thrown
the year long
down into the unknown

With a few years of German and a dictionary, I was happy to find I could make a half-decent translation of a poem that spoke to me. I felt like one of those thrown from cliff to cliff down into the unknown—but wished I could wander high in the light, gazing in still eternal clearness.

*

The Agony of Laughter

I felt drawn to get closer to Nature. My path would be to look inward and write from the source. For years I'd spent childhood summers with my family at our rustic cottage on Lovewell Pond. Now I went there alone, inspired by Thoreau to write in solitude. The little white cottage felt lost in the woods, its inside unfinished with unpainted boards nailed onto a frame of rough two-by-fours and simply furnished with used yard-sale items and faded white curtains. It felt empty without my mother, father, or sister. No one but me to make my own cup of chamomile tea, in silence. No creak of a door nor sound of a voice.

The steam bubbled up to a whistle and I poured the hot stream of water out over the teabag, limp as a little pillow, confined in the bottom of the porcelain cup with nowhere to go. Connoisseurs, I have read, call the turbulent encounter of dry leaves with boiling water "the agony of tea."

I sat on the screened-in porch, sipping hot liquid suffused with the aroma of chamomile and looking out through the lengthening shadows at the lake, where the cool evening breeze was stirring up ripples, disrupting the dim reflections of mountains on the other shore. Should I start tonight? What would I write?

I put the tea down on a small wooden table and went back to get my notebook and pen. Then I felt an intense, swelling pain in the lower right side of my belly, radiating through my torso. It became so strong I collapsed on the floor and began to writhe and roll back and forth.

147

After ten minutes the pain eased a bit, but then returned every hour or so in waves of exquisite agony. Was that hot dog I ate for supper spoiled? The whole night was like that, rolling in bouts of pain as I lay on the floor.

When morning came, something had to be done, so the next time the pain subsided I dragged myself over to a neighbor's house and knocked on the door. In a few moments the knob turned, the door creaked open, and motherly Mrs. Carney, in a drab workaday dress, said, "Chris, what is it?"

I whispered, "I need to see a doctor—can you give me a ride into town?"

"You look pretty sick," she said. "I'll get my keys."

When Mrs. Carney dropped me off at the local osteopath's office (MDs were scarce in this neck of the woods) the brunette receptionist at her desk gave me a registration form and asked me to fill it out. Pale and woozy, I stared at the questions for name, address, and medical history—wasn't it clear I was in no shape to fill out forms?—and handed it back: "I need to see... the doctor... right away."

"Oh." She looked at me again. "I'll get him."

Soon I was describing my pain to Dr. Burris: centered in my lower abdomen and radiating from there, it had come in excruciating waves through the night. Maybe the hot dog I ate was spoiled... And now the pain was coming on again. "I have to sit down," I said.

Soon I lay all the way down and began rolling slowly back and forth on the examination bed.

"You're feeling it now?" said the doctor, and I nodded. "Sounds like appendicitis." Without further ado Dr. Burris dialed the phone and briefed the Bridgton emergency room. Immediately he helped me into his car, peeled out of the driveway, and stepped on the gas. After about ten minutes of speeding on deserted country roads, I rose from my curled-up position on the front seat and soon was sitting upright, watching trees pass as we rode through the wind. "Feeling a little better?" asked the doctor.

"Yes," I said, and Dr. Burris, looking concerned, stepped on the gas even harder. We sped down the road and he said nothing more; uneasiness crept up my spine.

The small hospital near Bridgton was fairly new, with only one floor, a modern rectangular building with a spacious parking lot. As we rushed inside, I barely had time to notice the quiet and neat interior, with a small library of books. When the only doctor in Fryeburg arrived with his ailing passenger after driving 40 miles at 80 miles an hour, without any preliminaries the emergency nurse told me to undress and lie down on a gurney. She wheeled me down the hall, parked me near a wall, and left me there. Ten more minutes ticked by on the clock on the wall across the room. Then the surgeon strode in, took a look, and rushed off to get the nurse, who rushed back, apologized, and started shaving my pubic hair in preparation.

Soon I was lying on the operating table in fetal position, feeling naked and exposed. The surgeon, a dark-haired young Iranian doctor doing his residency in rural Maine, calmly stood over me and gently placed one hand on my shoulder and one on my legs. We both remained motionless for a few minutes, in silent communion. I began to relax under his touch, feeling this surgeon cared for me.

Then a spinal injection numbed my whole body from the neck down, but left me still awake. In that vague bodily numbness there was no pain, but I could feel the surgeon plucking my insides as if they were the strings of a cello. In the opaque glass lamp above the cloth screen that hid my abdomen, I could see a large splotch of reflected red and realized it must be the bloody, open incision. Then a sudden wave of nausea made me gag, about to throw up. Hands gently restrained me, a mask of general anesthesia was quickly placed on my face, and I disappeared into darkness and stars.

When I awoke, it felt like I re-entered my body, descending from somewhere near the ceiling to discover I was in the middle of talking to a nurse about who knows what. Dr. Burris, the osteopath, came in and said with a smile, "That hot dog was a red herring."

He explained they removed my appendix with no complications. Then Dr. Burris leaned toward me with an intense look. "When we were on the way here and you suddenly felt better, I sped up—because I was afraid your appendix had burst, relieving the pressure and spreading the infection throughout your abdominal cavity. It turned out there was only one pinprick spot where some pus spurted out, not enough to spread into peritonitis. You should be fine, just one day in the hospital to start your recovery."

As a boy I used to stay up late at night reading books with a flashlight under the covers—books like Jack London's *White Fang* and *Call of the Wild*. It was no surprise that after my appendix was cut out I spent the next day in the hospital reading a book from its modest library: Joseph Heller's *Catch-22*. It was an extremely funny account of the misadventures of one Yossarian, an American soldier in Italy, as my uncle Dan had been, during World War II. The problem for Yossarian, a B-25 bombardier, was that he didn't want to keep flying missions over German villages, bombing civilians. To get out of doing it, you had to be certified crazy. But if you *wanted* to get out of doing it, you must be sane—so you had to keep doing it. That was a Catch-22. It seemed that whenever a problem couldn't be solved, it was due to this mysterious regulation.

The unsolvable problem for me, the recovering reader, was that whenever I laughed, my stomach muscles contorted the healing incision, and I winced with pain. A big belly laugh was excruciating. I had to stop reading until I completely stopped laughing, but after the pain subsided, the temptation to go on reading returned. *Maybe I can restrain myself and not laugh too hard.* Gingerly I would start reading again, with the utmost restraint suppressing each chuckle, but sooner or later I could hold back no longer and again was convulsed in a fit—the agony of laughter. Reading the book itself was my Catch-22, and I could not resist. The ordeal went off and on for hours, until I completed nine or ten chapters of hilarious suffering. The line between joy and pain is thin, it occurred to me then. One can easily turn into the other.

The surgeon assured me the recovery regimen was working quite well, and my healing progressed very quickly. I was grateful for his calm, expert care, his compassionate touch that transformed the atmosphere.

After the day in the hospital, my parents arrived to take me back to Boston. I never finished *Catch-22*, and so was spared the horrors of the later chapters. But I'd read enough to feel, beneath the laughter, the brutal absurdity of war. And now the insanity was in Vietnam. With no idea what the next year would hold in store, I felt like a survivor, ready for anything.

*

Unstable Triangles

My appendix removed, I returned to town before the start of the fall term to look for an apartment to share, as I healed from the wound in my side, marked by a two-inch scar. The sun had set behind the trees by the time I walked up the steps, backpack over my shoulder, and knocked on the door of a brown Victorian. Soon I heard footsteps inside, the brass knob turned, and the door opened, revealing a woman in a long paisley dress. Her dark hair curled around her face, which was warm but plain, with no make-up. A few years older than I was, she had an air of quiet confidence. "Can I help you?" she said.

"I'm looking for a place to crash tonight. Bob said you might have an extra bed."

"Yes we do, if you don't mind a mattress on the floor."

"That would be fine."

"I'm Mary Sue," she smiled. "Come in and make yourself at home. We only have the apartment for a few days, until the new tenant arrives." We walked down the hall past two sparsely furnished rooms with bare floors and arrived at the kitchen. Sitting at a wooden table with a cup of tea was a young woman about my age with waves of auburn hair flowing down to her shoulders, a few freckles on her face, and a touch of red on her lips. "This is my friend Kathleen," said Mary Sue. "Will you join us for tea?"

"Sure," I said, and eased my pack down to the floor. Kathleen smiled politely and took a sip of peppermint tea. I stared at her, transfixed by the subtle aroma. She wore a tight orange dress with ruffled sleeves, and lifted the china cup carefully to her pursed lips. With her right thumb and forefinger she held the delicate handle, fingers partly curled and pinky extended, while her left forearm rested in her lap—with no left hand.

I held my breath for a second, then relaxed. The missing hand did not detract from her allure, I thought. In fact, it made her unique.

The three of us talked over tea for a while. Although I don't remember exactly what we said, I imagine it might have been something like this:

"Chris, did you see the Truffaut flick at the film archive?" ventured Mary Sue. "*Jules and Jim,* one of my favorites."

"Oh yes, a beautiful film. Two friends in love with the same woman. But the ending—why drive off a broken bridge into a pond?" I looked at Kathleen. "Did you see it too?" She nodded. "What do you think?"

"Oh, just another sad romantic movie." She scrunched up her face.

"But that was the point," said Mary Sue. "A triangle ending tragically."

"Maybe so," said Kathleen, stretching both arms in the air with a yawn. "I'd rather watch *The Hustler.* Anyway, I'm heading for bed." She stood up and walked towards her room. My heart beating harder, I caught up with her in the hall.

"Why do you like *The Hustler?*"

"Paul Newman," she smiled. "Have a good night." She stepped into her bedroom and closed the door behind her. I sighed, and trudged back to my room.

What happened next I remember well. Turning out the light, I lay down on the mattress with a wool blanket, to sleep alone with my fantasies. Then in the darkness I heard quiet footsteps. I looked up to see the shadowy figure of a woman in her nightgown approaching.

"Would you like some company?" whispered Mary Sue.

"Sure," I said, and she slid into bed beside me.

Mary Sue came back to see me again a week later, after I'd found an apartment. She was a congenial spirit, and we had something in common —it turned out she was a poet, visiting from upstate New York. I showed her my bedroom with a mattress on the floor and books piled everywhere.

We walked to a bookstore café and talked about poetry, then came back and made love again. She told me she was married, unhappily.
Her husband spent weekends drinking beer and watching football, and didn't understand her love for poetry. So she took the train to the city to go to readings and meet other poets. "Does he know you're getting involved with me?"

"Not yet, but he probably has his suspicions."

"Well, I guess it wouldn't be good for me to come visit."

"No, it's better for me to come here. He's used to me leaving on weekends."

I mulled over the situation, plagued by visions of her jealous football husband following her to the city to confront her young poet lover, who happened to be me. As we lay in bed the next morning, I said, "This has been great, but I don't think I want to go on with it. I need a steady girlfriend who lives here and isn't married, and the more involved you and I get, the less likely that will happen." She was sad but understanding. Mary Sue packed her bag and went into the living room. I lay there in bed wondering if I had made the right decision. When she came back in she gave me a poem she had just written:

> I said I would set the bird
> free, after seven days singing;
> on the eighth day, I said:
> "Bird, why do you not
> sing sweetly,
> as before?"

I thanked her for the poem. Later I thought maybe it would have been good to keep seeing her for a few months—we could have learned about love and poetry together—but then it would have been harder to break off, and I doubted I'd want to propose she get a divorce and marry me. We kissed goodbye, and Mary Sue left. We never saw each other again. But I kept her poem.

Chapter 9: Looking Inward

The Flamingos
Jardin des Plantes, Paris

In mirror-paintings like those of Fragonard
there is still no more of their white and their red
than if someone told you,
when he spoke of his lady friend: she was

still soft with sleep. When they rise in the green
and stand, upon pink stems slightly turned,
together, blossoming, as in a garden bed,
seducing themselves more seductively

than Phryne; until curling necks around they
nestle their eyes' paleness in their own softness,
in which black and fruit-red hide.

All at once an envy shrieks through the aviary;
but they have stretched out astonished
and stride, each one, into the imaginary.

—Rilke

Franklin Street, 1965

That fall I settled into my second-floor bedroom in a shared apartment,
with freshly painted white walls, faded green carpeting, and a double
mattress on the floor with a blue blanket pulled up to a pair of pillows, but
not tucked in. I had built a nest for two just in case. Beside the wall the
blonde wooden desk made from a detached door perched like a bird
horizontally on four black metal legs. On the desk, facing a brown folding
chair, was a big black Underwood typewriter—it clucked when I'd hunt

and peck to eke out a poem—flanked by a scattering of typed pages. A line of books, including the *Selected Poems* of William Carlos Williams and *Howl* by Allen Ginsberg, lay on the desk like fallen dominoes. On the opposite wall hung a large red-orange print of a big round face with dots for eyes and a tiny line mouth, signed in a lower corner by Paul Klee. Below was a stereo with speakers detached, beside a stack of LPs with *Another Side of Bob Dylan* on top.

There was also an elephant in the room: a large pile of books, papers, cardboard boxes, sprawled clothes, miscellaneous unidentified objects, and a bent hanger, in no apparent order.

One night I played my new Rolling Stones album up loud—"I CAN'T GET NO... SATISFACTION!"—and after a while, the phone rang. It was Alice in the room below, a single woman in her late twenties with a chin-length bob of dark hair. "Hey, can you turn that down? I need some sleep to get up for work in the morning."

"Don't you like the Stones? It's powerful music." I turned it down a bit, but not off. I liked Alice, but now that I no longer lived at home with my parents, I felt I had a right to play the Rolling Stones at midnight. Looking back, I must admit, sometimes I was absorbed in my own little world that I thought was big.

*

A Memorable Seminar

Robert Lowell, New England's premier poet, had in his book *Life Studies* infused the mundane matter of memoir with the energy of emotional art. So when Elena, a graduate student I'd recently met, invited me to an informal session with Lowell himself at a local coffee shop, I agreed without hesitation. Tall and lean, with curly brown hair, navy blue sport coat, and horn-rimmed glasses that framed his sculpted features, Lowell sat with notebook and pen amid a bunch of eager students around a table. When he asked us to introduce ourselves, I said Allen Ginsberg and the Beats had influenced me, and was a little surprised when he spoke of Ginsberg with respect. Apparently, despite their different styles, Ginsberg's emotional candor had influenced Lowell.

"What do you think of Bob Dylan?" I asked.

"The songs I've heard on the radio sound pretty good, but sometimes it's hard to make out the words," he said with a raised eyebrow.

When Lowell began discussing student poems, I wanted to contribute something, so I gave him a few lines I'd written about a dream. He read them intently:

> Where there's a will, there's a won't.
> The once-just-a-mouse
> is a fat, red-sweatered rat.
> No sweat, the guy in there got him;
> yet I keep on hitting it
> bam bam bam with a broomstick.

I feared it was too informal to be a serious poem, but Lowell seemed interested, calling attention to the rhythm of the last line. That was encouraging, but it still felt like luck when I got into his seminar.

Lowell had an ear and mind for striking lines. In Robert Penn Warren's anthology of English poetry he went through his top ten favorite pre-twentieth century poems, telling us what he liked about each. I'm not sure I can remember them all, but one was Wyatt's sonnet "Whoso List to Hunt," rumored to be about the poet's love for Anne Boleyn, wife of King Henry VIII. It ends with lines that for me, with their shifting rhythm, brought old poetry to life:

> Who list her hunt, I put him out of doubt,
> As well as I may spend his time in vain.
> And graven with diamonds in letters plain
> There is written, her fair neck round about:
> *Noli me tangere*, for Caesar's I am,
> And wild for to hold, though I seem tame.

In addition to Keats and Donne (for both he found it hard to choose only one poem) Lowell liked Ben Jonson's verse on the loss of his first son, William Blake's "London," and Thomas Hardy's "Wessex Heights." Marvell's "To His Coy Mistress" and Arnold's "Dover Beach" may have been on the list too. Another favorite was "Surprised by Joy," where the grieving Wordsworth turns to share a happy moment with his young daughter—but how can he when she is in her grave, "That spot which no vicissitude can find?" With a wistful sigh, Lowell said he wished he could write a line like that.

He went on to explain that he had turned away from his earlier tendency of striving to make every line brilliant, realizing that some lines were there for contrast or to prepare the ground. In any case, he could weave words together in evocative ways, like the final line of "Sailing Home from Rapallo," where his mother's name was misspelled on her coffin and her body "wrapped like *panettone* in Italian tinfoil." And I loved the conclusion of "Skunk Hour," where the spunky animal heroine sticks her head into a cup of sour cream and "will not scare."

Lowell was generous in his praise of poets he liked. Once after class I found myself alone with him in the elevator, with my green book bag slung over my shoulder and Lowell holding his brown leather briefcase full of poetry.

"Have you read Sylvia Plath?" he asked, pressing the button for the ground floor.

"No, I haven't read her, but I've heard of her."

Looking me straight in the eye he said, "Read *Ariel*—it just came out, and it's dynamite."

Sitting in front of the class in his tweed sport coat and tie, heavy dark-framed glasses, and rumpled hair, Lowell shared his enthusiastic dedication to poetry. He was polite and encouraging to his students—except for one incident in mid-semester that made me realize he had a harsh side too. We were discussing a poem by a student who always sat as close as he could on Lowell's left and spoke a lot, with an air of trying to impress. Lowell read several lines of the student's poem aloud and paused.

157

"What would you say about this?" he asked the class. No one responded. Lowell's comment was brief: "I would say it's pretentious." From then on the student was absent from class.

A few weeks later Lowell was absent too. Most of us had read his personal account of manic-depressive illness in *Life Studies*, but when Professor Alfred replaced him and told us about Robert Lowell's latest breakdown, it was a shock. Looking back I could see that Lowell had gradually become more manic in his intoxication with poetry, and his putdown of the pretentious student revealed an aggressive streak that could override his polite and friendly manner. Professor Alfred was a genial and valiant substitute, but I missed the fearless, refreshing intensity of Robert Lowell, an American bipolar paradox. In the spring, after recovering from his breakdown, Lowell returned to Harvard's Memorial Hall in front of a huge crowd to read a powerful poem protesting the Vietnam War.

*

Moonlight Panic Attack

The practice of writing poetry was becoming a daily habit. Inspired by Lowell's example, I would sit at my desk in front of the typewriter and delve into a hidden cavern of buried emotion, tapping out word by word whatever was there. I also kept a journal full of attempts at self-analysis. Sometimes at night I took a long walk by the river to ponder the nature of reality and where I might fit into it, as the country was torn over civil rights and the misguided war in Vietnam, which I had strongly opposed from the start.

One night while walking along the river's edge I heard the screech of brakes, then a loud bang and tumbling crash as a speeding car hit a lamp post and flipped over on Memorial Drive. When I walked toward the wreck its wheels still seemed to turn in the air in the moonlight. Sirens rang out, police cruisers pulled up, and an ambulance came. Medics put the driver's body on a gurney—alive or dead I couldn't tell—slid it into the back of the ambulance, and whisked it away. I kept walking alone in the dark, then stopped to look out at the leafless trees and the silent depths of the river. As I stood there my heart began to pound, filling my chest with spasmodic rhythm, seemingly out of control. Was this what they call a panic attack? I went back to my room, sat at my desk, and wrote.

Spoken as America

Straight out, where black meets black,
sharp lights cling to the exposed city
in peppered target patterns. Below me
the river snakes toward a moonstruck sea.
Here on the smeared grass
I stand both trapped and free;
I have come to meet my enemy.

Everything is past; I gleam like Christ;
the wind, inquisitive, fingers me.
What hides behind this fragile universe?
He strikes like ice cracking under me,
spreading a branching root-work of unease;
as the wind cuts in,
his cold nerves shoot through me.

Black metallic objects edged
with a blue tinge watch me walk the city.
Through concrete mazes
he has hugged my back;
crept into dreams; bugged my embassies.

Whether I know it or not
my enemy heads off each next thought.

Everywhere, in the opened night
his knife-eyes glitter…
My frog-heart beats full volume for release;
surrounded by the premonition of a shriek
I can hardly hold my form.
Inside, the hungry darkness waits
for me to be off guard.
I have come to meet my God.

When two weeks later Robert Lowell had his breakdown, I began to wonder if something like that might happen to me. After all, my Uncle Dan was schizophrenic. I went to Student Health Services, asked about psychotherapy, and was given an appointment with a therapist in his thirties at McLean Hospital, where I knew Lowell had stayed. When I arrived with several ink-blotted notebooks full of self-analysis, the therapist, tall and thin in a brown sport coat, looked them over and said, "These notebooks are not the solution. They're part of the problem."

Maybe it was true—I was too self-involved. I didn't stop writing in the notebooks, but focused more fully on poetry. After visiting my grandmother Millie I wrote these impressions:

At Grandmother's House

Reaching back into nothingness, the two-dimensional
past, my grandmother emerges as my eye into eternity,
pointing out a vase, or the table, inlaid mother-of-pearl,
her sea-captain grandfather brought back from Britain.

She talks, flaky with age, across the table, in the present—
and I hesitate to turn her back to memory's ornamented
pages: a true sense of time might close the book on her.
Yet she has no designs, and reads the record warm and clear.

This huge house, intricate with the possessions of centuries,
stands behind my flimsy life; I have ignored its potentialities.
Yet suddenly I don't want the plate with a nightmare face
she says she'll give me when she dies; my blank check
is a future which none of these things can write.

She investigates her genealogy, and confesses to an interest
in astrology; her ancestors settled the colonies, yet she feels
fate is up to us. I can't tell her I fear for my mind—
how can I flip, with all that past as ballast?

One ray of hope was my friendship with Elena, the poet who had
invited me to meet Robert Lowell. Five years older than I was, Elena was
divorced, with two kids, a young boy and girl. Except for the divorce,
her family structure echoed my own as a boy at Lovewell Pond in the
summers with my sister and mother, when my father wasn't there. Elena
encouraged me and gave me helpful comments on my poetry.

One night we slept together. The next day I walked down the street
riding a wave of euphoric awareness, with the sky, the trees, and even the
stoplights glowing with vibrant intensity. Later I told Elena about it.

"That's Eros," she said.

But when her ex-lover came by, I felt uncomfortable. He ignored me
and stood face-to-face close to her as they sparred in flirtatious arguments.
He was tall and strong, imposing both physically and intellectually,
a graduate student in History. As I stood watching from the sidelines it
seemed like he was a real man, and I, at 22, was a mixed-up kid.

Later, after he left, I opened up to Elena and shared my insecurities.
I knew she had been in analysis.

"I seem to be going through a psychological crisis."

"Tell me about it," she said. I began to explain, and responded to her
questions. After a while she asked, "Are you in therapy?"

"Yes."

"Good, you can work these things out. But for now I think we should stop making love, and keep on seeing each other as friends." And we did, now and then, for several months. But I felt a continuing sense of unease with her. Once I demonstrated a yogic shoulder stand and stood on my head in the dining room for several minutes while she went back to work in the kitchen. I hovered, suspended there with the world upside down, as it was when I lay on my bed as a kid, imagining what it would be like to walk across the ceiling and through the inverted door, as I listened to "Ghost Riders in the Sky."

*

24-Hour Potato

One afternoon in my shared apartment I walked through the kitchen and felt heat radiating from the oven. Turning the dial from "bake" to "off," I opened the oven door, knelt down in the bank of hot air, and peered in. There on the crusty metal rack was the russet brown potato I had put in to bake yesterday for supper and then completely forgotten. Amazingly it looked OK, its brown skin perfectly intact. I pulled out the rack and gingerly picked up the potato with a potholder. It was light as a wad of paper. I broke the potato in half and the interior was black cinder, riddled with tiny pockets of air. I tried to stick in a fork, but the skin, though still brown, was now brittle. Wow, I thought, a solid, heavy potato transformed into a featherweight ghost of itself through intense, continual heat. An inadvertent chemistry experiment—or even better, a work of art.

Pop art had been all the rage in the New York galleries for a couple of years now. But this could be the start of a new style—food art. I toasted a slice of bread and painted green stripes on it, then made a little exhibit on a side table in the living room with the russet potato cinder broken in half and the green striped toast—tongue-in-cheek symbols of culinary transformation.

Electric Rock

Bob Dylan's concert in late October, 1965, was held in the intimate
Back Bay theater. During the first half he played acoustic guitar in the
spotlight alone, singing poetic folk-style songs like "Blowin' in the Wind"
and "She Pretends That We Never Have Met." It was Bob Dylan from his
first few albums in person, the Bob Dylan I had listened to on the front
porch that summer at our cottage in Maine, enthralled by his streetwise
poetry.

Now with the plush red velvet curtain behind him and haloed in the eye
of the spotlight, Dylan fit the picture I had imagined—curly, shaggy
brown hair framing his thin craggy features, his black gambler's jacket,
white shirt with string tie, tight black pants and pointed boots. He was
laconic and seriously intent, but said a wry word now and then to
introduce each song, his voice trailing off with an almost-shy twang.
Yet when he sang a confidence gathered in him, his clothing seemed to
transport him to a realm where he held his guitar at just the right angle,
strummed it in just the right rhythm, blew his harmonica with Woody
Guthrie country boy authenticity. His outfit and poise seemed like a myth
he created and grew into, changing his name from Robert Zimmerman to
Bob Dylan. At first hearing his unique sound I had been a bit skeptical, but
the imaginative sparks of his lyrics and emotional vibration of his voice
drew me into the magic world he created in "Mr. Tamborine Man." Now
his songs were met with joyous applause in the small jam-packed theater.

After a short intermission the curtain opened on Dylan in front of his
rock band, the Hawks, with electric guitars, piano, and drums.
They launched into a raucous rendition of "Ain't Gonna Work on
Maggie's Farm No More." In a dramatic gesture, Dylan swung away from
the audience to face and lean toward his band, with his back to us,
rhythmically strumming and bending the notes on his electric guitar

through the wildly energetic set, his lyrics popping like a string of firecrackers set off by a rebel poet.

I'd heard he'd been booed by some purists at Newport and in the UK for turning from acoustic folk to electric rock. However, the youthful crowd in this theater had grown up with rock and roll too, as I had, and greeted his new style with enthusiasm. But like a jilted lover, during the second half of the concert Dylan kept his back turned and never said a word to or looked at the audience.

Then on November 5th the Rolling Stones played in cavernous Boston Garden. From our perch near a pillar in an upper corner of the huge hall, Mick Jagger and friends seemed like tiny puppets prancing around on the distant miniature stage amid flashing lights, as their high-powered electric rock, amplified to the max, echoed throughout the arena in "Get Off of My Cloud" and "I Can't Get No…Satisfaction." It was certainly loud, and the crowd went wild, but somehow the Stones jumping around in frustration on a tiny distant stage in the canyon of Boston Garden was a bit of a letdown. Their heavy beat was great to dance to, but acoustic or electric, I found more inspiration in the soulful poetry of Dylan.

*

The Blackout

A few days later, on the evening of Tuesday November 9th, my roommates and I were sitting around on the rumpled couch and well-worn chairs in the living room of our second-floor apartment, discussing the recent concerts over a few beers, when the lights became dim, flickered, and then went completely out. Did we blow a fuse? No, the lights were out in all our rooms. Was it just our house? We stepped outside into the gray light of the full moon, and the whole block was dark. And not only that— we walked down the block and as far as we could see, in every direction, not a streetlight or window was lit.

People were coming out of their houses and looking around in wonder. Could it be the whole city? We went down to the river and looked across at the looming hulks of the towering buildings of Boston, the spectral skyline dim in the moonlight, like a city of ghosts. Here and there on the riverbank people were listening to portable radios. Voices called out in the dark: "New York is blacked out too."

"The whole Northeast."

"Something tripped the circuit breakers of the power grid."

"It started in Ontario."

As the magnitude of the darkness sank in, a feeling of community began to bloom. Neighbors were talking to neighbors they never knew. We could see each other, dimly, in the peaceful presence of the harvest moon, hanging like a lantern in the darkness. If necessary, we could switch on our flashlights—but who really needed them? Save the batteries for later. We were all in the dark together, sharing a moment of history that was not a tragedy but a magical release from the mundane preoccupations of our ordinary lives, unplugged at least for one night, from Toronto to New York.

*

California Dreaming

As the fresh snow of December turned to dirty slush in the deep cold of January, and the clouds were gray, I trudged to class in a heavy wool coat and winter boots with a song to keep me warm, dreaming of California on a Cambridge winter day. I had sent in my application to the M.A. program in creative writing at San Francisco State; though I applied to other schools as well, the place I really wanted to be was the San Francisco of the Beat poets I'd read about in Kerouac's *The Dharma Bums*.

There were signs my fortunes might turn with the seasons. As I stood in an elevator in the new psychology building, a distinguished gray-haired man in a suit, his jacket unbuttoned, stepped in, and with a smiling open face reached out to shake my hand. It was a friendly gesture by a man I recognized but had never met—Erik Erikson, the well-known author of *Childhood and Society*. As a psychology major I was not allowed to take his general education course for non-majors—the only class he taught at the time. That he welcomed an ordinary student like me that way, without even knowing me, made a lasting impression. This was real humanistic psychology—being equal and open with everyone.

As spring birds appeared in the trees and I sat in the library supposedly studying, my gaze fixed on a young woman reading at a table across the room.

Vision

The young Japanese woman
fills the modern library
with a smooth stillness,
an unmoving motion
like milk pouring.

Her face looks recently
unwrapped from silk,
eternal as a china cup.

Any moment she may rise
and float in air,
her slow hair spreading

I had to admit my fantasy was influenced by the paintings of Marc Chagall. What actually happened was I turned back to my books and we both continued reading.

Then my roommates decided to have a party at our apartment. The glance and shy smile of a woman with light brown hair whom I'd never seen before drew me to Karina, and I danced with her. She was at ease in her body, smiling as she swayed in her blue dress. We danced and talked into the night and wound up in my bed on the floor. It seemed like a good match—she was an artist, and I wrote poetry. We fell asleep in each other's arms.

Karina and I kept seeing each other, usually at her place a few blocks away, a first-floor apartment with a front porch. She had the place to herself. Her old boyfriend had gone to Vietnam, and she didn't want to wait for him. She said she wanted a man who was there in person.

In early June she invited me to move in. I had to be out of my place by the end of the month anyway, so I began spending my time with Karina at her apartment. We listened to *Blonde on Blonde,* Dylan's new album, over and over, "Visions of Johanna" and "Memphis Blues Again," and danced to the Stones' "Let's Spend the Night Together" in the living room. Art, poetry, music—this was the life I wanted.

I wrote a long letter to Elena detailing what was not working in our friendship. I was tired of being a sidekick on outings to the park or the beach with her kids. It was time to move on. I had finally found a new girlfriend. Elena invited Karina and me over for tea, and I told her about a Super-8 movie I was making about a man who fell in love with a manikin. She listened attentively with her legs crossed, then took a sip of her tea and encouraged me to continue my creative endeavors.

That spring I was in a poetics course with Robert Fitzgerald, a tall congenial man with graying hair, an ex-naval officer, who had just published a translation of Homer's *Odyssey.* Each week we wrote a poem in a different form—sonnet, sestina, villanelle—and our final assignment was to abandon all forms and write in free verse. Mine was a rebellious fantasy:

Calling Off the Crucifixion
(a motorcycle saga)

Evening comes, as I ride
a Black Shadow out of Bethlehem.
My eyes light up in the setting sun.

The road maps in my saddlebags
weigh me down, so I throw them away.
The wind's an easy answer,
roaring through desert in leather,
black rubber churning the dust.

I skid to a stop
before an empty cross
here in the middle of nowhere.
The instructions say,
"Nail yourself up."

Fuck.
The old man is afraid
of my love.

*

Graduation

The night before graduation I slept at Karina's and was planning to go
back to my place on Franklin Street to meet my parents and sister when
they arrived. But before I got out of bed, there was a call from my
roommate. I reached for the phone with a groggy "Hello?"

"Your parents are here. Your mother walked up the stairs and opened
the door to your room without knocking—and found Molly and Carol
sleeping together in your bed. She looked a bit shocked. You better get
over here."

"Oh, shit. I'll be right there."

Five minutes later I arrived, alone and on foot, prepared to explain everything. My mother, father, and sister were waiting in silence, standing by their Ford station wagon parked in front of the gray, two-story house. I rushed over and blurted out, "Sorry I'm late. I was staying with a friend up the street." With a cool, wooden demeanor, my mother changed the subject. She did not not want to talk about it. My father and sister said nothing. We agreed to meet after the Class Day convocation, and I went upstairs to get ready.

Through some mysterious process I had been selected as Class Poet. That meant writing a poem for the occasion and reading it to the senior class assembly. Since it was 1966, for lack of a better idea I decided to write a sestina, a form with one of six words ending each line in a varying order.

Now it was time. I put on my black cap and gown, drank down a tingling shot of vodka, and marched in the procession to the convocation. When my turn came on stage at the podium, I looked out over the crowd of flat black hats tilting at various angles over young men in black robes and their families under a bright sun in the brick courtyard. I felt no fear—the vodka had knocked out my anxiety—and began reading aloud into the microphone, letting the rhythm of the poem carry my voice along. The audience listened patiently, and one line even got a laugh: "No longer / do undergraduates roll *tobacco* in cigarette papers." The final stanza made an affirmation: "There is magic still in words." The crowd applauded, and as I stepped down from the podium, trying not to trip on my robe, for once I felt accepted as a poet—at least by those who were there that day.

Karina and I had some good times together that summer. We went to hear the Beatles at Suffolk Downs, and could actually see them quite well, amid the screaming teeny-boppers, as they strummed and sang in light gray mod suits and brown mop tops just across the dirt of the racetrack. The excitement was palpable as they played songs like "She Loves You" and "If I Needed Someone." I was a little disappointed they didn't do something more recent, like "We Can Work It Out," with its hope of overcoming difficulties embodied in shifting rhythms. That afternoon the Beatles played a short set, and before long they stopped touring to work on studio albums like *Sgt. Pepper's Lonely Hearts Club Band.*

Despite our happiness, for Karina and me the summer was shadowed by a point of uncertainty. What would happen in September? Would we go together to San Francisco? She said if she didn't get a scholarship she could drop out of art school and come with me. But I was unsure about making that kind of commitment.

*

The Gazelle
Gazella Dorcas

Enchanted: how can the harmony of two
chosen words ever achieve the rhyme
that comes and goes in you, as on a signal.
Out of your forehead rise leaves and lyre,

and all your features already are metaphor
through love songs, whose words, soft
as rose petals, for one, who no longer reads,
to place upon his eyes, which he closes

to see you: transported, as if
each run were loaded with leaps,
only not fired off, as long as the neck

holds the head in listening: as when bathing
in the forest the bather pauses,
the forest lake in her just-turned face.

—Rilke

170

Part Four: Explorations

Chapter 10: New Life on the West Coast

Buddha

As if he listened. Stillness: a distance…
We keep on and don't hear it anymore.
And he is star. And other great stars,
that we don't see, stand around him.

Oh he is all. Really, do we wait
for him to see us? Would he need that?
And if we threw ourselves down before him,
he'd remain deep and indolent as an animal.

For that which draws us to his feet
has turned in him for millions of years.
He who forgets the things we learn,
and learns what points within us.

—Rilke

By the summer of '66, at least I had a direction: I would go to San Francisco, get an M.A. in creative writing and then find a teaching job. That seemed practical and down-to-earth—and also exciting.

San Francisco beckoned as a place away from the past where new things were happening, though I didn't yet know exactly what that might mean: poetry, music, protest—and Zen.

*

Karina and I ate our last meal together at a Chinese restaurant in Boston. When I cracked open my fortune cookie it said, "You are about to embark on a long and pleasant journey." In view of what was about to happen, I wish I could remember what Karina's fortune cookie said.

After a sad goodbye—we were not breaking up but going to school on opposite coasts—the next morning I climbed into the driver's seat of the used black Peugeot my father had given me for graduation. Buying a car for your son was a fatherly family tradition, and though generally set on defying my dad, in this case I could make an exception. "It was a good deal," he said, as he put his hand on the fender. "I had it checked by a mechanic. Don't smash it up."

It was the first car of my own. I liked the French look of the small sedan, and easing in behind the wheel, I put my foot on the clutch, grabbed the knob of the manual shift, and moved it through all four gears, to get the feel of it. Dave, my lanky biochemistry roommate with a crooked smile who was off to grad school in Wisconsin, sat in the passenger seat. Bob, an amiable acquaintance with short curly hair and an untucked flannel shirt, who, like me, was headed for San Francisco, shared the back seat with a few boxes of stuff and my stereo, complete with mid-sized speakers and crowned by its old reliable turntable. It was the beginning of September 1966, and the warm smell of adventure was in the air.

As we cruised through the green forests of western Massachusetts, Dave ran his fingers through his hair and looked out the window.

"This sure beats the hell out of taking the bus."

"Yeah," added Bob from the back seat. "On the road like Jack Kerouac, off to sit on a cliff above the surf and watch the sun set on Half Moon Bay."

"You're a poet," said Dave, who wrote poetry for his girlfriend Jean when he wasn't hitting the books or making a few extra bucks blowing glass pipettes for his father, a chemistry professor at Washington University in St. Louis.

"Nah, I'll end up selling real estate," Bob said laughing. "California, here I come!"

Many hours later, as we drove through the gathering darkness of Indiana toward Illinois, listening to a midwestern disc jockey play "That'll Be the Day" on the radio, I noticed a bright red spot of light glowing on the dashboard, next to one tiny word: *Generator*.

"Oh, shit." I turned to Dave. "We'll have to stop and get this fixed."

"Not yet—we can run on the battery," said Dave. "Until it runs out. We'll need the headlights, but not the radio." He turned the knob, and Buddy Holly went silent.

"Damn," said Bob, slapping his thigh. "Buddy's my man!"

Conserving our juice, we made it to Wisconsin on the battery, but it was Labor Day weekend and no auto repair shops were open. There was nothing to do but hang out in Madison.

After dropping out of school for a year, I had managed to finish college, and after graduation I moved in with Karina. She was an artist, spunky and spontaneous, with light brown hair she brushed from her eyes. For me, living together was a new experience, and that summer there were few responsibilities. We made art—Karina created some gracefully wrought etchings of reclining nudes amid swirling foliage, and I worked on my 8 mm film about a pudgy red-haired character with a crush on a discarded manikin, which I had installed in a corner. We danced to the beat of rock and roll in the living room. One afternoon in the rain we went for a walk through the grass down by the river, naked under wet raincoats, and sat there together, our bodies entwined, as raindrops fell on our hair and warm skin.

But the good times were not to last. That was the result of our one big argument. Karina wanted to go with me to San Francisco, but I hadn't known her long and if things didn't work out, I might feel responsible for luring her away from her art school program. As time went on and our feelings deepened, I was bogged down with indecision. I hated to be pressured, and when she bugged me one too many times, I burst out "I'm going to San Francisco—alone!" A week later, I couldn't bring myself to leave her, and went back contritely to ask her to come with me. She didn't look happy.

"It's too late," she said, shaking her head. "I got my scholarship."

I reached out to her. "Then let's stay in touch, and see what happens."

"Yes, let's wait and see."

That Labor Day weekend in Madison, I spent a few hours listening to records in the apartment of Dave's grad school friend. One LP I played over and over was *Chicago/The Blues/Today!* with the Junior Wells electric blues band featuring Buddy Guy on lead guitar, plus J.B. Hutto and His Hawks and Otis Spann on South Side piano. The rhythms were supple and visceral, with more heart and soul than most of the music I heard on the radio. This rocking, rolling, Chicago blues was a source for the Rolling Stones, and could truly be called "down home." The liner notes sparked my imagination with a description of how you could get off the elevated train at 40th Street and find live blues in clubs on the South Side. Well, tonight was Saturday night and Chicago was only a few hours away. I couldn't drive because the headlights would drain whatever juice was left in the battery—but there must be a bus.

"Hey Dave, want to catch a bus to Chicago and hear some blues on the South Side?"

"No, enough of the road already. Bob and I are going out for a beer at the Shuffle Inn. Why not stay here with us and have a Milwaukee brew? As they say: shuffle in, stagger out."

"Thanks, but this is a chance to hear the real electric blues," I said, strumming some air guitar. "When will I be near Chicago again on a Saturday night?" I lifted both hands, palms to the sky.

I knew I had to go, no question. So after several hours on the bus, I rode the elevated train to the South Side, where a few lamps in passing windows lit ramshackle wooden porches stacked on the backs of shabby buildings beside the iron tracks. I got off at 40th Street after 9 p.m. and walked down the metal stairway into the shadows. The street was quiet, almost deserted. On the corner, under a streetlamp, a lone black man in a loose beige shirt was lighting a cigarette.

After a moment's hesitation, I walked up to the stranger and said, "Hey man, where can I hear some blues?"

"Right over there." He gestured down the street toward a small nightclub with a dark red sign above the door: Turner's Blue Lounge.

"Thanks!" Relieved to find a blues club without wandering around all night on the South Side, I marched down the street and could hardly contain my excitement when I read the marquee: J. B. Hutto and His Hawks, the band I'd heard on vinyl just hours before. Now I could hear them in person. I stepped up, took a breath, mustered what composure I could, and reached for the smooth brass knob of the beat-up red door. Here and there the paint was worn and peeling, and the wood showed through. As I turned the knob the latch clicked, the door creaked open, and I stepped into the repeated thud of drums and the plaintive twang of electric guitar. The air was smoky, vibrant, and warm, alive with a chattering crowd sitting at the long bar to the right and gathered around tables spread through the room—except for a space at the far wall, not exactly a stage but a platform for the band. The drummer snapped his sticks in syncopation, the electric bass repeated a low, funky riff, and a wiry, intent, dynamic man swayed with his guitar, his mouth open in a soulful, piercing song that channeled generations of Mississippi blues singers, now alive and kicking here in Chicago. The blues today— electrified.

I took an empty seat at the bar and ordered a beer from the bow-tied, white-shirted bartender, who nodded, filled a tall glass from the spigot, and slid it in front of me. I plunked down some cash, picked up the cool foaming glass and turned to face the band, scanning the crowd. It was then that I realized I was the only white person there.

This was a new experience, feeling at one and the same time completely out of place, yet completely in the right place at the right moment, the place I most wanted to be. But I felt a twinge of anxiety.

Would they accept me? As I tried to relax and enjoy the music, a heavy middle-aged man wearing a fedora at a nearby table turned toward me. When he caught my eye, he smiled, then beckoned with his hand. "Come on over," he said in a deep voice. "With me and my friends. I'll buy you a drink." I slid off the barstool and crossed to his table.

We watched transfixed as J. B. shifted into a loping bounce, singing "Too Much Alcohol." Gradually he picked up the pace, repeating "Too much alcohol, too much alcohol," until it seemed he could no longer stand it and lay down on his back and writhed around, frantically strumming his guitar as he kicked his legs every which way and rolled his head around, singing "Too much alcohol" again and again until the words dissolved into anonymous syllables of pure emotion.

"Wow," I exclaimed, rising up from my chair, eyes riveted on J. B. in all his ecstatic glory. This midnight ramble with Chicago blues had made the broken generator worth it. I felt that from now on any difficulties I might encounter could lead to further adventures.

On Tuesday morning Bob and I left Dave to his graduate studies in biochemistry at Madison and drove on in the Peugeot with a rebuilt generator, heading southwest toward Colorado. After winding around foothills and up through the Rocky Mountains, at a high pass we crossed the Continental Divide. Pulling off the road, we stopped to breathe the thin air, feeling light-headed at 11,000 feet as we hiked around and gazed at the rugged peaks and valleys in all directions, exhilarated by the altitude, twice as high as the summit of Mt. Washington in New Hampshire, the highest mountain I'd ever climbed.

It was mostly downhill from there. Bob and I took turns at the wheel, driving day and night until we reached the ancient cliff dwellings of Mesa Verde, which I'd read about and was curious to see. On our guided tour the ranger explained that the Anasazi people took refuge here, climbing up long retractable ladders, safe from their enemies. Trash would simply be tossed over the cliff, where it accumulated in piles. Now, archeologists were sifting through it. With a nudge to Bob I whispered, "Much of what we know about ancient civilizations comes from their trash. What will future archeologists learn from ours?"

"Yeah," said Bob. "Why don't you write about that?"

I mulled it over. "It reminds me of Ginsberg's 'Sunflower Sutra.' He sat on a 'tin-can banana dock' with Jack Kerouac beside him 'on a busted rusty iron pole,' and among the dusty junk he saw a perfect beautiful sunflower."

"I gotta read that," said Bob, raising his eyebrows.

Following the ranger we descended a wooden ladder into a small round underground room, a sacred *kiva*, used by Pueblo peoples for ceremonies, rituals, and councils. It had no windows, just an entrance on top. I began to feel claustrophobic, crammed in with a gaggle of tourists in their sun hats and shorts. Their superficial chatter obscured any profound vibrations I might have sensed. My own superficial chatter didn't count, of course.

I was happy to climb back up out of the small room into the sunlight. Maybe Bob and I could do some exploring on our own. As the ranger talked to a lady with a wide-brimmed hat, sunglasses, and a thick Boston accent, I looked around for a way to ditch the tour group, but found nowhere to go—we were snug in the pockets of the cliffs, and the only way out was to climb back down.

Back in the car, we headed south through the dusty deserts of western New Mexico toward Gallup, a town where the people were mostly Navajo. I wanted to learn first-hand about the culture I had studied in college. But as we turned toward the road into the reservation, the red light on the dashboard lit up—yet again.

The generator had been rebuilt just well enough to last 1,400 miles, too far to go back to Wisconsin and complain to the mechanic. Instead we turned onto Route 66, leaving the Navajo reservation for another trip, and drove on the battery during daylight, pausing for a several-hour recharge at a gas station somewhere in Arizona. As we sat there baking in the desert heat, I reflected on our tenuous transportation.

Practically speaking, I thought we could make it without the generator. But I couldn't help wondering if these electrical failures were some kind of symbolic manifestation. Would the car my father had given me be up for this trip through the desert with no air-conditioning?

Back on the road, passing a row of red-dirt mesas and mountains defining the northern horizon, finally we crossed the state line at Needles, California, and sure enough saw some prickly cacti when we pulled into a campground near the Rio Grande. The next day my garden-like fantasies about California began to dry out as we sped through the hot Mojave Desert toward Barstow. Onward past Bakersfield to Fresno, Merced, and Modesto, the wide Central Valley slowly became more fertile and migrant Mexican farmhands worked the fields in the sweltering sun. When at last we turned toward the Bay Area, I felt some anticipation driving through the rambling hills. Then, as we descended, the air cooled precipitously, a fresh moist breeze to relieve our parched valley fever, and swirling clouds of fog rolled in from above. A tingling excitement surged inside me as the green trees of Berkeley welcomed us into a lush new world on the far western edge of the continent, the shore of the great Pacific.

*

Looking for Somewhere to Live

In early September, while staying with my friends John and Judy in Berkeley, sleeping on their sofa, I took the bus to San Francisco to check out possible housing. The first place I looked at was not very promising. Responding to a classified ad for a studio in what I didn't yet know was the Tenderloin, I rang the bell, and a buzzer opened the door. A stocky man in gray sweatpants and white T-shirt stood at the top of the stairs. Looking upward, I called out, "Is the landlady there?"

"She's dead," he said. There was a pause.

"I saw the ad—the apartment for rent."

"Come up and I'll show you around." The studio was plain and bare, and I had no furniture. Turning, he ushered me into his room across the hall and told me to sit in a chair. He casually locked the door, came back, and sat on his bed. Then he began to boast that he'd been in prison. Beside him was a new hardback book—*In Cold Blood* by Truman Capote.

His muscular build made me a little uncomfortable—especially when he said he'd show me his scar. He took off his T-shirt, turned around, and flexing his arms in the air with hands clasped over his head, rocked his shoulders up and down, so the long jagged mark of a knife wound writhed like a snake on his back.

"I have to go now," I said, as politely as I could, then got up and walked to the door, unlocked it, and left. The ex-con sat on his bed with a blank face and said nothing.

It took me awhile to find somewhere to live, and later discover the Zen Center. First I stayed for a month in an attic in Daly City, located near S.F. State but culturally on another planet. The house belonged to a deaf old man who lived with his mentally disturbed son on the floor below my attic room, rented to me by another son who didn't live there. I had to share the kitchen and enter up their stairs. Communication was difficult. The old man was too deaf to understand, and the son too disturbed to respond in a rational conversation. Through the floor I often heard him yelling at his father.

Meanwhile I went to a rock concert in a park with a small sign I made that said "Evil is Live Spelled Backwards." To me it meant that evil distorts the basic beauty of life by spelling "live" backwards, but some didn't see it that way. "I don't like your sign," frowned one long-haired guy. Later, I pondered his response. Maybe he thought I meant life is inherently evil? How interesting that one line could be interpreted in two opposite ways, like a figure-ground reversal, as I had experienced watching Andy Warhol's six-hour movie of a man sleeping.

In my attic room the situation was getting precarious. The disturbed son was often upset, cussing out loud. The family moved their father away for his safety, leaving me alone in the house with a wild man. One night he paced around shouting for what seemed like hours.

"Who took my glasses? That bastard, I'll kill him!" Did he imagine "that bastard" was me?

I checked the ads in the college paper again, and found one that said, "Hip, mature roommate wanted." That sounded more like it. Soon I had a room in a Victorian flat near Mission Dolores Park with the Amador brothers, recent Stanford graduates and explorers of the yet-to-be-publicized San Francisco scene. Rolando and Raphael had regular jobs— Rolando in social services and Raphael in Social Security. Rolando was outgoing, with a wide circle of friends, who often came over on weekends. Raphael was introverted, spiritual, and spoke very little. Another roommate was Lamar, an African American who lived 14 years in Japan after World War II. Trained as a Marine, he was now a pacifist with a warm smile, polite and good-humored. The brothers welcomed me to their weekend parties, and one night Lamar took me to Bop City, a laid-back after-hours club in the Fillmore, once known as the Harlem of the West.

Rolando sometimes used drugs, from marijuana to psychedelics to amphetamines. His brother Raphael abstained from intoxicants and devoted his spiritual explorations to a mysterious sect called Subud. Perhaps the fact that both had full-time jobs, and different views on drugs, set a tone in their group of friends that drugs were accepted for recreation and personal exploration, while avoiding the dangers of overdose or addiction, with no undue pressure to indulge or not. For Rolando, Timothy Leary's famous slogan would need to modified: "Tune in, turn on…" —but don't drop out. That approach suited me. I wanted to finish my M.A., and hoped to get a job teaching writing.

*

Good Vibes—for a While

Compared to my experiences on the East Coast, where the drug scene seemed like a furtive underground for misfits, the West Coast scene was more open and infused with a positive vision of social and spiritual revolution. And it was propelled by the creative energy of a powerful wave of new music. Every week in the park and at night in clubs like the Fillmore and Avalon you could hear good bands drawing ecstatic, dancing crowds—not just crowds of people dancing, but whole crowds dancing together—joining in lines, circling, holding hands with arms raised high. Psychedelic posters with swirling colors announced acid-rock groups like the Jefferson Airplane, with Grace Slick belting out "Somebody to Love" or the psychedelic anthem "White Rabbit" with its trip to Alice in Wonderland. And the Grateful Dead, with Jerry Garcia singing the mournful "Morning Dew," or jamming to the joyfully surging "Sittin' on Top of the World."

You could feel the good vibes walking down Haight Street, as passers-by greeted each other with "Hey brother," "Hey sister" on the way to free concerts in Golden Gate Park. The Diggers, a radical commune, gave out free food, and the Free Clinic cared for medical needs and came to the rescue when someone had a bad trip. I didn't consider myself a hippie, but buoyed by this intoxicating atmosphere I let my hair grow down to my shoulders, bought a dark blue Navy peacoat, and went to readings by wildly imaginative writers like Ishmael Reed and Richard Brautigan.

I began to get over my East Coast reserve in talking to strangers. Once on the street I struck up a conversation with a friendly dark-haired woman and invited her to join me in driving to Esalen, the new-age resort perched on a cliff above the surf at Big Sur. We couldn't afford the seminars, but sat on a little hill looking out at the ocean, sharing a smoke, getting stoned. As we drove back in the dark on Route 1, the winding coastal highway, suddenly a light brown doe jumped from a bushy embankment on the right-hand side of the road into the glare of our headlights, crossing our path, so close we were about to hit her. Amazed, I stayed calm. Time slowed down, like a movie in slow motion. The deer seemed to glide through an arc in the air. My foot pressed the brake just firmly enough to let her go by without throwing us off course. As she landed and leaped again into the bush on the other side of the road, time resumed its usual pace, and we continued on our way.

"Whew," I said, alive with the joy of relief.

Six months later the 1967 Summer of Love would transform the peaceful Haight-Ashbury into a media-generated carnival, attracting young people (and tourists) from all over the country. But the love didn't last. The deluge of runaways and flat-broke newcomers overwhelmed what there were of communal resources. Hard drugs and crime began to plague the Haight, and many of the original hippies left for communes in the countryside.

*

Long-Distance Breakup

Karina and I exchanged a few letters and postcards. I told her about my cross-country trip, the Chicago blues, and the San Francisco scene. We had not agreed to be faithful, nor had we agreed it was O.K. to get involved with other people. We were going to wait and see.

Then I began to hang out with Michaela, a long-legged, gentle young woman I met in a creative dance class taught by Anna Halprin, the choreographer. But when I thought about getting more intimate, I held back out of loyalty to Karina. That was my emotional paradox: I was still in love with Karina, but not ready to make a commitment either way.

After a while a letter arrived in a pale envelope etched with Karina's artistic calligraphy. I opened it slowly and read it carefully. She had found a new boyfriend in Boston, after I'd only been gone a few months. "I can't wait for someone who might not come back," she said, just as she had about her previous boyfriend who left for Vietnam.

I took a bus to North Beach, and went for a walk with her letter in my pocket, past old men playing chess in a beat café, a barker shouting for a topless show, and a lady on a bench tossing crumbs to a cluster of pigeons. Then I stopped and read the letter again. It was a chilly, foggy evening. The days were getting shorter, verging on San Francisco winter—no snow, but still cold without central heating.

The next day I dropped by during office hours to see my Keats professor, who seemed like a sensible man. I told him my story, and that I might drop out right away and go back to Boston to be with Karina. He paused, his hand on his chin. "You agreed to wait and see?" I nodded. "Then why not wait and see. Finish the year, or at least the semester, and see how things stand then."

"That might be too late."

In bed that night, lying awake, I came up with a compromise. I would wait until the December holiday break, then go back and see if Karina and I could work things out. If not, I'd return to San Francisco. The next day I called and told her I was going to drive across the country in the middle of winter to reclaim our relationship, and was ready to do it, too. There was a pause. "I'll have to talk to Jack," she said.

A few days later, as I packed for the trip, the phone rang.

"Hello?"

It was Karina. "I told Jack your plan, and he rolled his eyes." My gaze fixed on the breaking surf of an outdated August wall-calendar. She went on, "Coming back now would not be a good idea."

I sighed. While I made a brief effort to change her mind, somewhere inside I felt a growing relief. I would not have to act out my cross-country fantasy on the icy roads of winter. I did not have to be like Don Quixote charging at windmills, imagining himself as a gallant medieval knight, blind to the factual present.

That week I struggled to face it: Karina and I might be finished, done in by those 3,000 miles of the snow-covered continent, or to be more specific, her new boyfriend in Boston. Winter was a season I thought I left behind when I moved to California. But there's another kind of winter that can follow you anywhere. It's the winter in your bones, the chill winter cold of being alone. That was my winter in California without Karina.

For some reason, on Saturday I walked through the damp gray streets in the scattered rain toward the Asian Art Museum, at that time still in Golden Gate Park. There, among the evergreens, large wooden doors opened into an airy atrium full of Chinese stone sculptures of animals and

Buddhas, and smaller bronze ritual vessels encrusted with the green patina of centuries, the remaining relics of the early Han Dynasty. Somehow this museum, a storehouse of ancient objects created by humans in the far distant past, offered a perspective for me to begin to accept the loss of ephemeral love.

A heavy, rounded rhinoceros of darkened bronze splotched with crusty green seemed quite peaceful, as if it had just emerged from the water and shaken its massive bulk like a giant dog drying itself. But it was the Buddha statues that most caught my eye, from the small gray smiling one sitting over there with hands cradled in its lap to the fantastic Eleven-Headed Avalokiteshvara, the Bodhisattva of Compassion, a brass figure with eleven heads stacked in a cone above his shoulders and twenty-two eyes watching over the sufferings of countless sentient beings, in all directions, in every realm of the universe. I kept walking through the museum past Buddhas of different styles and cultures and came back to Eleven-Headed Avalokiteshvara as if drawn by an invisible magnet. It was Eleven-Headed Avalokiteshvara who would see through me, and Eleven-Headed Avalokiteshvara who would see me through.

*

Doing Time in San Bruno

The heavy-set deputy led me through the corridors of the men's county jail, several stories of concrete cellblocks surrounding an atrium. He ushered me into a square cell on the second floor, closed the iron-barred door with a clang, and locked me in, alone in a small barren room.

The walls were dull white. On one side was a bare porcelain toilet with no seat, and a small basin with a single faucet; on the other a metal frame bunk bed with a foam pad and one thin blanket. There was no rug on the hard concrete floor, just a small grated drain to wash the place down, with a faint smell of antiseptic. A bare bulb burned on the ceiling.

I sat on the bunk and enclosed my right fist in my left hand. As time flowed on, the cell made me feel like pounding the wall. How ironic, I thought, that I'm here by my own choice.

It started with a moving violation, a ticket for making a No Right Turn off Van Ness. Hoping to reduce the $25 fine, I decided to contest it in traffic court. After parking my car on the street behind the Hall of Justice, I sat in the crowded courtroom listening to how the cases went. When my turn came, I walked up to the wooden defendant's podium, wearing jeans, wire-rim glasses, a denim jacket, and hair down to my shoulders.

"What's your story?" inquired the judge, a middle-aged man with an air of authority that I hoped would be leavened by humor.

"Your Honor, I was distracted by a beautiful woman sitting beside me."

The judge jerked back slightly, then banged his gavel.

"Ten dollars or one day in jail!" he decreed.

Ten dollars was certainly reasonable. However, I'd never been in jail, even though I had tried. Back in Boston I'd joined a sit-in at the Federal Building, but by the time I was dragged off by the cops, the paddy wagon was full, and they decided not to bother with the rest of us. So I was curious what jail would be like, and here was a chance to try it, just for one night.

"I'll take the day in jail," I replied.

The judge clenched his teeth, annoyed by my response. "One day then! —at the county jail in San Bruno. Bailiff, take this gentleman into custody."

Oops, I didn't realize "one day" meant starting right now. The bailiff escorted me into a holding cell adjacent to the courtroom to join a few other new prisoners. I was allowed a single phone call to notify my roommates, and after an hour or so was loaded onto a bus for the short trip to San Bruno. There I went through induction, filling out a questionnaire and changing into an olive-green prison jumpsuit. The warden, after reading a note, said "We're not going to cut your hair, because you're only here for one day. The judge also wants you in a cell by yourself.

It's unusual that he sent you here—for a one-day sentence, ordinarily they just keep you in the jail at the courthouse."

Now locked behind bars on the second floor of the county jail in San Bruno, I looked out into the atrium and saw many of the cell doors were open and olive-green jump-suited prisoners were walking around. All except me had closely cropped hair. One who looked in his early twenties came up to my cell and grabbed the bars. "Hey man, some of us are wondering, how come they didn't cut your hair?"

"I'm only in for one day."

"What for, man?"

"No Right Turn. And you?"

"Dealing dope." He looked at me and paused. "Stay cool, man. Some of these dudes are troublemakers." As he walked down the line, the situation began to sink in. Among the hippie drug dealers and petty thieves, there must be some violent criminals here. I realized the judge had me locked in a cell alone for my own protection. And I was glad to feel safe behind bars. After a meager supper delivered to my door—over-boiled cabbage and instant mashed potatoes—the lights went down. I flopped on the bunk with my blanket and fell asleep to the distant sound of occasional coughs, footsteps, and voices.

The next day, free, wearing my jeans and jacket again, I rode the bus back, got off at the courthouse, and saw my Peugeot had a parking ticket under the windshield wiper. Ah, how unfair, I thought. I strode in, defiant, and made an appointment to protest the ticket. When the hearing came, with a different judge this time, I began to recite the tale of injustice I had rehearsed. But he cut me off with a bang of his gavel.

"Did you get this ticket while you were in jail?" the judge demanded.

"Yes."

"Case dismissed," he growled, and banged his gavel again, puncturing my self-righteous illusion.

*

Therapy Marathons

Not surprisingly, the L.A. version of the psycho-spiritual revolution was somewhat theatrical. Jianyu, our group leader, was an Asian American man with a shaved head, a therapist who dressed like a judo master and exuded an air of charisma. Indeed, his insights were illuminating enough to justify the respect with which he was treated at the encounter-group marathons he led at a mansion in Beverly Hills. Rolando, his girlfriend Sharla, some friends and I drove the six hours down to L.A. to experience a weekend intensive with Jianyu, all day and all night, sharing our inner lives as defenses dissolved and emotions emerged, going on and on without sleep. When it was my turn I told the story of how Karina and I fell in love and now were separated by the choices we'd made. When I finished Jianyu responded, "Sounds like you've been exploring the extremes of love and loss. No need for regret, you are learning a lot."

When we went back outside after the marathon, the light gray body of Rolando's Chevy was covered with a thin film of black dust particles. This must be residue of the fabled L.A. smog, I thought, as I swiped my finger on the fender and inspected the smudge on my fingertip.

Back in San Francisco, Rolando, who later became a diversity trainer, began holding marathon weekends with Sharla and some of his friends, where we encouraged each other to confront our mutual annoyances, angers, and jealousies with the aim of resolving them into intimacy. About that time I wrote a poem, beginning to process the loss of Karina:

Eclipse

The sun went down full on the sea
and set just right, red and wide,
as behind me lightning flashed
for you. Dawn was like china,
I was a soaring bird in the blue stillness.

But the days have all blinked by;
now moon and sun move on, apart.
Yet always, for a moment, they are one:
it bites into blackness with fiery hair
and the stars are revealed by a passing shadow.

*

Discovering Meditation

"We should always remain in beginner's mind. It means our experience should always be refreshed and renewed. It means always have the joy of discovering something. The same joy as children discovering something new."

—Shunryu Suzuki

Before long I found a part-time job delivering the Sunday *New York Times* in North Beach and the Marina, working for Intrepid Enterprises, a small independent business run by Gregory, an idealistic long-haired hippie who owned a head shop on Haight Street. Getting up at 4 a.m. each Sunday morning, I drove my old Peugeot to the distribution center and filled up the back seat with stacks of the hefty Sunday *Times*, then zipped up and down the steep streets of Telegraph Hill, making frequent stops to drop off papers. In mist and fog or morning sun, I breathed the cool, invigorating air of the bay as I trotted around houses perched together on the hillside. My route continued into a Marina apartment complex where I walked down halls delivering hours of Sunday morning reading for New York / San Francisco transplants and aspiring world citizens.

My new job meant sacrificing late Saturday nights, but somehow I met Jenna, a woman with strong features and wavy brown hair who wore long flowing dresses and seemed like a fellow spiritual explorer. On Saturday January 14th we went to Golden Gate Park for a Gathering of the Tribes.

Luminous Sky with Dragons

We drove in my old Peugeot
to Golden Gate Park for the Human Be-In
where Allen Ginsberg and friends
chanted mantras onstage,
the Grateful Dead played
and Owsley the LSD-maker
floated down from the sky
swinging from a great white parachute
into the wild and cheering crowd.

Then the acid kicked in
and my woman friend
in her long flowery dress and I
wandered into the woods,
looking closely at leaves.

As night fell on the beach
we joined a stoned tribe
drumming on pots and pans,
dancing and chanting
around a blazing bonfire.

From somewhere a quick hand
slapped in and out of the flames,
seeming to briefly touch
the glowing coals,
then lifted to show no burn.

Driving home I tried to focus
my mind on the task
and my eyes on the road,

in the shape I was in
not sure I could do either one.
We made it back, but the
acid amplified my anxiety
and I crawled into bed.

With eyes closed a vision
appeared like a bright neon sign
in big letters: FAITH
and I saw that one needed
faith to do anything,
even to walk one step,
and faith didn't have to be
faith *in* anything,
just faith in faith.

The next morning I got up with the rising sun and delivered a back seat full of the Sunday *Times* up and down a fog-free Telegraph Hill, stopping again and again to hop out of the car with a vision of wings on my heels, imagining myself as an avatar of Mercury, the messenger god, bringing the morning news to the world with effortless grace.

But soon my faith would be tested. One afternoon Harvey, Rolando's friend, wanted to borrow my car. "How long do you need it? I have a date tonight. Can you bring it back by six?"

"Sure. I just need to pick up something in Palo Alto." I was a bit leery, but wanted to be generous and live by the wisdom of my vision, with faith that things would work out.

"Make sure you get back in time," I said, handing him the keys.

At six he had not appeared. At seven I called Jenna to explain. She did not sound happy, but said she would wait. Harvey didn't get back until eight. When I finally picked up Jenna, she was silently brooding. I made some kind of wisecrack to lighten things up.

She rolled her eyes: "There's the clown."

Playfulness was important to me. The next week Jenna and I drove up Route 1 along the California coast. After an hour or so, somewhere in Sonoma County, I spied a sunlit pasture on a gentle slope looking out at the ocean and was seized by an impulse.

"Let's take a short cut," I said, turning right on a dirt road through the pasture. But the road petered out and we ended up stuck in the mud. I had to ask for help from a farmer in overalls, who grudgingly pulled us out with his tractor—probably the quickest way to get us wayward weirdos off his land.

We spent that night together at Jenna's apartment, and decided to stop seeing each other—we were just too different. But she told me about a Zen master who lived at a temple in nearby Japantown and held meditation at 5:30 each morning. For me, this was a great opportunity. I could learn from a master.

But the next morning I slept through the alarm. So I sat with my legs crossed on the floor in Jenna's living room, following her instructions to count my breath. Despite an ongoing avalanche of thoughts in my head, with the energy of desperate enthusiasm I intensely counted my breath to over a hundred in this first, informal session of meditation, something I never achieved again, even with years of practice. I soon learned you were only supposed to count up to ten and then start over again. Jenna smiled when I told her how my meditation went.

"Suzuki Roshi says that's beginner's mind," she replied, "open to everything."

Chapter 11: A Taste of Zen

This morning a monk
drinks tea in the quiet—
a chrysanthemum blooms

—Basho

Sitting at *Sokoji* Temple, February 1967

I sat facing the wall on a round black stuffed cushion, a *zafu,* on a flat black quilted pad set on a thick woven straw mat, fitted together with adjacent mats under a row of my fellow meditators, also quietly sitting, practicing *zazen.*

The silence was palpable, stirred only by the soft rhythm of breathing. As time inched on, the pain in my legs, crossed in half-lotus position, grew worse, then eased as they gradually numbed. With thumbs touching and hands cupped in a symbolic gesture, or mudra, at the navel, my connection with the universe, I followed the instructions, counting each breath up to ten, then starting over again—except most times I barely got to four or five before a bubbling stream of distracting thoughts swept me off into worlds of endless digression, probably something like this:

How much longer do we have to sit here?... I'll try not to look at my watch... that guy beside me has really good posture... better pull back my shoulders, stick out my chest, straighten up... ah, doing pretty well now... the woman in gray silk pants, she bowed with such grace... maybe talk to her later... hmm, better start over, remember my breathing... what will I have for lunch?

Eventually I woke up sitting there in the *zendo,* the meditation hall, with back sore and legs numb, and continued to follow the rhythm of breathing. The point was not to see how many breaths you could count, but to calm the mind enough to just sit. As time went on, moments would come, during and after meditation, when perception was clear, alive in the present moment, not so caught up in the stream of thoughts rushing by. It reminded me of how I felt lying on the soft grass of the riverbank, warmed by the sun of late spring after final exams.

But that first day as I sat there facing the wall practicing zazen, thoughts kept rising and stealing my attention again and again, with no end in sight, until the deep *bong* of the large brown bowl of a bell reverberated throughout the room. As the sound slowly dissolved, each of us placed our palms together in front of our chest, fingers pointing upward, and recited in unison a short prayer of dedication for the enlightenment of all sentient beings. Then a higher-pitched bell triggered a series of bows, towards our cushions and each other, and we filed out of the zendo, happy to stretch our limbs.

Suzuki Roshi, the Zen master, was not there. But a tall American in a black robe and shaved head, who I later learned was Richard Baker, looked in my direction with a clear gaze, then stepped toward me with barefoot poise and an air of being in charge.

He smiled and asked, "How was it?"

"Good. I could do this every day for the rest of my life."

*

Meeting Suzuki Roshi

Meditation opened my mind to a new dimension of awareness. At times clouds of thoughts swirled through my head, but now I knew that if I just sat and followed my breathing, eventually the inner weather would clear. Once on a walk in the park near Ocean Beach I lay down in the grass and got lost in obsessive thoughts wrapped in dark clouds of emotion. I watched all these thoughts and feelings flow through me like a passing thunderstorm. Later I wrote on the back of my worn denim jacket, "Thinking more now and enjoying it less? Try a little love, try a little peace, try a little quietness." Zen had begun to infiltrate my poetry.

Room at Night

Through the open window,
the city's rough harmony.
Far-off factories, traffic,
somewhere a howling dog.

The silent brightness
of the candle
dances in its
dancing shadow.
I breathe the richness
of incense in fresh air.

A car passes
through my ear
and disappears.

The sound of the mind
is like snow falling
in the wilderness.

My inspiration was Suzuki Roshi. That spring at the old Sokoji Temple on Bush Street in Japantown he often led zazen and sometimes gave talks in the small zendo above the large hall where the Japanese congregation met. Each meditation session began and ended with bells, signaling bows. In the mornings we chanted a sutra in ancient Japanese and bowed three times to the floor, facing an altar with a small stone Buddha. I was somewhat put off by the formal ritual, but Suzuki Roshi's presence gave the practice a profound meaning that I had to respect.

He was a gentle man, quiet but intense, with an imp-like sense of humor that sometimes crept in like someone peeking unexpectedly from around a corner. There was a presence about him, an inner stillness that permeated the serious atmosphere. Even though you sat facing the wall, you knew when he was there.

After one talk I asked a question. "Does Buddhism teach that we should enjoy life?"

"Mmm... yes," replied Suzuki Roshi, looking over at me. "The Buddha said we should enjoy life the way a bee takes nectar from a flower— gently, without harming anything."

After growing up with my father's drab work ethic, I was relieved and happy to hear this poetic image from a man who was kind and wise. My body and mind felt like green leaves basking in sunlight. Before long I made plans to attend the July session of the first summer training period at Tassajara Hot Springs, the property Zen Center had recently bought in the Ventana Wilderness, east of Big Sur in Los Padres National Forest.

*

A Narrow Path

Every day I drove over the hills of San Francisco at 5 a.m. to make it to morning zazen, so when I saw Erica's ad for a roommate to share her two-bedroom apartment in Japantown, I called right away. The only condition was to follow her macrobiotic diet, which didn't sound that hard, since fairly often I'd been eating brown rice and vegetables anyway, as Zen students often did, though few were strictly macrobiotic. And she would be cooking the evening meal. Balancing yin and yang, I thought, might be good for me.

But when I moved in I discovered just how macrobiotic Erica was, restricting herself every evening to short-grain organic brown rice and some limp, overcooked greens. She was a few years older than I was, dark-haired and graceful in vintage clothing, thin as Miss Twiggy.

We ate as we sat on mats on the floor at a low wooden table with a white tablecloth. Dessert, even fruit, was not on the menu—too yin. And no dairy products—too yang. Even water was limited to one cup a day.

As she stood at the sink scraping a carrot, Erica confided, "I'm having difficulty following this regimen myself, and I need you to support me by sticking to the diet 100% of the time, not only here in my apartment, but throughout the day, when you're away."

That was a bit more than I'd bargained for. I paused, then nodded reluctantly, "Well... I'll try."

Before long at school I found myself staring with yearning at a drinking fountain, slowly and guiltily moving toward it—then giving in and quenching my thirst with a plume of cool water kissing my lips. For the next few days I led two lives: strictly brown-rice macrobiotic in Erica's apartment, and secretly indulgent off on my own, drinking forbidden water and eating sweet potato pies. That seemed to me like a reasonable balance between yin and yang.

However, one day I bought a chunk of cheese and didn't manage to finish it before I got back to the house, so I slipped it, wrapped in white paper, into the refrigerator.

"What's this?" Erica was standing in the kitchen, frowning and holding up my small package of Gouda at a disapproving distance.

"Well... I support your diet for you, but in my case, I need a few supplements."

"You need to move out. *Now!*" she slammed the refrigerator shut and pointed to the front door.

"Okay by me," I said. No longer welcome in her Puritan Eden, I grabbed my cheese, took a big bite, and packed my bags, glad to be free.

I never met Erica again, but still think of her sometimes, for some strange reason. If I could see her now, with her fragile face and ethereal body grown a bit older and fuller, I might ask her why she had tried to live so strictly—and why she tried to impose that strictness on me.

"You don't understand," she might reply. "I had to do something to change my life—I'd been alone and depressed for too long.

Strict macrobiotics made me feel pure, and I hoped that someone could share my path. But you weren't sincere."

I might close my eyes, feel a slight tightness in my forehead, and take a deep breath. "I'm sorry, Erica. I should have been more open about needing to be flexible. I saw you as rigid and controlling. I had no idea how much you were suffering."

That spring I indulged my freedom. I took a film-making class and spent glorious days wandering around town with a 16-millimeter camera, filming everything that caught my eye, from wind in tall grass to waves breaking on the beach to showers of sparks as huge power hammers pounded red-hot glowing iron ingots into shape in a steel mill at the edge of the bay. I even found a woman, a dancer, willing to sway gracefully naked on camera, and double-exposed her image on dancing flames in a fireplace. My room in the Amador brothers' flat was still available, so I moved back in and hung curling film-clips of poetic scenes with clothespins on a line that sagged across the room, and glued them together into the chaotic rough cut of a black-and-white silent film.

*

Working with Fritz

In June I heard that Fritz Perls, the pioneer of Gestalt Therapy, was giving a weekend seminar at Esalen beginning with an introductory Friday night talk at a nominal fee. So before going to Tassajara for the training period I drove down the coast to Big Sur and took a seat in a hall full of well-off, somewhat hip people on padded folding chairs. On the bare stage Fritz, in a one-piece jumpsuit, with gray hair and a shaggy beard, spoke with decisive vitality. He began to talk about "losing your mind and coming to your senses"—dropping excessive thought and being awake in the present moment. It sounded a lot like Zen. When he asked for a volunteer to work with him as a demonstration, I raised my hand, and was surprised when he pointed to me. I came up on the stage, unsure about what I was getting into but riding a wave of deliberate action, and sat in the empty chair beside Fritz.

"Tell me about yourself," he began. I described the two sides of my personality, sometimes shy and insecure and other times bold and adventurous—one foot in the proverbial box, the other foot out, exploring.

"Notice the gestures you make with your hands," said Fritz. "Your right hand leads, and your left hand follows. Are those your two sides?"

"Yes, I guess so."

"Let each one speak."

I held up my right hand and made a fist. "I want to be strong." Then I held out my left hand and opened it. "I want to be loved."

"Now hold a conversation between them."

My right fist moved into my left hand, which closed around it. "My left hand says, 'You are strong, but I don't want to be dominated by you.' My right hand says, 'You are warm, but I don't want to be engulfed by you.' "

"And what is the solution?" asked Fritz.

I opened both hands and did what seemed natural: slid them together with interlocking fingers. Then speaking for both hands I said, "I don't want to dominate you or be dominated by you, but to intertwine with you on the same level."

"Now say that to the audience," said Fritz.

With a dawning sense of realization, I looked up at all their faces. "I don't want to dominate you or be dominated by you, but to intertwine with you on the same level."

Feeling the power of this insight from just five minutes with Fritz, I approached him later and said I might like to record him working with people on film.

"We have lots of footage already," he said. "But it needs to be edited. Are you interested?"

"Yes—but I'll be going to the Zen training period at Tassajara for a month."

His eyes lit up. "You could start after that." Then he paused. "The compensation would only be staff room and board at Esalen, nothing more."

"Sounds good to me."

I stayed around a few more days, long enough for a massage at the staff hot baths and to hear part of the Big Sur Folk Festival, with the pure high voice of Joan Baez ringing through the redwoods and the deep low rhythm when the Chambers Brothers played and sang "Wade in the Water" as surf pounded against the base of the cliffs. A friend told me that two years later her copy of Jack Kerouac's tortured novel *Big Sur* fell down the riverbank into the Big Sur river and drifted out to sea. Watching the irretrievable wet pages recede in the distance, to her it seemed ironic, perhaps more than just a coincidence. She felt some guilt that she lost a library book, and sad that she hadn't finished reading it—but somehow the book was where it belonged.

*

Tassajara: First Training Period

Sitting awhile
secluded behind the falls:
summer retreat begins

—Basho

From the calm inland vineyards of Carmel Valley a narrow road turned south into the foothills of the Santa Lucia mountains, gradually rising through thinning forest. The dusty road, etched in the mountainside by Chinese laborers in the nineteenth century, soon turned to dry, rocky dirt, rough and increasingly steep. Scraggly weeds clung to a rock wall for life, boulders piled up toward a mountain peak. But my old black Peugeot seemed to be doing fine. With its manual transmission I could dig into low gear and grind up around the steep curves winding through chaparral toward Chew's Ridge, past the cracked gray skeleton of a tree, to a rise where the view opened out over the rugged Ventana Wilderness to a distant wispy strip of the Pacific at Big Sur.

I stopped to take in the exhilarating view, feeling warm and glad I had come. Then the real challenge began. The road dropped precipitously like a twisting roller-coaster down into a deepening canyon. I used low gear to slow the car and save my brakes, but even so they overheated and began to slip. I had to pull over, stop, and let them cool. When I opened the door, stepped out, and looked over the narrow road's edge, below was a steep ravine, plummeting down to a patch of trees hiding a creek bed.

Beginning to sweat in my T-shirt, I stood there by the car as the sun beat down. The air on my skin was hot and dry. I took a swig from my canteen. Beside the road the tufts of grass were dried light brown. The air was clear, the rocks were warm. I had not seen another car since the road changed to dirt. It was not a good place for your car to break down.

Luckily, the old Peugeot with its low gear got me deep into the canyon to the end of the road at Tassajara Hot Springs, a cluster of wood and stone buildings beside a rocky creek. A steep hillside led down to trees leaning over the stream that wove through jumbles of stones. To either side of the road were even steeper slopes of dry brush, a few bent trees, and tangled vegetation. Serious-looking men and women, intent in T-shirts and shorts, walked around the courtyard and along the path toward the cabins beside the creek. I pulled into the dusty parking lot, turned off the ignition, and walked over to a door marked "Office."

The training period was about to begin, and I joined a group of newly arrived long-haired young men standing in the shade of a tree at the edge of the courtyard, discussing the first bit of guidance we'd been given. The Zen master, Suzuki Roshi, was not requiring us to shave our heads like traditional Japanese monks—but he was asking men to cut their hair short, no more than the width of two fingers. Of course there was no barber to do the job. A wiry guy with a rough-cut face said, "We might as well jump right in and shave our heads. That's the simplest thing to do."

"The most dramatic, too," said a round-faced guy with a smile. "A way to express our commitment—and by the end of training period our hair will grow back, and still be short enough to comply with Roshi's request."

"Better than getting a lousy haircut," added another, pulling on some strands of his hair, as if to take their measure. And so we went down to the baths, and before long our group of once-shaggy hippies looked like shaven-headed monks—by our own choice.

Revisiting that time, I gathered a few memories of Suzuki Roshi at Tassajara and the San Francisco center.

Moments with Roshi

The Zen Master is a gentle man
in a thin robe, who can move
large stones with his hands.
His light brush glides
in a smooth circle of black ink
on white rice paper.
Around him the air is clear.
When he sits, he sits unmoved.

At times he lives in a canyon
in Los Padres National Forest,
where he shaves his head
in a steaming hot spring.
Students come from all over
to study with him.
What do they learn?
"Nothing special."
"Not always so."
"Things just as it is."

Sometimes his laugh
reveals that the way things are
can be quite amusing.
When he walks back
from the zendo he stops
on the small wooden footbridge,
to look for a while at the creek
in the soft evening light.

At the city center, after zazen,
as we file out through his office,
he bows to each of us in turn
as we bow to him,
and only meets your gaze
when you are ready
to meet his.

*

Zen Practice

Visiting the Temple of Gathering Fragrance

Not knowing the Temple of Gathering Fragrance,
hiking in miles among cloudy peaks,
past ancient trees, with no one on the path,
deep in the mountains somewhere a bell.
The sound of a spring choking in treacherous rocks,
afternoon sunlight cools in the shade of green pines.
As evening sets in, by the bend of an empty pool
sitting quietly tames the heart's poisonous dragon.

—Wang Wei

The first challenge was *tangaryo*, the traditional sitting "outside the temple gate" for new students before being admitted to Zen monastic practice. In Japan tangaryo was five days or more; at Tassajara, it was reduced to three. The bad news: it was all day from early in the morning to bedtime in the evening, sitting in the zendo with brief breaks only for eating and necessary visits to the bathroom. The good news: formal zazen posture was not required. You could shift your numb legs around or even stretch them out before resuming meditation posture.

Tangaryo was a challenge I would have to accept. At least it was of limited duration, not physically impossible, and basically consisted of devoting all your energy to doing nothing. Hour after hour I looked at the wall, until the subtle patterns in the grain of the wood began to seem like faces of goblins, wise old women, and long-bearded men.

More difficult was following the regular schedule day after day, from the 4:30 a.m. wake-up bell to 9:30 p.m. lights out. The lights, by the way, were kerosene lamps with noxious fumes, as Tassajara was far off the electrical grid. After the wake-up bell came the periodic tock! of the *han*, a square wooden plank hanging from a tree branch and inscribed with mysterious Chinese characters. It was hit with a wooden mallet at shortening intervals culminating in a cascade of tocks. You were due in the zendo by the end of the second round. Then Suzuki Roshi would arrive, holding a small polished wood staff upright before him, walking quietly behind the rows of students sitting facing the wall, to take his seat on a low platform at the front of the hall—looking toward the meditating students, as did the stone Buddha statue on the altar behind him. Meditation began at the end of the third round, with the beating of a huge drum standing on thick wooden legs at the entrance to the zendo.

Forty-minute sessions of zazen alternated with *kinhin*, slow meditative walking, and morning service—chanting sutras, including the *Heart Sutra*, in Japanese and English, to the beat of the *mokugyo*, a large hollow carving of a squat writhing fish that produced a satisfying thump when hit with a padded mallet: *"Kan ji zai bo satsu gyo jin han nya ha ra mit ta..., "*

203

declaring that form is emptiness, emptiness is form, going beyond all concepts.

Then, continuing in the zendo with no break, came silent breakfast, a ritually elaborate meal where during the chant each student unpacked his or her *oryoki*, a finely made set of three black lacquered bowls nested inside each other and wrapped in a large white cloth napkin with utensils tucked in the knot at the top. Then food was served, one dish at a time, by student waiters who strode down the aisle holding the serving pots high, bowed to each student, and ladled rice, oatmeal, soup, beans, or vegetables into the appropriate bowl held out to receive them. After invoking the motivation to enlighten all sentient beings, we ate with quiet focus, knowing that we had to finish before the servers came back to give us tea and hot water to clean our bowls with a little padded stick that came with the kit.

After more chanting and bowing we finally filed out in our gray or black robes for a short break before a brief study period and the daily work meeting. As a new student I was assigned various tasks, from clearing brush next to buildings for fire prevention to trapping flies.

> Walking down the trail,
> a sting on the back of my
> hand—a black fly bites.

That summer flies were everywhere, ubiquitous insects alighting on anything edible, from a speck of food on a wooden table to your own exposed flesh. It was excruciating to be sitting in the zendo, peacefully breathing, becoming aware of tiny feet trickling across your cheek in little fits and starts, crawling toward the eaves of your nose. So a group effort was needed: during afternoon break a row of Zen students marched from one end of the zendo flapping towels, herding the flies toward the open doors and hopefully out. It was not perfect, but when done every day made a difference.

Flies on our food were a health hazard. There are mothers and children here, someone said. So I was assigned to tend the traps to capture and poison the flies in large glass jars. Wearing gloves, I emptied the jars of fly carcasses, which I buried in the dirt, and hung the jars with their bits-of-meat bait back on the wires. I felt irony and ambivalence: here I was at a Buddhist training center, following orders to exterminate tiny sentient beings, however annoying they might be. Why was I being asked to kill as part of Buddhist practice? Were they really an insidious threat to our health, or just a pesky pest to our peace of mind?

Being an exterminator made me uncomfortable. But for health, we had to be practical. The best I could do was learn to live with the paradox. So I said a prayer for the flies.

Once I was working with Phillip, built like a heavyweight boxer, who I've heard played the role of Captain of the Guards in *Planet of the Apes*. We were carrying a wooden bed frame, and I bumped it slightly against a stone wall.

"The bed can feel that," he said, even though we weren't supposed to talk during work period unless really necessary.

"What do you mean? It's not a sentient being."

"The whole world is a sentient being." I mulled that over for days. Did he mean that boundless sentience permeates the universe?

After three hours of work it was time for midday zazen, followed by ritual lunch and a forty-minute break before afternoon work period, punctuated by a short tea break, then more work in the hot sun until zazen, service, and ritual supper (often leftovers from previous meals). The day concluded with an evening break, then zazen again before retiring.

When Suzuki Roshi was there, he sometimes gave a talk that showed a different way to look at things. When a student expressed difficulty following the rules, Suzuki Roshi said the rules were like graph paper— when you have difficulty with a rule it points to where you are in your practice. In *Zen Mind, Beginner's Mind* he explained *shoshaku jushuku*, a saying of the great Japanese master Dogen Zenji that Roshi translated as "one continuous mistake." Zen practice could be seen as years of one mistake after the other, meaning years of single-minded effort. In our very imperfections we find the basis for our "way-seeking mind." The mistakes we make tell us what we need to work on. Difficulties are part of the path.

As someone who had spent many years nurturing the desire to do what I wanted as much as possible, following the Tassajara schedule day after day was a challenge. On days with 4 or 9 in the date, there was no work or midday zazen, which gave some time to do laundry by hand or go for a walk. But I wished for a free day more often.

Once on a day off in the warmth of late afternoon, returning from a walk down the creek I saw Ted, who I'd heard had some Zen experience, submerged up to his neck in a pool among smooth stones, under a shady tree. We began to talk, and I asked him, "To become enlightened do you have to lose your ego?"

"Yes."

"But how can you function without it?"

"Actually, you don't really need it."

Pondering his response, I continued down the path toward supper. If enlightenment, what Roshi called "big mind," includes everything, do we really need to cling to the small mind of identifying with an illusory self-image? Later, on top of a stone wall near the meditation hall, a fearless Steller's jay, with blue body and black crest, tilted its head and looked at me quizzically, then turned and bounced away.

Though I did my best to be a good student and follow the schedule, it felt claustrophobic. After two and a half weeks of rigorous routine I began to fantasize about taking a break for a few days and driving to Monterey, just to regain my sanity, then returning for the conclusion of the practice period. Finally I went up to Richard Baker, the head monk, in the courtyard, and told him my proposal, emphasizing that I was not quitting but just needed a little flexibility, to take a short break.

He looked at me with a steady gaze. "Zen is not for everyone," he said.

After thinking it over, I decided to stay and tough it out. Actually, it got easier after that. Maybe confronting Richard let a little steam out of the pressure cooker. By the time we reached the four-day intensive *sesshin* (all day practice) for those who were leaving at the end of the month, I was energized for a strong finish.

During a study period I browsed through the small Buddhist library and came upon a thin green hardcover book that listed many different techniques of meditation. One in particular caught my attention. It was a meditation on sound, listening to sounds in the environment and then turning the ear inward to listen to the sound of listening. I decided to try it during zazen.

Gate

Going nowhere,
riding on a horse of air,
breathing, breathing.

Turning the ear inward,
listening to the sound
of listening.

In between the particles of silence
a whole is opening.
Through, on through, riding through.

When I turned my ear inward, my mind dissolved in a rushing flow through an inner tunnel vortex, and came out clear on the other side. Perception was bright, vibrant, luminous, continuous with the texture of silence. The air seemed to shimmer in the pale yellow room with its cohort of sitting Zen students. After a while some thoughts trickled by in a faint stream underneath my otherwise placid mind. Is this enlightenment? Not quite, I thought—this flickering doubt shows that. Nevertheless, I felt transformed, mentally clear, and happy to be alive.

The next day, in the morning sun a mountain towered above as patterned shadows of leaves speckled the wide dirt path.

When I came upon Richard Baker outside the office, he turned to me and asked, "Are you glad you stayed?"

"Yes," I nodded and smiled.

Then I drove out of Tassajara on the rocky, winding road in bright sunlight, heading toward San Francisco before starting my new job at Esalen, with the windows wide open to let in the breeze. As I picked up speed, suddenly there was a loud flapping sound from below the rear window, on the shelf above the back seat. Looking in the rear-view mirror, I saw a book wide open with pages flapping and crackling in the brisk wind. I pulled to a stop, climbed into the back seat, and reached for the book. It was the Bible, bound in black, that I'd been given in Sunday school many years ago, and had brought with me along with some other spiritual books. The Bible had blown open to a colorful picture of Daniel in the lion's den, a lone man calmly confronting great tawny cats with snarling jaws and thick manes. It felt like a message from the universe. There would be trouble ahead, and like Daniel, I would need faith.

> In a lightning flash
> one is not enlightened—
> very significant!
>
> —Basho

Chapter 12: Journey Through Dark and Light

Ancient Airs, No. 19

In the west I climbed up Lotus Blossom Mountain
and far off saw the Bright Star.
In her white hand she held a lotus flower
as she walked on air through pure emptiness.
In a rainbow robe, trailing a broad sash
fluttering in the wind as she strode toward Heaven,
she invited me to climb the Cloud Terrace
and pay homage on high to immortal Wei Shu-ching.
Then in a dazed rapture I went off with her,
riding a wild swan into the Purple Dark.
When I looked back down at the Lo-yang river,
vast ranks of Tartar soldiers were marching
past fresh blood spattered on the wild grass
while wolves and jackals were wearing officials' hats.

— Li Po (Li Bai)

After Tassajara

When I got back to San Francisco, now with short hair, I sat zazen in the living room. My mind was mostly clear and spacious, certainly different from the rush of thoughts that had held me in its grip before.

Soon I headed back to Esalen to begin my job with Fritz Perls. Fritz greeted me warmly in his comfortable office, and told me of his interest in Zen. Then he broke the news that I would be working with Jason, a tall folk guitar player who was experienced in video recording and had made the most recent unedited tapes of Fritz's sessions. Jason was proficient at playing and singing "Digging My Potatoes" and other songs by Big Bill Broonzy, one of my favorite blues musicians. But despite our mutual interests, Jason did not want my assistance on what he saw as *his* video project, especially given that my editing experience was only with film and he would have to train me to use the video equipment.

"You're no help at all," he said.

"I can edit. I just need to learn how to work with videotape."

I began organizing a catalogue of tapes, but the training session with Jason never happened. I got the impression he had cultivated a close relationship with Fritz and saw me as competition. Once I noticed them smiling and hugging when Jason came up to Fritz in the dining room.

Otherwise, I enjoyed being at Esalen. I remember some wild dancing and an interesting conversation with Sarah, a level-headed, open-minded journalist, who sat with me over tea and asked about Tassajara, which she planned to visit for a book she was writing about the California new-age spiritual scene.

One evening Fritz found out I played chess and challenged me to a game. When he beat me decisively, he chuckled, "Sometimes aggression feels good." I was left wondering how that fit with our therapy session when he had guided me toward integrating my aggressive and receptive sides like intertwining hands.

As time went on Jason continued to avoid me. It was clear he did not want to work together. One afternoon Fritz gave me a lift up the hill in his little blue Fiat and I told him about my problems with Jason. "I think he's jealous," I said.

"Oh no, that can't be," replied Fritz. "He's such a nice guy." I was a little taken aback that Fritz dismissed my input. But I wasn't surprised a year later when I heard they had a falling out and Jason had left. Meanwhile, for almost two weeks I'd felt useless and bored by what had turned out to be a non-job.

A few days later I decided to leave. I walked up to Fritz's cabin, but he was not there. So I wrote a short note—something like "Thank you, but this is not working out"—and put it on one of the medical oxygen tanks near his door. I hadn't realized he needed them. Then I packed my bag, got into the Peugeot, and drove south on Route 1, the road that wound along the cliffs of Big Sur toward San Luis Obispo. Sarah had mentioned a commune down the coast at Gorda that might be worth a visit.

Gorda turned out to be a ramshackle group of buildings tucked in the hills just up a rough dirt road from the highway by the cliffs. The large stone house held a makeshift kitchen, some old furniture, and plenty of space. I opened the door and walked into the surging rhythm of conga drums and found a crowd of long-haired hippies dancing in flowery clothes, swirling around the room in undulating lines that linked together and spun apart. As I stood there taking in the scene, a young man in a floppy tan cowboy hat came up and held out a hand with a small sugar cube in his palm. "Howdy, brother," he said. "Help yourself."

"Acid?"

"Sure thing, man. Enough to fly to the moon."

"Thanks." I took the tab and put it in my pocket, figuring I'd take it at a time of my choosing. He smiled and went on swaying to the music.

After a night in my sleeping bag under the stars and a free oatmeal breakfast from the communal kitchen, I took a walk in the cool of the morning fog along a network of little trails that criss-crossed the woods, connecting the makeshift cabins and shacks that formed the encampment. Under a twisting tree, a little apart, I found some scattered piles of weathered lumber. It was a nice spot, with a view of the ocean. On my way back I saw a long-haired man sitting on a bench carving a walking stick and asked him whether the lumber was available for me to build a shelter. "Yeah, go ahead," he said. "A brother was gonna build himself a shack, but who knows when he'll be back."

"I'm not sure I'd want to be using his lumber when he gets back."

"No private property around here," the folksy hippie replied. "Use it or lose it."

Later that afternoon, sitting in the sun watching a shaggy dog, a mongrel collie, frolic in the brush near a tree, I put half the dose of acid on my tongue and let it melt into my nervous system. Laying back, I closed my eyes. There were no hallucinations, but when I opened my eyes again the tree was vivid, the air was clear. I looked over at the dog, and she looked back with a sparkle in her eye, prancing as if she wanted to play. It seemed we could feel each other's consciousness, as if we were long-time friends. I picked up a stick and threw it for her to chase. She brought it back beaming, and when I didn't throw it again, lay down and set about satisfied chewing. Then a little boy appeared with a wide open face and an aura of magical innocence. Later that afternoon I sat under a tree and wrote about him.

The Acid It Floated Me High

The forest delivered its child to my eyes, a child so clear in his there-ness, he stood tip-top and a tiny triumph on the windowsill of his mind, wondering aloud to the birds. Clasped in his soul were eight tiny reindeer, and a clear idea of his destiny. I stroked the fur of an African cat and awaited his every word. None were said, but many passed silently by. The most of his moments were so bright I astonished my might with his wisdom. Could this be explained without love? His hand held an invisible talisman, no harm could come to his eyes. Flecked with expectation, he stood and looked at me as I was, a human with plastic fabrications. Had the best in us cruised to the blessing of his island, notion would have it we truly escaped. Traipse as you will, the sky encloses more openings than letters in alphabet soup. Little child, you are here, so near to the sparkling water of life. Letting go of this vision, we both live.

The boy began to play with the dog, and I went for a walk in the woods, marveling at the beauty of each tree with its intricate branches and spreading leaves, savoring the ocean air with each breath. Following a trail towards the ridge, I met two middle-aged men in colorful short-sleeved shirts and Bermuda shorts, with close-cropped hair, walking from the other direction, looking like brothers. "Hello," said the taller one, wearing sunglasses. "Nice day, isn't it?"

"Hello. Who are you?" I said, pretty sure they were not part of the commune.

"We're monks from the Benedictine hermitage, not far from here," said the other man matter-of-factly. His face was smooth and tanned.

"Oh," I said. "I'm stoned on acid. I thought you might be from outer space." They both laughed. "No, we're from inner peace," said the first, serenely.

Soon we were deep in a philosophical discussion about God, Zen, LSD, and spiritual experience. The Catholic monks seemed open-minded and interested in what I had to say, but I had no idea what I was saying. My consciousness had moved down to somewhere in my belly, looking up at my head from within as my mind spun a train of incomprehensible thoughts with a wagging tongue.

"That gets profound," said the taller monk.

"Zen and prayer have something in common," said the other.

My consciousness returned to my head, but I was dumbfounded. What were they talking about? "Well, I need to get back to reality," I said. "Thanks for the conversation."

Returning to the commune, I sat down to reassemble my psyche. For a endless minute I watched an ant climbing carefully along a twig. Then I wrote in my notebook:

> Poetry on acid
> is no more than an ant
> or all that is

It seemed like it might be profound at the time, and may be still. Or maybe you just had to be there and high as I was.

*

Across the Border and Back

After coming down from the trip I decided the Gorda commune was at the other extreme from Zen—too disorganized—and resumed exploring the southern California coast. My next stop was at Long Beach, a bit south of L.A., where suburban development stretched out on one side of the road and a long white beach stretched out on the other. It was late afternoon, and several beach parties were going on. I pulled over, parked, and approached a line of tables with young people and beach bums wandering about, eating food from a grill, drinking beer, and some smoking pot. An amiable young guy with shaggy hair and mustache, white T-shirt and jeans welcomed me.

"Help yourself," he said. "There's plenty for everyone."

"Thanks." Not yet a complete vegetarian, I grilled a hamburger. When I told him of my travels and that I was looking for a place to crash that night, he invited me to sleep on the couch at his house—his family wouldn't mind. His name was Alfie, and he seemed naturally friendly in a non-assertive way. When we got to his house, a modest one-story suburban dwelling where most rooms opened onto the yard or the patio, he introduced me to his father—a grouchy gray-haired figure in khaki shorts with hairy legs who did not get up from his chair—and his mother in her apron, who was too busy in the kitchen to say more than a brief hello. They seemed less than thrilled about Alfie's adventures smoking pot at the beach. When his older brother Alan came home, however, it was a different story. Alan was a handsome, accomplished pianist, and he introduced his new girlfriend, an attractive redhead with black net stockings named Gloria.

As we all listened to Alan play a sonata, it seemed to me Alfie was overshadowed by his older brother, and the family dynamic was driving him into the counterculture. He didn't have a car, so the next morning I invited Alfie to ride with me on a brief trip to Mexico.

"Cool," he said. "Let's go and get stoned."

214

We drove down to San Diego, were waved across the border, and continued past Tijuana to Ensenada, where Alfie directed me along the Punta Banda Peninsula to La Bufadora, "the snorter," a sea geyser— an underwater cave that catches the crashing surf in a notch between massive rocks and shoots up a white plume of spray, sometimes 100 feet in the air. That afternoon the spot was almost deserted except for us. We leaned against the metal railing, feeling a periodic sprinkle from the geyser in the breeze.

"This is great," I said. "Like a whale in the depths of a sea-cave, spouting triumphantly."

"Want to smoke some hash?" offered Alfie. "I brought a little with me." He reached deep in his pocket and pulled out a tiny packet. "It's pretty strong stuff."

I was reluctant to get too high because I was driving, but watched Alfie roll a joint, blending the resin of hash with herbal cannabis, and took a few drags along with him. By the time we got back in the car I was definitely stoned. Keeping my eyes on the road, I started driving further south into the dusty farmlands of Baja California.

"There's a checkpoint ahead," said Alfie. "See that little building near the side of the road? They'll turn us back if we don't have visas."

"Not if they don't see us," I replied, swerving to the right onto a dirt road through the barren fields. I was feeling adventurous. Keeping out of sight of the checkpoint, we bumped along back roads until we could return to the main route about a half-mile beyond it and continued on our way. The landscape was dry and deserted, and a few miles later I pulled over, having second thoughts.

"Where are we going?" murmured Alfie.

"I don't know," I said. "I'm starting to get paranoid. Now that we're beyond the checkpoint without papers, carrying dope, we could wind up in a Mexican jail." Paranoia crept into my mind, took root, and grew, until I feared the checkpoint might have called ahead and the Federales were waiting for us down the road with fixed bayonets, hungry to bust some hippie tourists.

"Yeah," said Alfie. "If you want to turn back, I'm OK with that."

"All right then." Retracing our shadowy route around the checkpoint, we turned back toward Ensenada and the border. After a while we stopped at a gas station to fill up and buy something to munch on. "What about the hash, and the grass?" I said.

"I've got a little bit left."

"I may be paranoid, but we could get busted for smuggling at U.S. Customs. It happened before, to a friend of mine. The State of Texas impounded the car."

"I've gone back and forth several times, and they never checked me in San Diego. I hate to waste the hash," said Alfie. "It's really good stuff." He walked around until he found a secluded spot and smoked the precious remainder. I waited at the car, still paranoid.

We crossed the border without incident, coming in late at Alfie's house, and I slept on the couch another night. By the morning my paranoia was gone. I thanked Alfie for putting me up and drove my old Peugeot back toward Interstate 5, heading north through the wide Central Valley.

At the sign for Porterville there was a slight upward slope and I thought I'd shift to a lower gear, but inexplicably dropped it all the way down to first at forty miles an hour—with a resounding clunk that abruptly jerked the car back. The transmission was shot. I could only crawl in first gear. The other gears didn't work.

Shit, I thought. If I can't afford to get this fixed, I'll have to sell the car. I felt a hole in my stomach. My father bought me this car just last year. I put-putted to a repair shop on the outskirts of Porterville and showed the broken Peugeot to the husky mechanic.

"How much to fix it?" I inquired.

"Foreign car. Probably have to order a new transmission. Maybe $500 or more."

"I can't afford that." Then a pause. "How much will you give me for the car?"

He stood there with his hands on his hips and thought it over.

"No market for a car like that around here. I'll give you $50 for the tires."

I sighed. My father would not be happy to learn the fate of his gift. What else can I do, I thought. Maybe it's time to leave his legacy behind, once and for all. "OK," I said. "I'll take the $50. You can have the car and the tires."

In the gas station a big red and white thermometer read 105 degrees. I was stranded in the middle of the desert in mid-August. Already my T-shirt was damp, my throat was dry, and my skin felt ready to burn. Instead of waiting for hours in the heat at the side of the road, trying to hitchhike back to the cool gray fog of San Francisco, I decided to use my $50 to take the bus.

*

Return to Sokoji

Sometimes a cloud
gives one a rest from
watching the moon

—Basho

When I got back to San Francisco after the trip to Esalen, Gorda, and Mexico, my zazen was no longer as clear as it had been. Obsessive thoughts had returned. My Zen practice had lapsed, the glimpse of peace had been temporary. Slowly I pulled myself up the long stairway toward Suzuki Roshi's office with heavy steps, pausing to lean on the railing, feeling remorse. I was disappointed with myself, and wanted to confess to him—to be encouraged and forgiven. Just as I reached the hall at the top of the stairs, he came striding out of his office in his informal robe, staring stone-faced straight ahead. Briskly he walked right by me without a glance, as if propelled on a mission. Without looking back he strode down the hall and disappeared around a corner.

I was left to stew in my own emotions. Was he just preoccupied by something else? Was he angry at me for letting my practice lapse—

or for not taking the loss of my glimpse in stride, and instead getting upset about it? I had a feeling he could sense what was in my heart and mind. If this was a teaching, what did it mean? In any case, I walked back down the stairs and resolved to continue my practice.

The fund-raising campaign to purchase Tassajara had attracted more new students to the modest city zendo. We met in a room behind the balcony of the large Sokoji auditorium that was used by the Japanese Buddhist congregation. In a new policy, the zendo doors were closed at the start of zazen at 5:30 am and 5:30 pm so that late-comers would not disturb the silent meditation once it had begun. If you were late you took a seat on one of the black cushions set on a line of thick straw *tatami* mats next to the wall on the balcony. You sat facing the wall in the rafters with the cavernous hall behind you.

One evening when I was late (which I admit was rather often) I was sitting on one of these seats beneath the eaves about halfway through the 40-minute zazen period, quietly trying to follow my breath amid a flow of distracting thoughts.

Suddenly, the ear-splitting sound of an organ hit me at point blank range. My shocked senses jumped into full alert at the sonic blast. Then it dawned on me that this must be organ practice, and the pipes were right up here in the balcony. Very Zen, I thought. The shock of the now. I sat full of majestic organ music for several minutes until it abruptly stopped.

When Suzuki Roshi got angry it came like the blast of that organ and dissolved without a trace. Once at morning zazen he was making his usual rounds, walking ceremoniously behind the row of students sitting facing the wall, holding his polished wooden stick upright before him. As he passed, even though we could barely hear him and only see him with peripheral vision, quietly coming, each student would raise both hands and place them together palm to palm pointing up at heart level to acknowledge his presence and greet him with a bow, a *gassho*.

That morning, about fifteen feet before he reached me, Roshi suddenly shouted "GASSHO!" Then again, even louder, "GASSHO!"

I peeked over to see what was happening. The student Roshi had shouted at was looking back at him with a puzzled expression. The young man must have been new, unfamiliar with the ritual, and didn't know what "gassho" meant. Roshi's expression suddenly changed from fierceness to kindness. He stepped toward the student, bent down beside his ear, and whispered, "I'm sorry." I was touched by his sudden complete change from anger to compassionate, caring presence.

*

Because It Had a Touch of Style

The navy-blue peacoat with fine leather cord on its lapels and cuffs chose its owners carefully. That's how it came to wrap itself around the young man with long brown hair and black wide-brimmed hat who walked down Geary Street with collar turned up high and hands hugged close in spacious pockets through the foggy cool of evening toward the Avalon Ballroom. A lost hippie with torn shirt, beads, and makeshift vest accosted him: "I really like that coat—will you give it to me?"

Taken aback, the young man said, "No, I really like it too," and then walked on.

In the Avalon, as the Grateful Dead began to play and the stoned crowd filled the floor and danced as one to a solid rocking rhythm embellished with the intricate explorations of Jerry Garcia on electric guitar, the young man carefully folded the peacoat and placed it under a chair back in row G for safe-keeping.

Several hours later, after Jerry's mournful voice intoned the final chorus of "Walk Me Out in the Morning Dew, My Honey," the young man went back to get the coat, but it was gone—a loss he ponders even now whenever he feels attached to something much too beautiful.

*

A Walk in the Park

One day at Zen Center I ran into Sarah, the journalist I met at Esalen. She introduced me to a friend of hers, a slender fellow with well-trimmed straight brown hair and plaid Bermuda shorts. "This is Tom Wolfe," she said. We shook hands. I'd heard of him as the author of *The Kandy-Kolored Tangerine-Flake Streamline Baby,* about customizing cars in L.A. Looking back, I realize he must have been in San Francisco doing research for *The Electric Kool-Aid Acid Test,* his account of Ken Kesey and the Merry Pranksters, creators of psychedelic happenings with the Grateful Dead. Wolfe later claimed he never took LSD, only notes, during his time with that flamboyant crew, but from the tone of his prose he must have been on a contact high. When we met, he seemed content to ask no questions, and soon excused himself.

Sarah and I went out for coffee and then for a walk in Golden Gate Park. She was curious to explore the San Francisco scene, and took notes on much of what we saw—the man holding up a Bible and shouting at hippies sprawled on a hillside, the sari-clad dancers chanting "Hare Krishna" to drums, dronc, and finger symbols, the jazz-rock band playing to introduce a man who took LSD and believed he was the Messiah in league with aliens on flying saucers. We talked about how dropping acid could lead in some cases to spiritual insight and in others to confusion or superstition. I said the flying saucer Messiah made me want to subscribe to *Scientific American.* "Suzuki Roshi says you can't get enlightened through intellect alone, but it's better to have a good intellect than none at all. I guess your experience on acid depends on what you bring to it."

At the edge of the meadow Sarah wanted to check out a man standing on a small stage with a microphone, amplifier, and speaker. He had curly brown hair and beard, and like Tom Wolfe, was wearing Bermuda shorts. His name, Austin Brightly, and P.O. box address were displayed on a neatly hand-lettered poster beside him. Well-spoken and sounding rational, he was asking the crowd to help him resolve a problem with his ex-girlfriend, who had rejected him and married someone else. He wanted to remain friends, but she did not. He wouldn't want to break up her marriage, but if only the people in the crowd would contact her and let her know he still cared for her, maybe she would relent and give him some sign that she still cared for him too. Then he asked if there were any questions.

Learning to cope with rejection was a trip I'd been through, so I raised my hand and asked, "Why don't you give up? Why don't you let go and move on?"

"I could give up on marrying her," he said, "but I couldn't forget about her. That would be impossible. I wrote a song in my songbook for her." He read out her name and address and pleaded once more for people in the audience to get in touch with her. "If only twenty-five of you would write a postcard to her, preferably this afternoon, that might change her mind."

Just then three anonymous teenage boys in blue jeans crept in beside and behind Austin Brightly, holding up a big white sheet painted with bold black letters proclaiming VOTE FOR ME. I had no idea where they came from. Sarah looked up from scribbling her notes, and we glanced at each other and smiled. Now, years later, I see that could have been me up there.

Another day, at Ocean Beach, I used a broken stick to write a poem in the sand—close enough to the crashing waves so I knew at high tide it would wash away. In the long run, nothing lasts. And by now I've forgotten the poem. Let's face it. There's nothing to do but let go and live your full life in each moment.

Then why am I writing this memoir? To remember that.

*

Hippie Goodbye

I never really identified as a hippie   I was a grad student, not a drop-out—but the San Francisco hippie scene influenced me with its ideals of peaceful community and creative freedom. Curious, I moved to a room in an old Victorian on Haight Street for the month of May, as the Summer of Love was about to get underway. Young drop-outs and runaways arrived from around the country with their backpacks and beads, looking to get stoned, and some crashed on our living room floor. Soon they were panhandling the crowds clogging the sidewalks as tourists peered at the hippies through the windows of cars and tour buses crawling slowly down Haight Street.

Several of those who hung out at our pad regaled us with tales of brazen shoplifting. Then one day I noticed a blank check was missing from my checkbook, which I kept in my bureau drawer. When the cancelled check arrived in the mail at the end of the month it was made out in a strange hand to Mnasidika, a Haight Street boutique, for about $26, with my signature forged. I never locked my door—part of the hippie ethos—so what had happened was pretty clear. Only one check was gone —probably not taken by a professional thief but a crasher who wanted to stay under the radar until moving on, parading down Haight Street in a colorful flower-pattern shirt.

When I returned to the neighborhood after spending the Summer of Love at Tassajara and Esalen, I ran into Gregory, the long-haired, craggy-faced founder of Intrepid Enterprises, the *New York Times* delivery service I'd worked for not long before.

"Haight Street has changed," said Gregory, holding a steady tone. "The Mafia moved in, and took over the drug trade. Now there's violence at night. My best friend was stabbed, and died in my arms." His face broke with emotion, and he seemed close to tears. "I'm closing up shop and moving to Mendocino."

Overwhelmed by too much too soon, hippie paradise had become urban hell. The Diggers, the underground commune that tried to practice the slogan "freedom is when everything is free," no longer gave out free food in the park. The Free Clinic's medical section closed, denied funding by the city. Ken Kesey moved to his dairy farm in Oregon. Joan Didion wrote her vision of hippie anarchy in *Slouching Toward Bethlehem*. Even the Grateful Dead got busted at their Ashbury Street house and left the Haight.

222

Old-time hippies were urging an exodus to northern California, and the Diggers decided to hold a "Death of Hippie" funeral procession. On October 6, 1967, the first anniversary of acid becoming illegal, about a hundred people marched from Buena Vista Park down Haight Street bearing an open wooden coffin with signs that proclaimed the end of the media-generated hippie era. They made their way to the Psychedelic Shop, which was going out of business.

"Hippie" had just been a label; it was time to move on.

*

Stop the Draft Week

By October the Vietnam War had escalated, and thousands of young men were being drafted. Many in the Bay Area anti-war movement felt a need for dramatic action. Instead of the usual protest march—of which there had been many—they would shut down the Oakland Army Induction Center for as long as they could, actually interfering with the draft itself. Posters were put up around Berkeley and Oakland declaring October 16-20 as STOP THE DRAFT WEEK.

The week began on Monday with a peaceful sit-in, following the principles of nonviolence used in the civil rights movement. Protesters sat blocking access to the entrance of the Induction Center on Clay street in downtown Oakland, where buses full of draftees from all over northern California arrived. Many protestors were arrested, including the folksinger Joan Baez, and were escorted to paddy wagons without resistance, as had been worked out with the police beforehand.

When I read the news of the sit-in the next morning, I wished I had been there, and took a bus across the bay from San Francisco to join in the second day. But Tuesday was very different. I arrived just in time to see a phalanx of burly policemen in dark blue uniforms marching through hundreds of sitting protestors, swinging riot clubs left and right, bashing people's heads and shoulders. Blood began to flow, people raised their arms in self defense and struggled to escape the onslaught as the police marched on, beating them all with flailing clubs, mowing them down, reporters and photographers too.

That was a mistake. The next day's papers had pictures and graphic descriptions of "Bloody Tuesday," and the police got a lot of criticism. Outraged, I resolved to come back for the next big protest day. So did a lot of others. Hundreds filled the streets around the Induction Center. But the tactics had changed. Instead of sitting and waiting to be beaten, we were quick on our feet, retreating whenever the police marched in and regrouping to blockade another intersection, pushing trash cans, parked cars, whatever we could find, into the street to obstruct the path the induction buses would have to take. When the police came in to clear one intersection, we escaped to block another, staying out of reach yet reappearing everywhere. It was an exhilarating feeling, fighting back non-violently but creatively, outfoxing the police, breathing with a deep sense of freedom.

But I knew we had leaped over the boundary of disciplined protest in a way that could lead to deadly violence, as it eventually did at People's Park in Berkeley. I still wanted to do a purely nonviolent sit-in in accord with the spiritual principles of Gandhi and Martin Luther King. The next morning no mass protest was scheduled, so I went to the entrance of the Induction Center alone at 4:30 a.m., before the first buses would arrive. The glass double door was locked, but lit from within. I sat down in meditation posture blocking the entrance, back toward the door, my legs crossed, hands in my lap, following my breathing. Gradually one bus and then another arrived, and a line of draftees began to form in front of me, waiting to get in. They looked young, just out of high school, quiet and uncertain, maybe scared about where they were going. One crew-cut kid in a navy blue zippered windbreaker asked me, "What are you doing?"

"Protesting the draft," I said. No one objected. We settled into the quiet of Oakland downtown before dawn with its deserted streets and empty buildings. Following its own sense of inflexible time, a lone stoplight slowly changed from green to yellow to red, and back to green.

Then two strong deputies in gray uniforms appeared inside, unlocked the glass doors, and pushed them open, shoving me forward onto the concrete. Without a word, they brusquely picked me up, carried me out of the way, and dumped me on the sidewalk. I figured they didn't arrest me in order to avoid more unwanted publicity. Instead the deputies directed the line of draftees to enter the building.

As the young men walked in, uneasy but obedient, I picked myself up, a bit sore but uninjured. I had not expected to stop them. But maybe our protests had some effect. According to the historian Howard Zinn, by May 1969 more than half the draftees ordered to report to the Oakland Induction Center did not show up.

When I look back I wonder what happened to those young men in that line, waiting to meet their fate? How many would be killed in combat, maybe shot by a sniper while on patrol at Khe Sanh? How many would be wounded, maybe trying to save a buddy caught in an ambush during the Tet offensive, and receive a Purple Heart? Or would any kill a civilian because enemy soldiers did not wear uniforms, and Americans did not always make a distinction—some even killing old men, women, and children at My Lai? Would any men of conscience try to stop the atrocities? How many would survive the war but succumb to post-traumatic stress from the horror they experienced? And how many would come home and settle down with a wife, children, a house, a car, and a decent job? In October, 1967, there was no way to know what lay in store for them.

My thoughts drift to a poem by Tu Fu (Du Fu), written in China a thousand years ago.

Thinking of My Younger Brothers on a Moonlit Night

From the garrison, war drums signal no more travel;
through the frontier autumn, a wild goose calls.
From tonight on the dew will be white frost;
the moon back home too must be luminous.
My brothers are all scattered,
no family to ask if they're still alive.
The letters I send never get a reply;
as of yet there's no end to the fighting.

*

Good for Body and Soul

From the fall of '67 through the spring of '68 I lived on Lyon Street, on
the edge of the Fillmore district, across the Panhandle from the part of the
Haight where I later learned Janis Joplin had an apartment. Late one
afternoon I was returning from S.F. State, waiting at a trolly stop for the
N Judah streetcar. There was only one other person waiting, a woman in a
paisley dress and embroidered jacket, standing with one knee slightly bent
and her hand on her hip. We began to chat. Her name was K.V., and I
noticed she seemed comfortable using the F-word repeatedly in casual
conversation. I wondered if she was trying to tell me something.

I once loved a woman who made great lasagna,
good for both body and soul.
She lived in an old apartment building
where you walked from a skeleton elevator
down the dark red carpets
of wine-bottle halls.

But her room was fresh and pleasant
with a big double bed
that when you touched it just right
rose up and turned into a wall cabinet.

She had a passion for second-hand clothes.

The first night
we kissed in the doorway of an antique shop
and got so turned on we almost
took the bus to Eureka, California.

Instead we took a bath by candlelight
and washed each other's bodies
in billows of foam.

I came to visit her often.
Every morning I felt like a new man.

As the December holidays approached, K.V. informed me she had
received a letter from Thomas Bailey, an ecological writer who lived in
New Mexico. He was married, but last summer when he came to San
Francisco they had a brief affair. Now his wife was out of town and he
wanted K.V. to visit. Along with the letter he sent her an airline ticket.

K.V. said she wasn't in love with him, but didn't see how she could turn
down a trip to Santa Fe. Would it be all right with me? I wasn't happy
about the idea, but respected her honesty. After a pause, in the spirit of
"free love" I said "If that's what you want to do, OK." But I knew it meant
we were willing to risk our relationship. I wasn't ready to say I was really
in love with her, but for me our affair had been an adventure. Could I trust
her, or would this be another fling that didn't last?

*

A Spiritual Struggle

While K.V. was gone, I threw myself into Zen Center's December sesshin—physically, mentally, and emotionally. I wanted to make up for my lack of follow-through after the experience at Tassajara by conjuring up another spiritual breakthrough to release me from suffering. Following the demanding schedule with passionate intensity, I gathered up all my frustration and practiced out of desperation—completely ignoring my teacher's instruction to practice "with no gaining idea."

This all-out assault on "enlightenment" came to a head during the final day's meditation. Practicing with utmost intensity, I sat stock still until my body began to shiver, then tremble. Soon I was convulsed with a wave of emotion, my arms and legs shaking, my face breaking into a grimace. I looked toward Suzuki Roshi at the front of the room. He sat there calmly and patiently, seemingly unconcerned.

Weathering the emotional storm, I made it through the concluding ritual and dedication. After we filed out of the zendo, a small group of students gathered around me. Trevor, who I knew had a profound experience at the July sesshin that summer at Tassajara, asked "Was it *kensho*?"

In truth I didn't know what it was. But I wanted so much for it to be a glimpse of enlightenment that I looked down and murmured, "Yes."

"Roshi does it every time," said Trevor, as if welcoming me to the club.

Then I realized that despite its emotional power, my meltdown was brought on by forceful striving for enlightenment and lacked the insight of expanded awareness of my glimpse at Tassajara. I felt ashamed that my answer was not really true. Grasping at my previous experience had not brought it back, no matter how intensely I threw myself into it. Now at least I could see the way forward: to practice with patience and "no gaining idea."

When K.V. returned, we gradually drifted apart.

"Free love" had left me feeling alone.

*

The Antique Wilderness

My train broke down
in a ghost town.

At dusk in the deserted
streets of the desert
I lost my way
to an old hotel.

Everything was still
so well arranged.

The dust was a
fine touch,
it swore
that no one had been there.

I stood on the threshold
as if in a field
of new-fallen snow.

This
is the antique wilderness—
traditional, original.

Here death has the freshness
of living alone.

Chapter 13: Traveling East and West

How many cloud peaks
have crumbled, leaving it clear—
the moonlit mountain
—Basho

Zen, Poetry, and Nature

I turned to combining Zen practice with writing poetry and communing with nature. Under the spell of Basho's haiku and his far-ranging walks through old Japan, that spring I took two short backpacking trips, jotting down my impressions along the way. First I hitched through Marin toward Point Reyes, and in a couple of days hiked out to the coast.

Point Reyes March

soft throaty growl
big gray pussycat
crouched just off the trail

we stare at each other
without moving

silent agreement
I detour left
the bobcat disappears

redwoods
still for centuries
the buzzing of a bee

woodpecker
up there somewhere
but where?

madrone
big body
smooth skin
long limbs spreading
from trunk and belly

pines
down the mountainside
whole forest up in arms

Point Reyes
from Mt. Wittenberg
in late afternoon
a long-necked bird
flies out to sea

climbing from the valley
high on the mountain
hear the ocean roar

Feeling alive in the footsteps of Basho, Thoreau, and John Muir, I went next to Muir Woods and slept in the bush on the side of Mt. Tam.

Mt. Tamalpais April

the stream climbs down
a shady canyon
beside the mammoth rock

and an old bent tree
with a bird's nest
cradled in its crotch

stopped
by a steep rock face
I look over my shoulder
a hawk
leaps from its jagged temple
alive in high blue air

butterfly
beside the rocky trail

two flies in a
dogfight
dive

Inspiration Point
a sign so weathered
the words float broken
through wooden ripples

up the last climb
even without a pack
I must carry myself

then into the open sun
wow
look down at the mountains

on East Peak I find a nest
among the rocks to eat my lunch
unseen by tourists
and there below
is a rock strange as an Aztec goblin
staring right at me

these grandfather rocks
with beards of moss
have mouths
if they could talk
the stream rushes down
into deep green pools

old giant redwood
though the creek has half-eaten
the earth out from under it
still tall as the canyon

approaching dusk
one tiny violet flower
its small mouth
a trap for flies

just finished poem
a jet cracks across Cataract Canyon

the setting sun
big orange lantern in a tree

wearing a spiderweb
the water fountain
I used awhile ago this morning

The ever-changing power and beauty of Nature creates life and death as it turns through the seasons. It is mother and father to us. We must find ways to live with Nature in harmony.

*

Choked with Emotion

The assassination of Dr. Martin Luther King, Jr. in April 1968 left us in shock. Where would the nonviolent movement go now, without its spiritual heart? Riots rocked many big cities, ghettos erupted in raging grief, but so far the neighborhood where I lived, on the edge of the Fillmore, seemed, if not calm, less chaotic.

Early one afternoon I was standing alone on the corner eating a hot dog, waiting for the bus. Very few people were out on Lyon Street, with its weathered Victorian houses, when a middle-aged black man in a derby hat and unbuttoned coat walked up and stopped in front of me. "Give me a bite of that hot dog," he said firmly.

I had been mugged in the neighborhood before, but this was a different approach. Maybe he just wanted a symbolic gesture of sharing. "All right," I said. "Here, have a bite." He took my hot dog with both hands, bit into it, chewed and swallowed, then returned it to me.

But that was not enough. Staring straight ahead without meeting my eyes, the man lifted both hands again, in slow motion, and grabbed me around the neck. At first his grip was not tense—then he began to squeeze, grimacing painfully, as if gripped by an inner conflict.

His hands gradually tightened around the tendons of my neck, while threads of fear curled in my stomach and thoughts flashed through my mind. I could struggle to break free and try to fight him off. But his grip, though strong, was still restrained. He must be grappling with the throes of anger over the death of Dr. King. Maybe if I stayed calm he would relent. I took the chance. Was I really the white man he wanted to kill?

"What are you doing?" I said.

"Agh-h-h-h…" He grunted. His grip tightened a little more. Then it released. The man turned and walked away without another word. Relieved, I stood there, still holding my hot dog, glad that my mind had stayed calm.

Evening

The dim light
of dusk in the city
weaves me into a
forest of shadows.

Only a tinge
of color left.
Afternoon flies,
trapped by my
almost closed window
stumble against the sky.

Looking back
at pen and paper,
it takes my eyes awhile
to become soft enough
to write this poem by.
Now it is finished.

Like an animal howling
deep in the forest,
it cannot be seen.

*

Violence on Top of Violence

Paul, my one-time college friend, showed up shortly after the assassination of Robert Kennedy. He had been working on the campaign, and was there in the ballroom at the Ambassador Hotel in L.A. when Kennedy gave his victory speech after winning the California primary— and while leaving through the kitchen was shot in the head. We sat on the floor of my living room and Paul described what had happened, something like this, in the words of one who was there:

"The room was crowded, full of excitement. Kennedy had just said 'On to Chicago!' He joked about bringing his dog for good luck, and left to a roar of applause. We were on our way down to another room for a celebration, milling around in the lobby, when a woman cried out, 'They're going to kill him like they killed his brother!' We all looked up. What was she talking about? Amid a commotion the police hustled a thin young man down the stairs. Who was he? What happened? A rumor filtered through the crowd that he had just shot Kennedy, who was still alive, but in critical condition. A friend of mine had brought a fifth of whiskey for the party, and when he heard the news he drank it down and was still on his feet. We were in shock. People were punching the wall or hugging each other and crying. When we got out to the parking lot, a man collapsed on the hood of his car and started sobbing."

"First Martin Luther King, and now this," was all I could say. "Kennedy might have stopped the war." Then after a pause, "It must have been hard for you to be there."

"Yeah, it was all too much," said Paul.

As our conversation went on, both of us in a state of emotion, eventually I brought up something that was still bothering me, hoping to resolve my anger by acknowledging and expressing it directly, as I'd learned to do in encounter groups. I said to Paul, my voice rising, "You know, I'm still angry about that night a few years ago when you got knock-down, drag-out drunk. While I was falling asleep you came into my room and stood up straight as you could on the foot of my bed, and fell on me like the trunk of a tree."

"What?" said Paul, looking surprised. Had his drunken stupor blacked out the memory?

"It shook me up. It felt like a physical attack, so I threw you out." I paused. "Why the hell did you do that?"

"You're pretty harsh," he said. "I was just drunk." From his tone I knew he was hurt. To him it was a drunken episode he could hardly remember. Looking back, I feel sad for Paul, and wonder what happened to him.

*

Forward or Backward?

That spring I began to go out with Anna, a graduate student in fiction writing from New York City. She was thin, intense, with dark, medium-length hair, and played jazz piano. You could say we had an affinity, even though she smoked and ate meat, both of which I was trying to avoid. Our personalities just clicked—and maybe that was the scary thing.

Later that spring I heard from Karina that she and Jack had split up. If I still wanted to, I could come visit. Maybe I should have known better, but I was haunted by the idea that without Jack in the picture, Karina and I might get back together. Before I got more involved with Anna, I could go back to Boston and see.

After a cross-country bus ride I arrived at Karina's place to discover she was already driving around with a classy new boyfriend in a red Triumph convertible. So much for that. We were still "friends" and had some long talks, but I slept on a couch in the hall. Finally the end, I ruefully thought, of my deluded romantic fantasy.

Wondering if I could help support myself with writing, I mimeographed a few pages of my poetry and gave them to summer school students relaxing or studying under trees around campus, saying "Free, or whatever you can afford." Most of them gave me a quarter, and after a few hours

I had about eight dollars—but I felt like a sellout, and never did it again.

Then I went to visit my grandmother Millie in suburban Reading, and indulged in a midnight snack in her kitchen.

Senses

Midnight becomes
a finger covered
with peanut butter,
which I put in
my mouth and lick.

The kitchen's a mess
too good to get out of,
a silence full
of the fly's buzz.

The time I tried
to see the sun,
the sun was in
my eyes.

*

The Way Inside

Willy was not tall but rugged, with unruly dirt-blonde hair and the weathered look of a one-time street urchin turned self-possessed mountaineer. We had met a few days before, at Karina's apartment. It was the summer of '68, and we walked backwards down broad Mass. Avenue toward Central Square, hitching to Newport to hear Janis Joplin at the Folk Festival.

"Karina said you're into Zen," Willy remarked as he stuck out his thumb. "Rock climbing is like Zen, but more challenging—you have to focus in the face of danger."

"Yeah, but Zen is more than just focusing."

"Then what is it?"

"Zen masters don't often explain. You might say it's a moment-by-moment practice of awareness—but it's also a spontaneous insight that can't be described in words."

Just then a big red slightly decrepit Cadillac convertible pulled up and the two African American men in the front seat made it clear, in their half-ignoring way, they were stopping for us. Glad for the ride, we hoisted our packs and piled in. "We're headed for Newport," I said.

The big man in the passenger seat turned and grinned. "That's where we goin' too," he said with mock savoir-faire. "I'm Sugar Bear... this here is J. C." Sugar Bear was the name for him all right. He was huge, but he carried his weight with ease, smiling and smooth in every move. J. C. was big too, but lean and grim, with no soft edges or trace of humor. An air of subdued violence hung over him like a sentence ending in the sharp scar that cut his cheek like an exclamation point.

"We're brothers, me and J. C.... half-brothers," smiled Sugar Bear. "It's amazin' we get along well as we do, but we do get along, just stoppin' now and then to beat each other's ass."

J. C. refused to comment, with a look of disgust.

"You got to watch him—he can be mean, that J. C." Sugar Bear laughed, as if recalling a practical joke. The big Caddy rolled down Mass. Avenue and across the bridge to Boston. It was sky-blue July and sailboats heeled up slightly in the gentle waves of the Charles. But instead of heading for the highway south, J. C. turned down Tremont Street into Roxbury's black ghetto.

"Where we goin'?" Willy asked carefully.

"We got to cash a check here—but don't worry, we goin' to Newport," cooed Sugar Bear through his usual smile. "Can't be takin' such a long ride without no gas money."

We pulled under an MTA trestle and both Sugar Bear and J. C. slammed their doors and disappeared into Joe's liquor store. Willy and I sat there for a moment before either spoke. "Well, we got the ride we were looking for—all the way to Newport," I said with a wry smile.

Willy scoffed. "I'm not afraid of those guys," he said, clearing a path with his hand through his thicket of hair. A young black man in a windbreaker walked by, stopped, and looked at us through his dark-framed glasses with a puzzled expression.

"You know who you ridin' with?" he said. "They mean trouble, those fellas."

I shrugged and flipped up both hands. The young man turned and walked on. Willy was impassive and waited in silence until our benefactors returned.

Sugar Bear strode out of the store carrying an entire case of beer in his meaty arms. He threw it in the car and urged "Let's get *out* of here!" under his breath. J. C. jerked the car back, then turning, peeled out like a teenage punk leaving rubber. Careening around corners and cutting across lanes, we sped toward the wide highway. Willy sat back and lit a cigarette. I held on with my arm over the side, feeling a surge of anxiety and a certain thrill at the speed.

All at once I was staring at an off-white front fender inches from my elbow. An abrupt swerve barely avoided impact, but behind us was a station wagon full of men gesticulating. They zoomed along in pursuit, shouting and waving through rolled-down windows. One guy gave us the finger. The chase was on, like something out of a silent comedy, everything hopping a little faster than ordinary reality. The Caddy had power, and J. C. poured it on, pulling out into the free lane ahead.

Before long, behind us the growl of a motorcycle began to close in, and a blue uniformed cop waved both vehicles over. J. C. looked like he might just keep going, but Sugar Bear glared at him and shouted something and he pulled up on the shoulder. The station wagon had stopped several lengths behind, and the cop parked his bike about midway between the two cars and walked back to talk to a group of white men in T-shirts and jeans. After several minutes of waiting-room silence, the officer methodically approached us and inquired as to what was going on.

"They were tryin' to run us off the road," volunteered J. C., nodding to the rear.

"Well, slow it down." The cop was writing on a pad, but didn't give us a ticket—instead he said "Wait here," and walked methodically back to talk with our pursuers again. They had more to say than we did, but the cop finally turned and with "OK, you can go," waved us on.

J. C. took off without hesitation, restrained only slightly by the warning. Within five minutes we were sailing again, breaking out our case of beer and passing the cans around. We were riding high, but I was still nagged by anxiety about the casual way J. C. wove down the road. Meanwhile Sugar Bear was delivering an animated monologue about how "That cop was too scared to do nothin' but raise his eyebrows and open his mouth," as he drained another can of beer. Willy, unperturbed, was putting away as much as he could while it still was available. I decided that words of caution would not carry much weight, and I might as well relax in the faith that we might very well make it to Newport alive.

Soon we swooped in at a sign that said GAS and everyone got out to take a leak while the Cadillac drank its fill. J. C. hit us up to help pay for gas. Willy and I scraped together a few bills, aware that it was unlikely we could afford concert tickets anyway.

Inside the station I noticed Sugar Bear was inspecting the cheapo sunglasses rack with the eye of a connoisseur. When we finally got ourselves together and back on the road, the roly-poly giant pulled out the pair he had lifted and donned them with a display of the utmost cool. But Willy was ready. Reaching into his pockets he pulled out three pairs of sunglasses and passed them around. Clearly he thought he had one-upped our hosts.

In response, Sugar Bear just opened another beer, and J. C. continued his reckless driving. Perhaps it was no big surprise when he drove off the road. The surprise was that we merely plowed harmlessly up an embankment. After a moment of silent contemplation, we backed down

241

and started off again, all of us wearing our shades. This time when J. C. resumed speeding and weaving down the road, I felt impelled to speak out. "Hey man, slow down," I ventured. But J. C. drove on as if he hadn't heard me.

Then to my surprise Sugar Bear began to preach. "J. C. what are you *doin'*? What is the *matter* with you? I *know* I'm goin' to hell—but I don't wanna go *that fast!*"

J. C. pretended to ignore this also, but it did seem to deter him from getting even more carried away. Whenever he would begin to speed up, Sugar Bear would make a similar speech, and without much decrease in speed, J. C. would compromise a little by not weaving around so much. Willy and I became more subdued by the need to calm J. C.

By this time we were approaching Newport. It hadn't taken long. Exiting onto a narrow road leading to the festival grounds, we were suddenly bogged down in traffic, a long line of cars inching their way along. The necessity of patience was too much for J. C. He saw an opening—the opposite lane was momentarily clear—and he wheeled the big Caddy out into that space and stepped on the gas. There we were, making an end-run, and oncoming cars were approaching, astonished, head-on. There was no room to get back in the right lane, but J. C. did not appear to be interested. He was heading for the first car, challenging, accelerating. The other driver took the better part of valor and went off the road. The next one followed him into the ditch. Sugar Bear was yelling and grabbing at the wheel.

We came to a halt at the feet of the cop who was supposed to be directing traffic. He motioned J. C. out of the car and took him aside for a private talk. Sugar Bear said nothing, Willy said nothing, and I said nothing too. This time J. C. had a ticket for sure, and when he returned to the car he and Sugar Bear settled into a wordless depression. J. C. drove slowly to the nearest supermarket parking lot. He parked, got out of the car, and went into a phone booth.

"What's happening?" I asked Sugar Bear.

"He got to make a phone call." Sugar Bear talked like the ball game was over. "Too many tickets. He'll lose his license, maybe lose parole," the big man said quietly.

J. C. and Sugar Bear dropped us off at the Festival grounds and drove slowly away in a cloud bank of gloom.

When I think of it now, I feel sad for them. They had to deal with the consequences of the wild ride they had taken us on, and our presence may have encouraged—while Willy and I went scot-free to continue our Newport adventure.

And one thing led to another. We walked toward a large fenced-in area on a slight hill, where crowds of people were pouring out of the gate down toward us. Evidently the afternoon concert had just ended, and Willy and I realized this was our chance to get in. We fought our way upstream through the river of humanity—like salmon, I thought, or maybe like people who had forgotten something. Sure enough, there was no guard at the gate, and turning sideways, dragging our packs, we squeezed through. Inside was an open grassy space with concession stands and portable toilets, sloping down to rows of seats and a large stage, the whole area enclosed by a high chain-link fence. People were slowly making their way out, while some still stood in groups talking.

Willy and I wandered around looking for a place to hide.

"PLEASE CLEAR THE GROUNDS. WE HAVE TO PREPARE FOR THIS EVENING'S CONCERT," the sound system announced. "THANK YOU."

Willy nonchalantly led me behind a trailer truck and sat down, leaning back against the big double wheels. "Just act like you belong here," he said.

The sound system continued urging people to leave. Willy and I made small talk until someone who looked official poked his head out from the window of a house trailer and said, "Get outta here!" We got up and moseyed in the general direction of the exit, looking for the long way around. There were only a few stragglers left inside the enclosure now.

243

"PLEASE CLEAR THE GROUNDS. ANYONE WHO DOES NOT LEAVE IMMEDIATELY WILL BE ESCORTED OUT BY GUARDS."

At that moment we were rounding a surprisingly large bunch of bushes behind some concession stands. Without saying a word I dived in. Willy followed, and after him another guy who'd been looking for the same opportunity. We crawled into the midst of the brush and lay low on our bellies and did not move.

After awhile it was clear we had not been seen. I moved a little to get more comfortable among the rocks, roots, leaves, and branches. The dive had just happened all of a sudden, with no plan—though perhaps inspired by the spontaneity of our recent wild ride. I had to admit I was proud I had taken the lead. Yet it seemed ironic that my ego took credit for something that had just spontaneously happened without its assistance.

Now it was down to silent waiting. I lay there in the thicket, occasionally shifting position to adjust for the sticks and stones that kept gnawing at my prone body through my T-shirt and jeans. No one had a watch. Time passed at its own pace. It felt like hours that we lay there, sweating in the late July heat. Gradually noises and voices began coming from the direction of the stage. It sounded like a band setting up, though it was still too early for the evening concert. There was joking around among the musicians, the twanging here and there of electric guitars, and a high-pitched cackle of laughter that sounded vaguely familiar.

At last there was a "One... two..." and "TAKE IT! TAKE A LITTLE PIECE OF MY HEART!" Boom, boom, boom, "BREAK IT!—" The band screeched to pieces and onstage everybody broke up laughing.

"Janis!" whispered the guy who had jumped in the bushes with us.

We lay there listening, feeling lucky to be the secret audience at this brief rehearsal. Janis Joplin and Big Brother and the Holding Company never got beyond one song that afternoon, nor did they manage to finish even that, but they did a great job of loosening up.

The music stopped, although sounds of miscellaneous preparations gradually increased. The light became grayer, and soon we could feel the soft cooling warmth of a summer dusk. The voices increased steadily, and were all around us now. The concert crowd was coming in.

"Let's get up," said Willy.

"Let's wait a little longer, just to make sure."

"Well, I'm getting up." Willy crawled over to the edge of the bushes and crouched. Then he stood up and walked away. I waited for sounds of him being discovered, but there were none, only the mild chaotic buzz of the crowd. I crawled to an open spot and peeped through. The place was alive with people. Everything was cool.

I stood up and walked straight ahead to become just one of the crowd. Willy and I sat on the grass and waited for the concert to begin. It felt as if we had always been there.

*

Smashing Through

When I came back to visit my parents after two years on the West Coast, they had moved to another house, smaller than where we had lived before. As we sat around the mahogany dining room table, finishing our vanilla ice cream and apple pie, cabinets were crowded together along the wall, displaying china dinnerware and crystal glasses, my grandmother's gifts to my mother. Was there still room for me here, sleeping in the tiny guest room? Our conversation may have gone something like this:

"How do you like living in a smaller place?" I asked, waving my hand around the room.

My father finished chewing his mouthful of pie, swallowed, and wiped his lips with a white napkin. "Now that your sister's at college and you're hanging out with the hippies in San Francisco, there's no point paying for space we don't need." He looked pointedly at my shoulder-length hair. "By the way, why don't you get a haircut? You won't find a good job with hair like that."

245

"I'll get a job when I get my M.A. Meanwhile, I'll wear my hair how I want."

"And I'm footing the bill for you to hang out all day and smoke pot."

I paused and looked down at my melting ice cream and flakes of piecrust. "I don't need your money. I'm ready to support myself right now. I'll get a part-time job and work my way through school. Then I won't have to listen to this every time I come home."

"You'll listen when I speak to you," said my father, pointing his fork in my direction.

"When I finish my M.A., I can get a part-time teaching job at a community college—"

"Not part time, full time, so you earn a good living."

"I want time to write—"

"You can write in the evenings. There's no reason you can't find a job that will give you financial security."

"But I want—"

"You need to think of the future, of supporting a family." He was waving his fork.

"But right now I need—"

"Don't sacrifice security. It's irresponsible."

I hated how he interrupted me. Whenever we had an argument, he always interrupted me. My father believed a man should be king of his family. He cut in with strong words to enforce his rule. I didn't like how he dominated my mother, and tried to dominate me as well. I began to rise from my chair. "Irresponsible? How can you say—"

"You need to settle down and get your life together." He stood up, facing me.

"But—"

"No ifs, ands, or buts."

I clenched my fists. "That's a stupid cliché! Don't you see—"

"That's enough, young man, no more excuses."

"Stop interrupting me!" My voice was rising.

"You're just afraid—"

"*Stop interrupting me!*" Now I was shouting.

His eyebrows went up as his mouth opened. "The way you react shows that *I'm right!*"

That was all I could take. I grabbed my empty glass from the table—smooth to the touch—stepped back as I lifted it in the air, then smashed it hard on the floor. It exploded into pieces that scattered across the faded oriental carpet, as if fleeing the impact, and came to rest, spread out in chaos.

My father and mother stood there, aghast. I turned and strode into the guest room, where I sat on the floor in the dark with my back to the wall, breathing hard. I had made my point, but at what cost?

*

Searching in the Dark

Later that summer I went to visit my other grandmother, Nana, in the small town of Clinton, Massachusetts. There I discovered a wood carving of a Mallard duck done by my uncle Dan, then in the veteran's hospital for shell shock from surviving a battle where his buddies died in the snow-covered mountains of Italy during World War II. But when I got off the bus and crossed Main Street, a traffic cop with panic in his eyes at the sight of my shoulder-length hair fumbled for the walkie-talkie on his belt and made a frantic call for backup.

I proceeded up a side street, hoping to avoid confrontation, but within two minutes three speeding police cars with lights flashing converged on me, two of them jumping the curb and pulling up on the sidewalk, blocking my path in all directions. Gleaming black doors opened, several officers quickly stepped out to surround me, and the one in charge ordered, "Put up your hands."

He patted me down and then took out a pad of paper and pen and began the interrogation. "Where are you going?"

"To see my grandmother."

"Where does she live?"

"703 Prescott Street." This information was methodically noted, and after a few more questions I was allowed to go on, walking alone through the dim, tree-lined streets.

Half an hour later I sat watching the news on TV with Nana, my proper, tea-drinking grandmother. She was upset to see footage of a protest march.

"Oh dear, what are they doing?" she sighed. I didn't ask her about my father's younger sister Beverly, who had her child born out of wedlock given up for adoption, and according to my mother, died from pneumonia after running out into the winter cold with wet hair.

Uncle Dan's artistically painted duck-hunting decoy, with bottle-green head, brown and gray body, black tail, and white collar around its neck, floated peacefully in my lap, its yellow bill forever mute to all family secrets.

And then the bright conical beams of multiple searchlights from dark police cars began to explore the hedges and bushes of my grandmother's carefully tended yard.

They would see no sign of what haunted my father: the unmentioned deaths of his sister and brother, who could find no place in our world, two sensitive people who did not survive.

*

At the end of the summer, as I hitchhiked back to the West Coast, many Vietnam War protestors at the Democratic Party convention in Chicago were violently beaten and jailed in what ought to be called a police riot.

Ancient Airs, No. 14

The Tartar Pass abounds in wind and sand,
a bleak and lifeless place since ancient times.
Trees have lost their leaves, the autumn grass is brown.
We climb up high to watch for the western enemy:
a deserted fortress in the vast empty desert,
in the village beside it, not a wall remains.
White bones lie through a thousand frosts
in abrupt mounds covered by hazel brush.
If you ask who opposed and mistreated whom,
Heaven's Men, full of pride and maliciously warlike,
sparked the outraged anger of our Holy Emperor.
He ordered the army to beat the war drums;
harmonious strength turned into a murderous wind.
He dispatched soldiers, causing turmoil in the heartland:
three hundred and sixty thousand men.
Widespread sorrow, tears like rain—
disheartened, they had to go.
How could they farm their fields?
Without seeing the men who served there,
how could you know the bitterness at the mountain pass?
General Li Mu is no longer here.
Frontier men were fed to tigers and wolves.

— Li Po (Li Bai)

Part Five: Taking the Path of Zen

Chapter 14: Turning Toward Dharma

Reply to Vice-Prefect Chang

In late years I only love quiet,
worldly affairs are not my concern.
Looking inside, there's no long-term plan,
only empty knowing returns me to this old woods.
Pine winds blow through my loosened clothes,
the mountain moon shines as I strum along.
You ask for an explanation of the cosmic pattern?
A fisherman's song, deep in the cove.

—Wang Wei

Wild Bird

Back in San Francisco I went to S. F. State to register for the fall
semester and ran into Anna, the fiction writer from New York I'd been
dating last spring. She looked more attractive than ever, with her dark hair
parted in the middle, falling around her face. "How was your trip to
Boston?" she said coolly, studying her nails.

"Well... things didn't work out with Karina. By the time I got there she
had a new boyfriend."

Anna glared. "Well, the hell with you!" Then she walked away. I stood
there dumbfounded, so taken aback I didn't follow her. Nor did I call her
later, after her anger might have had time to fade. Maybe I feared our
artistic affinity would lead into conflicts over other issues like smoking
and Zen. Or maybe I was just not ready for a possible deep commitment.

By that time I had moved into a communal apartment in an old gray
Victorian with some other Zen students across from the Bush Street
center. We ate together and (for the most part) woke up early to cross the

street for morning zazen. One morning on the balcony an unfamiliar student strode in, and moving with militant intensity, bowed, sat down, and crossed his legs in full lotus. After zazen, when Suzuki Roshi walked in, the newcomer bowed with gusto, and Roshi bowed in return.

It turned out he was a poet whose work I admired who had just come back from studying traditional Zen in Japan. I thought he might be interested in sitting in with our informal weekly poetry group of Zen students, so I found out where he was staying nearby and knocked on the door. When the poet opened it, he seemed more reserved than he was at the zendo. I invited him to drop in on our group. He looked at me without expression and said "No." That was that. Maybe he wanted to protect his privacy, but it was disappointing.

One night, feeling my own identity was too small and confined, I wrote a poem transforming myself into a symbolic being, untamed and free, called Wild Bird. I was shy about reading it aloud to the poetry group with full force because it might seem overbearing. Kurt, a tall guy from Colorado who drove a panel truck, had no such compunctions, and offered to read it for me—which shamed me to go ahead and read it myself with the intensity it demanded.

Wild Bird

Christopher Lennox,
that plodding follower
of crucifixions,
has been transformed.
I am the air,
alight upon the headstone of the Word,
with diamonds in my eyes.
I am the flying Bodhisattva,
you heard me.
I live in Eternity.
My name is *Wild Bird*.

As I read I felt the power of my new poetic identity. I could imagine my feathery wings spreading out in the air of the room, exulting in freedom.

*

Bush Street, Fall 1968

I liked living in our communal household, in a flat up the stairs with a small porch and rooms off the hall leading back to the kitchen. Our diet was vegetarian. We baked bread and made yogurt, warming it overnight with a lightbulb under a cardboard box, and ate the occasional omelet. But some wanted to follow a strict macrobiotic diet of only brown rice and vegetables—and they were often the ones who would sneak out to gorge on jelly donuts. I disliked fanatic adherence to rigid rules, especially when done with hypocrisy. When a couple of these guys gloated over their pastry adventures, recalling fierce Zen stories I threw an empty donut carton at them across the table and shouted, "Zen is not about donuts!"

Awareness of eating is part of Zen practice, though discrimination about what one eats is not encouraged. But sometimes it may be necessary. Once at communal dinner I was about to chomp on a forkful of lettuce when I spied the point of a thumbtack sticking up through a torn green leaf. How did *that* get there? Maybe it just dropped in. The big wooden salad bowl sat on the table against the wall, right below the bulletin board.

My bedroom was small and dull white with a wooden floor, planks painted dark brown. In an alcove under the stairwell was a single thick straw tatami mat with my dark red sleeping bag stretched out toward a small pillow. Against the wall a long narrow table made of wide unfinished boards lying across two used wooden wine boxes supported a Japanese rice-paper notebook with an elegant flower on the cover, a blue fountain pen, and a few slim books of Asian thought and poetry, such as *Zen Flesh, Zen Bones*; Basho's *Narrow Road to the Interior*; and *Old Friend from Far Away*, Chinese poems translated into free verse.

In the center of the table was a fine blue cloth under a dark brass Buddha statue about six inches high, seated on a lotus throne with hands cradled in a mudra upon crossed legs. Before the Buddha was a single white candle, unlit, with a slight scent of burnt wax. To the left lay a small bamboo flute. On the opposite wall hung a "God's eye," a diamond pattern of purple yarn woven on crossed sticks. There was no chair in the room, only a zafu, the round black kapok-stuffed meditation cushion where I sat looking out toward the light shining in through the bare, partly-open window.

*

Breaking an Icon

Even though practice at Sokoji was not as demanding as a training period at Tassajara, I still felt confined by what seemed like the rigid formality of traditional rituals imported from Japan, with frequent bowing, precise postures, and emotional restraint. Once, looking out across the street from my window, I saw the old temple as a huge alien monster with its arched mouth waiting to swallow me, as the whale had swallowed Jonah.

I wanted to rebel, just as I had defied the social conformity of the fifties. I was even clinging to forms myself, with that inexpensive Buddha statue on the little shrine in my bedroom. Why was I bowing to this hollow statue when the real Buddha was formless and transcendent, beyond representation? For centuries the early Buddhists had refused to make statues or paintings of their great teacher, only going so far as to represent his footprints.

One morning my frustration came to a head, literally. Recalling a Zen story about "killing the Buddha"—not clinging to his external form—I grabbed the Buddha statue and smashed it on the floor. Then I looked down at what I had done. The Buddha's head was broken off. A foot away was the headless body, lying on its side on the wooden floor.

Then I knew that I loved my Buddha statue, simple as it was. Even if it was only a crude representation, bowing before this little Buddha was a way to express my gratitude for the teachings. Filled with remorse, I carefully picked up the pieces, glued the Buddha's head back on, and placed the mended statue on my shrine.

*

Front Porch Poems

It felt good to meditate peacefully at Zen Center each morning, starting the day with some clarity of mind and a positive feeling. I had finished my coursework for the M.A. in Creative Writing, so I rarely had to take the long bus and streetcar ride back and forth to the campus. All that remained was to read for the oral exam and write a Master's thesis, both due in June. For the orals I chose William Blake, Henry David Thoreau, and Gerard Manley Hopkins, three spiritual writers of very different styles. I began with Blake, writing notes and short quotes on 3x5 cards, starting with a poem that seemed in tune with the Buddhist idea of non-grasping:

> He who binds to himself a joy
> Does the winged life destroy;
> But he who kisses the joy as it flies
> Lives in eternity's sun rise.

The Master's thesis was another question. It was to be a book of poetry, and I had never written anything near that long. I decided to build on the regularity of Zen discipline: each day, whether the weather was foggy or sunny, I would sit on the small front porch at the top of the stairway leading up to our front door and wait until I had an idea, then write it down in a rice-paper notebook I'd bought in nearby Japantown. For example, this poem took shape when I sat on the porch after taking a morning walk:

The Archeology of Spring

On the way to the library
I take an abrupt left turn
into a vacant lot
surrounded by mounds of dirt,
overrun with rich grass.
Here and there the foundations
of what used to be a house
are lying around like huge cement crumbs.

An easy chair with the stuffing coming out,
its inner springs exposed to the sun,
sits back with a piece
of packing crate in its lap:
"State Textbook Warehouse
Sacramento, California."
With archeological intuition
I've stumbled upon an ancient ruin
right in the middle of San Francisco.

A pipe sticks up, its eye
at the elbow joint,
like a periscope above the waves of grass.
The dead are watching us
from submarines
that move with the speed of eternity
beneath the earth.

Maybe I could live
in this graveyard of pale dry Christmas trees,
in the little cave I see
that looks like a dragon's mouth.

In these lush bushes
I could be at ease;
on that chunk of cement
I could sit and smell the wildflowers,
feel the breeze.
Something real is happening here:
I trust the patience of the grass.

*

Escape with Your Life

One morning when I walked down the hall toward the front porch with my notebook and pen, the quiet of our communal household was shattered by the loud *Crack!* of a gunshot from the street outside. *Crack!* Another shot ripped through the silence. I looked down the hall at the wood-paneled door, eyes and ears alert and body tense. What was happening? Would there be need for a witness? I walked to the door and paused, cautious but curious. For the moment the shots had stopped. Slowly I turned the knob, gingerly opened the door a crack, and peeked out.

A yellow cab had stopped near the curb at an angle with doors flung open. The burly white driver in a brown leather jacket and gray cap stood in the middle of the street, feet planted apart, his right arm straight out, aiming a stubby pistol at a lanky black man frantically sprinting along a red brick wall, his gray suit flapping in haste. *Crack!* the next shot rang out as he disappeared around the corner.

The cabby stood stock still, erect, holding his pose with arm extended, aiming the pistol at eye level. His aviator jacket hung open in front around a hefty belly and chest, and his face was set in a scowl. When the fleeing man did not reappear, the cabby deliberately lowered his pistol, still gazing toward the brick wall, then tucked the gun in his belt, climbed back in the cab, and drove off in another direction.

He never looked at me, with my head poking out from the partly open door. But I recognized him. I once rode in his cab in south San Francisco, and remembered his taciturn toughness, his jacket and cap, and how he drove the long way around to my destination. Those were the days when the big neon Hamm's beer mug graced the skyline, filling up over and over with a glowing amber brew topped with white foam. I used to watch it, entranced, from my window.

After the cabby left, I walked across the street to the corner along the brick wall, wondering if the fleeing man had been wounded and needed an ambulance. There was no sign of the man, except for a bullet scar on the bricks and the three-inch spot of blood on the sidewalk.

This sobering experience brought home to me the cruelty and futility of violence. The inner peace of meditation was not all I felt in those days, on the front porch or anywhere else. But it helped me ride though the tumult.

*

The Hexagram of Revolution

By this time, with the occasional exception of smoking a little pot when visiting non-Zen friends, I had pretty much given up drugs, with their risk of bad trips, in favor of the slow but sure path of Buddhist practice. I also turned away from paths that might lead to political violence, seeing social and spiritual evolution as necessary for true political change.

After the assassinations, riots, and clashes with police in the spring and summer of '68, some felt the winds of revolution stirring the air. That fall college students across the country organized protests not only against the Vietnam War, but also over the way their schools were run. The academic establishment had to stop collaborating with the war effort and change the curriculum to allow black and third-world students to study their cultures.

There was plenty happening at San Francisco State, as I saw when I ventured on campus. One slightly surprising demonstration was a crowd surrounding what appeared to be a naked hippie couple sitting together on the grass. Were they making love? It didn't look like it, though I couldn't see well through the tightly packed crowd, and basically felt so what—was the custom of wearing clothes in public really a problem?

Meanwhile, the Black Student Union and the Third World Liberation Front were spearheading a movement to change the curriculum in fundamental ways, with detailed demands to establish an Ethnic Studies department and bring in more students and faculty of color. I wanted to do something to support the teach-in I heard was planned, so I made a pile of Xerox copies of the hexagram for Revolution from the ancient Chinese book of divination, the *I Ching,* and included excerpts from the commentaries that advised undertaking a revolution only when absolutely necessary, waiting until the time was ripe and you had the support of the people, making your demands clear, persevering, and after succeeding not pushing beyond what the people could accept. In other words, revolution, but with sage advice. Arriving early at the teach-in, I put a copy of the Revolution hexagram and commentary on each seat in the auditorium until my supply ran out. I didn't expect this action to have much effect, but wanted to make a gesture in a constructive direction.

The S.F. State protests culminated in a five-month strike, with daily demonstrations and teach-ins. Administrators called in the police, who tried to break up the demonstrations and arrested students on several occasions, but the strike went on. It finally ended in March with a compromise that included most of the students' demands.

Organizing, demonstrating, negotiating—and going on strike when necessary—had achieved some progress toward equal opportunity, at least in education. Today, more than fifty years later, in a new host of ways the struggle goes on.

*

Right Livelihood

Meanwhile, I needed a part-time job to support myself. I hoped to find work that was not too boring and had some meaning—or at least did no harm, in accord with the Buddhist notion of Right Livelihood. So I looked through the classified ads in the student newspaper. Years later I wrote a poem about what happened:

Albert the Opera Fan

I answered an ad for a part-time job
to help me get by while finishing school:
"Reader/companion for man
paralyzed with multiple sclerosis."
I went for an interview
and met Albert in the Veterans' Hospital,
awkwardly folded into his wheelchair,
his facial movements spastic,
his smile a distorted grimace, with a slight drool.
Groaning sounds were all he could manage.
I can't do this, I said to myself,
and turned down the job at first,
but the next day called back:
"I have to do this."

Once Albert had played the piano.
Now I read to him from *Opera News,*
and moved on to *Sons and Lovers.*
Communication was a challenge.
Eventually all he could fully control were his eyelids,
so I would list letters of the alphabet
until he blinked at the right one,
slowly spelling out telegraphic messages.

If I'd asked, "Should I sit
on the other side of the bed?"
"W-H-Y-D-I-D-T-H-E-C-H-I-C-K-E-N
C-R-O-S-S-T-H-E-R-O-A-D"
he might have blinked in reply.
He cracked a big crooked smile
when I got his jokes.

A high point was our field trip
to see Mozart's *Don Giovanni*
at the San Francisco Opera.
Albert's brother rented a van
and got us box seats, wheelchair accessible.
The aides dressed him up
in white shirt and dark suit
and we rolled through the fancy hall,
up the elevator and into a luxury box,
where it seemed we were hardly noticed.

By the climax when Don Giovanni
fell down into hell with a musical swoon
and disappeared in a chorus of flames,
Albert was in heaven.

And he lived on, even beyond
his brother, a Stanford scientist
and family man, who died of a heart attack.

For years the job of reader/companion
was handed down from Zen student
to Zen student, and in his own way
Albert became a teacher.

A Modern Primitive Rite

It was around the time of the struggles over People's Park when I read that a rare Bergman film made for Swedish television and not widely released was being shown that afternoon on the Berkeley campus. Maybe I could see the film and also check out the protests. When I got off the bus from San Francisco at Shattuck Avenue and walked up Bancroft, I was struck by the unusual quiet, the lack of traffic. As I got close enough to see the corner of Telegraph Avenue, the usually busy street seemed almost empty—until suddenly a chaotic crowd of students came pouring out of a drifting gray cloud and dispersed in all directions, chased by blue-clad policemen swinging clubs.

Pop! a projectile arced toward me over the heads of the scattering crowd, hit the pavement with a thud, and burst, releasing a churning cloud of pungent gray gas into the air. It was wafting my way, so I hustled to take a shortcut across campus, away from the turmoil. There in deserted Sproul Plaza an abandoned pickup truck was perched at an odd angle, smashed into a tree. The contents of a metal trash can burned with wildly dancing flames.

It felt like a war zone. There was no one to be seen. A sandwich-board sign still stood alone by the entrance to Dwinelle Hall, holding a colorful poster for the film now eclipsed by events—Ingmar Bergman's *The Ritual: A Modern Primitive Rite*. The box office and building looked empty. I figured I'd already witnessed a modern primitive rite, and walked back across campus through the stench of lingering tear gas.

*

Getting Another Degree

Despite the upheavals of the time, living across the street from Zen Center allowed me to cultivate a life that was quiet and regular enough, for the most part, to complete my poetry thesis and prepare for the orals, while working a few afternoons a week with Albert. The M.A. seemed within reach. But I did not expect the ordeal that awaited.

Shortly before the thesis and orals were due, I came down with a wicked case of the flu. Rolando's girlfriend Sharla was kind enough to use her skillful fingers to type up my thesis, and I dragged myself down to the campus to hand it in. In the quad I ran into Robert, the shaggy-haired professor I met with monthly to discuss my reading for the orals, as he was parking his motorcycle. When he asked how the reading was going, I said "OK, but I'm sick with the flu."

A week later I received a notice from the administration: my thesis was unacceptable because it was not on parchment paper. Oh shit, I thought, I forgot to look at the official requirements for submission. I had to redo it on parchment, but didn't want to ask Sharla to type it again. Gwen, a Zen student next door, stepped in and saved me from having to hunt and peck the whole book while sick, and I managed to get the thesis in on time.

Then I lay in bed for a week, recuperating and reading over my notes for the orals. When the exam day came I sat down with two professors: Mel, my friendly advisor, and Stu, an accomplished poet. Robert was supposed to be there but sent word he couldn't make it. The orals went pretty well—being sick I'd had nothing to do but study and write. Mostly we discussed what I thought about Blake, Hopkins, and Thoreau. But Stu, who evidently knew his stuff, came up with a very specific final question: "What was the name of Blake's engraver, the man who did his illustrations?"

I paused and stared straight ahead, mentally flipping through notecards. Luckily the name popped up. "Basire," I said, "James Basire."

Mel and Stu looked at each other and nodded. "You've passed," said Mel. We all stood up and shook hands.

The good news was, I'd completed the thesis and passed the orals for the M.A. The bad news came in my grade report in the mail.

For the Directed Reading tutorial, Robert had given me an Incomplete. The notice said I had to complete the course and would not get my degree in June. It was true that I missed our final meeting, but I had told Robert I was sick. And he missed my oral exam to boot! Why was that motorcycle-riding, seemingly hip, shaggy-haired professor acting like a persnickety perfectionist teacher?

I was really angry—so angry I sat right down and wrote him a letter featuring several choice four-letter words, expressing my outrage at this injustice, then stamped it and dropped it in a mailbox. When the letter fell in and the metal lid closed, I felt some satisfaction—which soon turned to dread. After getting that angry letter, would he ever revise my grade? It seemed too late to turn back. Had I just thrown away the degree I'd been working on for three years?

I rushed back home and called him on the phone. Luckily he was there. "Professor, about that Incomplete. I told you I was sick. But I want to apologize in advance for the angry letter I just sent you. It was pretty ugly."

"No problem," said Robert. "I understand. I'll change the Incomplete. And when the letter comes, I won't even read it. I'll toss it right in the wastebasket."

"Thanks," I said, surprised he so easily changed his mind. Maybe asserting his power over my fate was enough, and he could relent. I got my degree after all, but sometimes wondered whether he actually resisted the temptation to read my angry letter.

Was sending that letter a mistake? Maybe, but regretting it dissolved my anger and spurred me to call Robert and solve the problem. What a mistake is may depend on your point of view.

My M.A. notice arrived in the mail soon after Apollo 11 landed on the moon and Neil Armstrong stepped down into the primal gray dust of the Sea of Tranquillity. The picture looking back at the blue earth from that perch in space gave us a new perspective on our problems.

*

Not Altamont

That summer I had considered going to Woodstock, but decided the long hot dusty cross-country trip was not worth it to sit in a field in a crowd of hundreds of thousands and listen to music blasted by giant amplifiers from a tiny stage in the distance. Besides, in the Avalon Ballroom I'd heard the Grateful Dead play their long, improvised jams—what could be better than that?

But when word got around about a big free concert with not only the Dead but the Rolling Stones being planned that fall in the Bay Area, a kind of Woodstock West, I was thinking of going. After several delays from difficulties in finding a suitable site, the concert was announced for Altamont Speedway on Saturday, December 6th. But that was the date of a one-day sesshin, a meditation retreat I wanted to attend. So my growing commitment to the spiritual path collided head-on with residual Deadhead devotion to stoned rock-and-roll hippiedom.

One factor was my slight disillusion with the Rolling Stones. I liked dancing to their funky blues-based rhythms, but some of their edgy songs like "Under My Thumb" and "Sympathy for the Devil" pointed in a different direction from the quasi-spiritual jam-band ecstasies of West Coast acid rock I'd discovered in San Francisco. And the Hell's Angels, the outlaw motorcycle club, had been hired to provide "security" for $500 worth of beer.

So I decided not to go. Later, I heard the concert disintegrated into chaos. The Angels parked their bikes in front of the low stage to fend off the surging crowd, got in fights as the Stones played "Sympathy for the Devil," and beat up an 18-year-old African American art student high on methamphetamine. Enraged, he pointed a gun in the air, and a drunken Angel stabbed him to death. Due to the violence, the Grateful Dead decided not to play. In any case, I was glad I chose meditation instead.

*

Laissez-faire at the French School

Come now, children
as you run, I'll walk
among the hailstones!

—Basho

Tucked beneath the shining gold cupola of the Russian Orthodox church was the little traditional French School, founded two years before with an immersion program of all day in French except one hour in English. It was that hour, in each of two classes, first grade and second through fifth, that I was hired to teach.

When I arrived for day one, the headmaster, a heavy-set man in a gray suit, led me into an empty classroom and gestured toward the teacher's desk. Then he went out on the playground where children were playing catch and jump-rope, blew a whistle to end recess, assembled the older kids in an orderly line, and marched them into the classroom to stand at their desks in silence, facing us.

"Say good morning to Mr. Lennox," he said.

"Good morning, Mr. Lennox," the children responded in unison.

"Good morning," I said. With military precision they all sat down at their desks and looked up at me.

Their faces were open and curious, but a prickling unease spread over my skin. I didn't realize the *Ecole Francaise* would be so formal. At my initial interview, when I asked what to teach, the headmaster shrugged and said, "Do as you wish." But it was San Francisco, 1969—did he realize I wrote wild poems and sometimes smoked pot with friends? My long hair was trimmed—but would I fit in?

The students' orderly behavior lasted precisely until the headmaster left the room. Immediately they began to turn to each other and chat, giggle, and fool around, waiting to see what I'd do. Actually I had no idea what to do, never having taught before, and the students could tell. At first it was hard to get control of the class. It seemed like the rigid discipline of their

French classes was a pressure cooker, and in English, with a new teacher, the lid was taken off, explosively releasing the pent-up steam. Not believing in strictness myself, my attempts to establish control lacked follow-through. In frustration, I'd raise my voice and shout "Quiet!" to get a minute of peace, but that soon would unravel. I was uncomfortable being a disciplinarian. With my own ambivalence toward authority, what would I do now that I was the authority figure?

Remembering my best experiences in school, and drawing on what I'd read of the hands-on Montessori method, I changed my approach and re-organized the class around a group project: writing and editing an informal newsletter in English. The students would compose stories, reports, jokes, gossip, and comments on their activities, and put them into a few pages that I would help edit and print on the school mimeograph machine and distribute in class to be read and discussed—*The French School Weekly Update,* or something like that, with articles like "Charlotte Loses Her Homework."

Then Monique, a bright-eyed, enthusiastic little girl with bows on her pigtails, arrived directly from France. She couldn't speak English. I couldn't speak French. How to work with her individually and still teach the rest of the class? I assigned the two oldest girls, Sophie and Danielle, to sit with Monique in the back of the room and teach her to speak English, starting by pointing at things and naming them. Beyond that, they could come up with their own ideas and learn how to teach in the process. Young kids can pick up language fast—in a couple of weeks Monique was speaking enough English to follow along with the class.

When it came time to prepare for a small assembly with their parents before the winter holiday break, I asked the students if they would like to write and perform a short play. They jumped on the idea and decided, like Shakespeare, to borrow a plot—the story of Rudolph the Red-Nosed Reindeer. I did little in the way of direction. When the assembly came, the French portion consisted of selected students standing up on cue and reciting passages from classic French literature. When the English part began, I sat back and watched as Santa (with a pillow under his red jacket) came in with his reindeer (on hands and knees with cardboard antlers and home-made costumes, including a red nose for Rudolph), speaking and acting the lines they had written.

"Hi Rudolph, how come your nose is so red?"

"I colored it red with my mother's lipstick."

"If she sees it you'll get in trouble."

"No, it was her idea."

I didn't have to do anything but watch. The parents and teachers were pleased. It was all so American. I realized that French pride in tradition included respect for creative freedom as embodied in New World lassez-faire.

The first-grade class was different, with students all about the same age. They were constantly squirming around at their desks, whispering to each other—except for one quiet, self-contained little boy, Édouard, who sat attentively to the side near the back and never said a word, like a pocket gopher peering out of his burrow. A teacher told me he was always like that during class.

Getting the first-graders to focus their attention on a big project like a newsletter seemed out of the question. First they needed to learn to write words and sentences. So I gave them the freedom to draw pictures of whatever they wanted on paper with crayons—after all, writing began with pictures—while I walked around and talked to each one, helping them spell out some English words about what they were drawing. Nevertheless, sometimes the kids I wasn't engaged with got distracted.

Once, to get the attention of the whole group, I suddenly leaned toward them in a slight crouch, with arms half-raised as if holding the air in my hands, and said, "Would you like to hear a *story*?" The class became quiet, with all eyes on me. To keep their attention, I made up a tale of a magic tree with birds of bright colors perched on its branches and a zipper that went all the way up its trunk. "One of the birds with its beak unzipped the zipper and out leaped a bunch of white and brown rabbits. Purple frogs jumped up and down. Then along came an elf with a bushy gray beard

267

sitting on an orange elephant's trunk. The elf asked who had the most fantastic trunk, the tree or the elephant?"

"Now it's your turn, kids—imagine what you think is the most fantastic trunk and draw a picture of it. Then under the picture write some English words about why you chose it."

Later when I asked the kids if they had finished writing on their pictures yet, no one raised a hand. Then in a loud, firm voice, Édouard said, "*No!*"

The room froze in silence. The children looked at him with eyebrows raised and mouths open, amazed. Édouard had spoken. A little shyly, he smiled, then resumed his silence and picked up his crayon, and we went on with the class. From then on Édouard spoke rarely. But he had shown that he could.

A week later, when the parents came to visit, his mother, an engaging woman with black hair and a long dress, shook my hand and said, "I'm so happy that Édouard spoke in your class. He told me all about it. He has no problem talking at home, but in school he was afraid he might say something wrong."

When his mother learned of my interest in Buddhism, she said, "You've got to read this Russian mystical book called *The Way of a Pilgrim*. Salinger mentioned it in *Franny And Zooey*." Later she gave me a translation of the Russian book, about a wandering monk who recited the "Jesus prayer" like a mantra. It turned out the Russian Orthodox and Buddhist mystical traditions had some similar practices. "East meets West" is nothing new. Travelers got around back then on the Silk Route.

That spring I asked the headmaster if it was OK for me to find a substitute for a week so I could go to a sesshin coming up at the Zen Center. He nodded his head: "As you wish." A few days later in the auditorium at S.F. State I ran into Anna, the woman I'd dated before going back to Boston for the summer. Her anger seemed to be gone, and I asked if she would like to sub for me at the French School.

"Sure, I'd love to." We talked a bit more, and Anna asked, "In your Zen group do they have a restricted diet—like, is it vegetarian?"

"Yes, at least at the Center," I said, "Though it's not a requirement otherwise." I suppressed the urge to add that they didn't allow smoking, knowing that Anna smoked.

"Maybe it's just as well we didn't get together," she said.

I nodded, then slowly slid my fingers together. "Yeah, I guess so," was all I could muster. I still liked her, but had to agree we were headed in different directions.

Before I left for the weeklong retreat I told the older class what I was going to do, and at their request, showed them how to meditate. Before long, several students were sitting on top of their desks with their legs crossed, hands in their laps, quietly trying to follow their breathing. Some of the older girls who were taking ballet even managed to sit in full lotus —legs crossed with each foot over the opposite thigh—something I could not do for more than a minute. When I returned from the retreat a week later, one little boy proudly announced that he had meditated at home every day I was gone—sitting in his closet with the door shut.

*

Page Street, Spring 1970

By that time Zen Center had moved to a beautiful big brick building on Page Street, with a courtyard, meditation hall, kitchen, dining room, and living quarters. I found a shared apartment with some other students on the second floor of a green Victorian house a little way down the hill. This was the beginning of a new chapter for Zen Center, with an urban residential center in San Francisco as well as the retreat center at Tassajara over three hours away.

I still had a lot to learn about Zen in daily life. Ellen, a tall and friendly young woman, asked me what was my favorite dessert, and when I said strawberry shortcake, offered to make me some. But when it appeared on my plate and I took my first bite, it tasted different from the strawberry shortcake I was used to. The strawberries were fine, but the thick, heavy whole-grain biscuit was nothing like the light spongy stuff my mother used to make.

"What's wrong? Don't you like it?" Ellen asked.

I tried to explain. "It's not bad, but it's not what I expected."

Ellen looked crestfallen. Attachment to the fluffy spongecake of my childhood kept me from appreciating the healthy cake of the present moment, and the woman who made it.

For over a year I had been in psychotherapy at Mount Zion Hospital through a low-income program, believing that therapy could be a helpful complement to Zen. My therapist was a sympathetic, attractive, dark-haired middle-aged woman who was open to my interest in Buddhism. My intuitive trust in her eventually allowed my distrust of authority to manifest during therapy in a simple request: would she be willing to exchange seats with me and let me sit in her chair behind her desk for just a few minutes, to see what it felt like? At first she was reluctant, saying we should maintain the formal boundaries of therapy. But at the next session she said, "OK, let's try it." We got up and exchanged seats. I felt the support of her swiveling chair and looked at the things on her desk—papers, folders, a pen, the telephone—without touching anything. I wanted to respect her privacy. Sitting there felt a bit strange but no big deal.

"Now what?" she asked, smiling, from the client's comfortable chair.

"I don't know," I said. "I guess I just wanted to see what it felt like. And whether you trusted me." I paused. "OK, we can switch back now."

After the move to Page Street I asked my therapist's advice on dealing with a problem I had with a strange guy who kept coming by to hang out in our living room. Maybe he wanted to meet women or eat our food, but it felt like he was intruding. I didn't want to get angry at him, but didn't want our politeness to let him push us around. My therapist suggested something she called "friendly distance"—firmly keeping a distance while being nice at the same time. I tried it, explaining to the interloper in a friendly way that we needed our space, and it worked. He left.

While I slowly made progress in dealing with daily life, my practice on the cushion was not as focused as I wanted it to be. Stories, gossip, and creative speculation still constantly welled up in my mind. Meditation had become somewhat old hat, a comfortable habit that kept me from going bananas, but without the enthusiastic energy of open beginner's mind. Sometimes reciting a mantra I learned from Sonam Kazi, a visiting Tibetan translator, helped me focus.

In June a Tibetan teacher, Chogyam Trungpa Rinpoche, came to San Francisco. The spiritual grapevine was alive with stories about him— how he was a powerful Buddhist master, a *tulku* or reincarnated lama who had escaped from the Chinese occupation of Tibet, studied at Oxford, given up his monk's robes to become a layman, and married a young Scottish woman. He was said to drink alcohol, and once crashed a sports car into a joke shop, leaving him with a limp. His book *Cutting Through Spiritual Materialism* was full of the penetrating insight that, along with his playful sense of humor, enthralled large audiences of spiritual seekers and established practitioners on his American tour.

I joined a group of Zen students going to hear his talk. Trungpa Rinpoche arrived an hour late, made his way to a polished dark wooden chair on the stage, and sipped from a glass of clear liquid that may well have been saki, as he spoke with the cultivated diction of an educated Englishman. But what blew me away was his sheer spiritual presence. Watching and listening to him, my mind opened and I felt high, in touch with a plane of pure awareness.

After the talk, riding back in a car with some Zen students, I tried to describe my experience. "When something like that happens, it's better not to talk about it," one of them said. I thought it over, and a few weeks later, decided I needed to deepen my spiritual practice by going back to Tassajara, for a longer stay this time. Suzuki Roshi would be there.

Chapter 15: Intensive Training

View from the Great Peak

The ancient sacred mountain—what is it like?
To north and south the greenery never ends.
Creating intense and mysterious beauty,
shadow and sunlight split at dusk and dawn.
Breathing hard, emerging from a layer of clouds,
eyes open wide at returning birds—
the only way is to climb to the very top:
then all the other mountains will look small.

—Tu Fu (Du Fu)

Returning to Tassajara

No longer driving my old Peugeot, in the summer of 1970 I returned to Zen Mountain Center at Tassajara Hot Springs for further intensive training. If I'd flown in a helicopter and looked east from above Big Sur, I might have seen the rough-hewn ridges of the Santa Lucia range rise 6,000 feet to Junipero Serra peak, above a rocky, corrugated landscape of mountains and canyons. But I was riding in the back of a four-wheel drive Dodge Power Wagon, rumbling along the bumpy, winding dirt road over Chews Ridge toward Tassajara canyon, hidden deep in the midst of wilderness peaks, its location reflecting the profound practice of Zen.

*

Teachings on the *Sandokai*

The last two lines of the *Sandokai*, an ancient and melodiously rhythmic poem by Sekito that we chanted each morning, were similar to those carved on the han, the wooden board hanging outside the zendo, hit with a mallet in a gathering rhythm to summon us all to sit zazen. Both urged us, in view of impermanence, not to spend our time in vain.

When I returned to Tassajara, Suzuki Roshi was completing a series of teachings on this seemingly paradoxical text, which he referred to in English as *Oneness of One and Many,* understood as "one whole being that includes everything."

During one talk Roshi stood pointing to a line on the portable blackboard in the gray stone zendo, leaning forward in his robe with his face alight: "Hearing the words, understand the meaning." If we focus on a finger pointing at the moon, we won't see the moon itself.

That made sense. The harder part came next, when he said that at Tassajara we should follow Tassajara's rules, not make up our own. The rules are not the point, but they point to the real teaching.

I remembered Roshi had said that rules were like graph paper— the lines show you where you are and what you need to work on. I resolved to try. I would do my best to follow the Tassajara schedule and learn from my encounters with the rules.

Suzuki Roshi's final talk on the *Sandokai* was a real lesson for me about grasping after enlightenment, which had been a problem, especially after my first training period. "Practice is not a matter of far or near." When you strive to attain enlightenment, you think you are far away from it or getting near to it. But enlightenment is right where you are. When you practice with "no gaining idea," that is enlightenment. How to give up attachment to a goal, and yet keep going? The key seemed to be: keep going in the right direction.

*

The Reckoning

To be ordained or not, that was the question. In August, Suzuki Roshi would offer a simple ceremony in which his lay students could commit themselves to the Buddhist path. Commitment had been a big issue for

273

me, both in career and relationships. I had a tendency to follow my enthusiasms and infatuations until they wore thin, then discard them like old clothes. My fear was of being trapped in an unsatisfactory situation. I was devoted to meditation as my spiritual practice with Suzuki Roshi as my teacher, but did I want to become officially a Buddhist?

What was a Buddhist anyway? A follower of the Buddha. And who—or what—was the Buddha? The Awakened One, who had seen through delusion and found deep inner peace. He embodied both wisdom and compassion, which I found inspiring. But how much of his story was legend, like the tales of Paul Bunyan? I began to read a book on the historical Buddha during morning study period. The answer seemed to be that the Buddha lived so long ago, about 500 BCE, that very few specific facts about his life could be confirmed by historical research. But that was not the point. However much they may have been embellished over the centuries, the basic elements of the Buddha's story had something more important than historical details: the ring of truth.

The Buddha lives on in his legend—as the son of the wealthy king of a city state in ancient northern India, he grew up protected from the material sufferings of ordinary people. But he found that privileged life superficial and unsatisfactory, and left home, shaving his head and sewing a robe out of patches of cloth, to live as a wanderer in search of the ultimate spiritual truth. And when he found that truth, sitting under the Bodhi tree—the descendant of which is still hallowed in Bodhgaya—despite the fact that the truth went beyond words and was difficult to communicate, he devoted the rest of his life to teaching it.

Most importantly, the Buddha lives on in his teachings, passed on for centuries through oral recitation and later through written scriptures. In his first teaching he described the Four Noble Truths: *dukkha* (suffering or dissatisfaction), the cause of suffering, the cessation of suffering, and the path to the cessation of suffering. With this diagnosis and prescription, he showed a way to heal what ails us.

I could relate to the Buddha's story and teachings, and found them inspiring, so what was the problem? For one thing I wasn't sure I believed in rebirth, a seemingly indelible part of the Indian cultural context. And growing up as a Unitarian, I was skeptical of complex formal rituals. But Zen did not seem to emphasize belief in rebirth, and its rituals, while formal and somewhat austere, were quite elegant. The main point in Zen was the practice, both sitting in zazen and maintaining the presence of awareness in daily life. So what was holding me back? I requested an interview to see if that could help resolve my doubts.

Suzuki Roshi's cabin was neat and simple, with a small, low table of dark polished wood on a floor covered with firmly woven tatami mats. A striking example of Zen calligraphy hung on the wall. I sat on a cushion across from him as he carefully cut up a green apple with a small paring knife. He offered me a section, then plopped another one into his mouth. After we each had a piece of the sweet crunchy fruit, he asked "How are you doing?"

"I have a problem. I'd like to take lay ordination, but I'm not sure I'm really a Buddhist."

I explained my various reservations. Roshi paused to finish chewing another slice of the apple. Then he said, "Why not go ahead and get ordained? If you ever have any regrets, you can blame me." And he smiled like a fellow conspirator.

"OK," I said with relief. The next day I joined the group of students each learning to sew a *rakusu,* a dark blue scale model of the Buddha's robe, about a foot square, sewn together with invisible stitches, which is worn like a bib around the neck of an ordained lay person in the zendo and on ceremonial occasions. Roshi's wife (*Okusan* in Japanese) was the patient instructor. Contrary to my expectations, I actually liked learning to carefully sew with stitches so precisely hidden behind the turns of the cloth they could not be seen.

During these days of preparation I had time to reflect on the five basic precepts for Buddhist laypeople: do not kill; do not steal; do not lie; do not commit sexual misconduct; and do not get intoxicated. Not to steal and not to lie seemed pretty straightforward. Sexual misconduct had been defined differently for celibate monks or nuns and married laypersons, and in modern Japan even priests can marry. For us it seemed to mean not to cause harm through our sexual conduct.

Suzuki Roshi explained the spirit of the first and fifth precepts in ways that went beyond simple rules for behavior. Not to kill a sentient being intentionally ultimately meant "Do not kill Buddha nature," the basic awareness we all share. And do not get intoxicated meant don't get intoxicated by *anything*, not only alcohol or drugs but also thoughts and emotions.

If I looked at these precepts one by one, applied to my life up to then, I had to confess that as a kid I killed a number of fish, often white perch, then cleaned and ate them (my mother usually did the cooking) during summers at Lovewell Pond. But I always felt bad about the killing part— watching the fish's last twitches as I "put it out of its misery"—and had long since given up fishing. Dealing with mosquitos was a challenge. It's hard not to swat an insect inflicting a bloodsucking bite on your arm. And our immune systems kill invading microbes to keep our bodies alive. In such cases I could focus on the deeper meaning of the precept, not to kill Buddha nature, the potential for enlightenment in all sentient beings.

Aside from lapses like twice stealing a book in college—one poetry and the other with a Buddha on the cover—to see what it felt like (the answer was guilty), plus a few regrettable lies and ill-advised one-night stands, the main challenge for me was "Do not get intoxicated." Even though my drinking and drug use, except for a few explorations, was quite moderate, my problem was that I didn't need drinking or drugs to get intoxicated. Ideas and emotions were all it took.

For instance, if Karina hadn't told me not to come, I would have driven cross-country in the middle of a stormy winter to confront her and her new boyfriend in Boston—and possibly dropped out of school. Blinded by romantic fantasies and not wanting to lose her, did I really know Karina very well after that one intoxicating summer? Maybe the summer of happiness was not the problem, but the winter of grasping to get it back.

Clearly I still had some work to do on that last precept, learning how to deal with intense energies without getting swept away.

*

Spanish Dancer

As in the hand a sulfur match, tipped white,
before it comes fully into flame, on all sides
stretches out flickering tongues—: beginning
in a ring of spectators quick, bright, and hot
her circling dance flares up and spreads itself out.

And suddenly it's completely in flames.

With a glance she ignites her hair
and whirls all at once with daring art
her whole dress in this burst of fiery heat,
from which, like startling snakes,
her naked arms stretch out, awake and rattling.

And then: as if the fire might be scarce,
she draws it all together and throws it off
imperiously, with haughty gestures
and looks: it lies there furious on the ground
and more and more it flares and won't give up—.
Yet triumphantly sure, and with a sweet
greeting smile she lifts her face
and stamps it out with small firm feet.

—Rilke

*

Work Period—and Days Off

Except for dates with the number 4 or 9, which we had off, every day after morning zazen, service, and breakfast we would change our robes for work clothes and gather in the courtyard for a meeting. I was assigned to a team digging a ditch for a water pipe by the side of the road, which was not easy, especially at first, because it meant unearthing rocks, and even cracking through big ones with a pick before digging out the pieces with a shovel. Not being used to such physical labor, it took me a while to get into shape, but as I got stronger I came to enjoy it, swinging the pick and digging with the shovel until I was bone-tired and covered with dirt. After a while I was tapped to be foreman of the ditch-digging crew, which given my thin build, I'd never expected. What it really meant was reporting at work meetings on our progress. Our team worked together as equal partners.

Later I got a work-study scholarship and became the garbage man, driving an old Ford pickup around Tassajara collecting the trash and unloading it at the dump and compost pile around the Hogback toward Grasshopper Flats. Cleaning up garbage was sort of an honor in Buddhist thinking—getting right in there with the clutter of trash, the smell of refuse, and the rotten remains of vegetables to purify oneself and the community. I also have to admit it was sometimes interesting to see what my fellow monastics threw away: empty bottles of herbal and conventional medicines, foil wrappers from chocolate bars, and the occasional used condom. In an old Zen koan, a monk asks "What is the Buddha?" The master answers, "A shit-scraper." In those days, before toilet paper, they apparently used a carved wooden stick.

When we had a day off from work, after morning practice, service, and breakfast we were free to climb around boulders down the creek to the Narrows and swim in a deep pool, or bushwhack through the brush up the mountainside to take in the view. When I found a nice spot I might sit for a while, and sometimes jot down a poem.

Wilderness Retreat

a fawn and her doe
nibbling grass
chewing leaves
I sit
not moving
the breeze

a bird like a dark hand
opening and closing
reaches through morning air

Climbing Hawk Mountain

the steep meadow
keeps getting steeper
and always another hump
looms from behind the last
until out of the tough
thickets of brush—
I must be near the top—
giant granite teeth jut
and it seems I've climbed
a dragon's back

but up in the midday sky
surrounded by prehistoric ridges
I curl up into a
shady cradle of rock
to rest
and eat and drink

and echo the canyon
with a bamboo flute
in double octave notes
that leave my ringing ears
near peace

a high silence
known by hawks
pilots of solitude
and mountain peaks

then on the way down
like the one I lost a year ago
I find a blue fountain pen

To Tassajara Creek

A long day along the creek
I lay me down to rest
in hairpin canyon

the sun behind the cliff
silhouettes one yucca plume
right on the brim

*

Struck to the Heart

When the city center was still at Sokoji temple, I remember Suzuki Roshi, dressed in a dark robe and holding his carved wooden Zen Master scepter, giving a talk in the back of the large hall where the Japanese congregation met. I think he said something about not getting too attached to our habitual pleasures and comforts. Everything changes, and when things change we may suffer. He asked if there were any questions, and senior student Richard Baker's hand went up. "What if there's something you're *really* attached to, like strawberry shortcake?"

Everyone laughed, including Roshi, at Richard's revealing enthusiasm.

I looked around and saw that Stephen Gaskin, the long-haired leader of the Monday Night Class, a psychedelic philosophy seminar I once dropped in on, was smiling as well. Recently I read that Gaskin said Suzuki Roshi was an honest man, whose every action was an expression of truth. As wild as things were in San Francisco back then, Stephen felt safe because he knew Roshi was there.

At another lecture I sat near the front to the side and listened as Roshi talked about how many young people were turning away from their parents. It was not good, he said. They felt lost, with no family. We should treat our parents with respect and gratitude for having brought us up.

These words struck my heart. My face crumbled in sorrow. This means me, I thought—but it's my parents who cannot accept me. I felt the hidden pain of my life with them—how they often didn't understand me, didn't know how to show love, feared talking intimately, and tried to impose conventional ways on me. With sadness in my heart, I looked down and held my head with my hand. Roshi had touched my most vulnerable point, my alienation from my family, especially my father, and our mutual inability to find each other—leaving me, underneath my wise-cracking exterior, lost and lonely as an orphan.

Could Roshi really understand, with his different cultural background? Maybe not the circumstances of my specific case, but the fact of my suffering? As I gazed up through the liquid blur in my eyes, I saw that

Roshi was looking at me. Not smiling or frowning, just noticing. Then he continued his lecture.

Later, when I was living at Tassajara during the summer guest season, my parents drove around the country on a camping trip in their Ford station wagon and came to visit me. My father was freaked out by the long drive in on the rough dirt road over Chew's Ridge. With their automatic transmission, they had to stop again and again with overheated brakes.

It was also weird for them to see me with a nearly shaved head, sometimes wearing a robe, living in a community of similar people walking around in meditative silence in this remote mountain canyon, bowing when they passed each other. Mother and Dad stood under a gnarled oak tree and said little—pale, subdued, and bewildered—as if they feared we were some kind of alien cult from another planet. They didn't stay long—in fact, my father couldn't wait to get out of there.

After they left, a fellow student told me he'd been present the week before when my parents visited Zen Center in San Francisco and were introduced to Suzuki Roshi.

"At first Roshi was welcoming, until your father leaned over and confided his opinion: 'Of course, Chris is immature, not like you and me.' Suzuki pulled back from your father and became distant. I thought you should know that."

Later, when Roshi returned to Tassajara, while we were all having tea in the courtyard, he came over and gave me an unexpected hug, something he'd never done before, and I felt his unwavering compassion.

*

Healing Spring

At Tassajara I heard stories of how the hot springs had once been a site for sacred healing. One day several of us walked up the Hogback and held a brief ceremony for the Esalen tribe of American Indians who used to come here to soak in the springs and feel renewed.

Sacred Ground

not a small hill
but a lookout toward afternoon
sky beyond mountains
where the wide wings of a great cloud
span the horizon

a few well-placed stones
bring the spirit home
in the space between young willows

dappled shadows
where the path turns over a rise
then down by switchback
to the rocky bottom

across the open canyon
by a dry waterfall
the cliff does its slow dance

from all directions
the creatures of earth and air
come here and pass on

Father Sky
Earth Mother
let the sun return

the wind breathe full
through trees
the root unknown
tonight the fruit will be stars

Failing to Master the Art of Monastic Living

Despite my appreciation for the elegance of formal Zen rituals, I still felt rebellious when I thought they were too rigid or restrictive. For example, we had to finish eating before the hot water for cleaning was poured in our bowls, and the time allowed was never enough, meaning we had to chew vigorously and not take too much food. The point may have been to discourage daydreaming, but only allowing about five or ten minutes for actually eating seemed overly strict.

Once my medium-sized bowl was still full of beans when the hot-water servers came striding down the aisle. Beans need to be chewed, and there was no way to finish in time. Rather than panic I carefully picked up the red and black lacquered bowl brim full of beans and placed it on the straw mat beside and behind me, taking it out of action. After completing the ritual without it, I reached down and picked up the full bowl and held it perched on the fingers of both hands like an offering, raising it slightly when I dipped my head to bow, then held it up with defiant concentration as we walked out of the old stone zendo in single file. Outside, I sat down on a wooden bench and ate my beans, glad to find a way out of the bind.

Formality got even stricter when Tatsugami Roshi, the former master of ritual at Eiheiji monastery in Japan, came to lead our training periods, with the suspected mission of shaping things up. Tatsugami Roshi was built like a heavyweight wrestler. He looked tough as Sitting Bull, with a face like crushed rock. When his solid presence entered the zendo, it was clear he could not be pushed around.

His specialty was ritual discipline. He spoke in brief grunts and staccato Japanese sentences. All told, Tatsugami Roshi was the perfect target for my authority figure projections. And maybe because of that, I kind of liked him.

When I was assigned to make the ritual offering, he was sitting on the platform in front of the altar like a block of stone. I stood at the back of the hall with a dark red cup of special green tea on a black lacquer tray, held head-high with the fingers of both hands, awaiting the moment in the chant when I would walk forward ceremoniously and place it carefully upon the altar. There were two possible aisles to walk down, one on either side of a low partition, where students could sit on both sides. As a rule one walked down the aisle on my right, but on this day there were fewer students than usual and they all sat on the aisle to my left. Should I adapt to the situation and walk down the aisle where everyone was sitting, or follow the right-side convention even though no one was there? I chose to adapt, and began my stately walk on the left past the group of students.

Suddenly a burst of unintelligible Japanese shot like a bark from the motionless Tatsugami Roshi, and I knew I'd picked wrong. I stopped, embarrassed, but maintaining the stately pose, turned around and returned to the back of the hall and began again on the right, striding slowly past the empty seats to place the ritual offering on the right side of the altar, where it belonged.

No one criticized me about this mistake—maybe because the correction was immediate, and nothing more needed to be said. But to me it stood for two different approaches to life: creative adaptation to the present situation verses strict adherence to tradition. My heart was with creative adaptation, and Tatsugami Roshi, in his shaved head and robes, was the imposing enforcer of tradition.

In the *shosan* ceremony at the end of a practice period, students confront the abbot one by one and ask dharma questions. Possessed by a reckless impulse inspired by a few Zen stories, when my turn came I walked up to Tatsugami Roshi and expressed my pent-up frustration by shouting as loud as I could in his face:

"AAAAhhh!" His head moved back slightly, absorbing the sonic impact. Then with a half smile he said calmly, "Take it easy."

At that time I was training to be one of the chant leaders. We would stretch out our voices by going way up the creek and shouting as loud and long as we could into the echoing canyon. I'd heard about Primal Scream therapy, and thought I might give it a try. Once I shouted alone for almost an hour, until powerful anger surged up through my screams, anger at my parents for all the ways I felt they betrayed my trust. But the more I screamed the angrier I got, with no end in sight, until a moment of insight: anger itself can be addicting, and I didn't want to get stuck in it.

Caught, or Not?

In my rough wooden cabin
a bee worked herself into a knothole
and then for about an hour
kept frantically buzzing and scratching.

If I poked something in to help her out
I feared it would only hurt her.
When I banged on the wall to knock her loose
she shut up for a while,
then went on scratching and buzzing.

My persistent bee friend, were you stuck?
I couldn't sleep with you in my thoughts.
Now with my mind at rest,
I see you were likely a
carpenter bee, carving out a nest.

*

For a while I served as the shopper, each week driving the white Dodge Power Wagon with its big rear cargo compartment over Chew's Ridge to Carmel Valley and Monterey, to load up with supplies from the supermarket and do any needed errands, including some limited shopping for students—especially for chocolate.

Bringing in Supplies

a drift of mist
above the frosty pines
gray, deep green,

touches of white
on the mountainside
a steep drop
to the valley below

driving around the topmost bend

first snow on Chew's Ridge
damp from light rain

still the enchantment of winter

pine whiskers
cold fleece

stopping the truck
beside the road

we roll up two big snowballs
to take down to our friends

*

Practice in the Dark

Secretly at night
a worm, under the moonlight
bores into a chestnut

—Basho

It was a custom at Tassajara that every night one student slept in the zendo, as an informal guardian. After the winter practice period and before the summer guest season, that spring several leaders of Tassajara left for a few weeks and went to the San Francisco center. I was appointed de facto *Ino*, in charge of the zendo, and that included making sure we had a student volunteer to sleep there each night. There was no problem until one time a fellow student woke me up around midnight with an air of urgency. He said his roommate assigned to the night watch had "heard strange sounds near the shrine and saw a ghost, an old man with a white beard, then left the zendo and won't return. I'm willing to step in and do it, if you'll be there with me."

"OK," I said, feeling responsible to deal with the situation, and also curious whether the ghost would appear to the two of us. We took our sleeping bags and both retired for the night on tatami mats near the back of the zendo. We lay there alert, unable to sleep. "Did you hear that sound?" whispered my companion.

"Maybe a creaking branch," I said. "Could be the wind." We watched and waited and finally dozed off. The ghost never appeared.

But something did happen later in June, when I was on duty guarding the hot spring baths. People from off site sometimes tried to sneak into the baths at night. I decided to sleep on the narrow wooden bridge across the creek that led to the entrance, a way to make sure that no one got through. As I slept very soundly on the well-fitted planks of the arc, suddenly something came crushing down on me and I woke up shouting "Yaaaaah!" as I leaped up grabbing a stranger who'd just stepped on my chest.

We shared a moment of fear that dissolved when we saw what had happened. The young man was apologetic. "I'm sorry, I didn't see you."

I escorted him and his friends back to the office and they left before dawn, as the sound of the han, in a gradually quickening rhythm, summoned all beings to morning zazen.

*

Late Summer

At the Deer Park

Empty mountains, no one to be seen.
But hear, the echo of someone's voice.
Returning sunlight enters this deep forest
and shines again rising on the green moss.

—Wang Wei

We knew Suzuki Roshi had bouts of poor health for a while. The past two winters he had severe flu, and in March his gall bladder was removed. When he was well, he came back to Tassajara to teach and work with renewed energy. He loved it there—immersed in nature, among his students, where intensive Zen practice found a home.

One day in late summer he gave a brief unscheduled talk in the zendo. Sitting in front near the altar, he suddenly got up from his cushion, took a few steps across the platform, and stood beside the shrine. He said he would like to live ten more years to complete his work. Then he paused, and said in a strong, heartfelt voice, "I want disciples who will follow me through life and death."

I was moved, and a bit shocked at the import of what he was saying. I wanted him to live at least ten more years—but something about the way he spoke implied that he might leave sooner. In my cabin I had a small wooden incense box with a Chinese character stamped on the cover. I thought it meant "long life" but was not completely sure. Later that afternoon I went to Suzuki Roshi's cabin, showed him the wooden cover with the Chinese character, and asked what it meant.

He looked at it and said, "Long life."

"It's for you," I managed to say, and gave it to him.

He smiled ruefully and nodded. "Thank you very much."

*

Farewell

As autumn nears
our hearts draw together
in a small tea-room
—Basho

It was a day off, and I was doing my laundry by hand in a big galvanized basin. For the first time, I washed my rakusu, and was dismayed to find Suzuki Roshi's brushwork and seal on the back were beginning to fade, as I'd feared. Just then Roshi himself walked past on the dirt road. "What shall I do if your writing on my rakusu disappears?" I asked him in consternation.

"*You just try* to make it disappear," he said with a grin as he walked by.

That fall we learned Suzuki Roshi had cancer, and by late November his condition was dire. Many of his students assembled in San Francisco for the transmission ceremony to install Richard Baker as the new abbot of Zen Center. The hall was crowded with students and teachers in formal black robes. All waited in silence, until in the hush the sound of a staff hitting the floor, the rings on its handle jingling, came from the hall, and Suzuki Roshi entered. He was barely able to walk, his skin dark brown, his body emaciated, bravely striking his staff to the floor with each step, as his Dharma heir followed behind. Sadness pervaded the crowd in black robes, written on every face.

Later I learned that when Suzuki Roshi was in bed, shortly before he died, Richard asked him where they would meet. Roshi raised his arm and extending his finger moved his hand in a wide circle embracing the universe, then placed his palms together, fingers upward, and bowed.

Suzuki Roshi was a spiritual father to me. It felt too soon to lose him, yet this was his teaching: we must find our own way to go on.

*

Reflections at Dusk

black branches
break up the moon

down in the stream
the pieces are
dancing together

Chapter 16: Moving On

In the mist and rain
can't see Fuji all day long—
how intriguing!

—Basho

The Path of Traveling Light

After more than a year and a half of sitting each day in a black robe
facing the wall at Tassajara, on a warm April afternoon I was hiking on
a winding path through small scrub and over a rocky rise toward the vast
Pacific Ocean, quietly chanting a mantra under the widening sky. As the
sun went down behind a ridge, the trail led into some woods, and I found
a level spot surrounded by trees to lay out my sleeping bag.

Back at Tassajara, when the weather was good, sometimes I slept out
under the stars. There on the hillside above the cabins, far from the city,
the Milky Way spread like a starry river across the night sky. And one time
when walking back from evening meditation, I looked up awestruck at the
brilliant galaxy of stars—woven with luminous gas of the cosmos brewing
wild seeds of life—when a sudden yelp made me realize I'd stepped on the
tail of my sleeping friend Noah, the dog.

Now settling into the wilderness, after a quiet peanut butter sandwich
I lay back in the dark and looked up through the trees. Just a few stars.
While I eased into sleep, one by one the stars disappeared as clouds drifted
in.

I woke up with rain on my face in the gray light of dawn, and lay there
listening to falling drops land on my sleeping bag. Quickly packing my
gear, I set out a bit damp, draped in a blue nylon poncho, bought on sale at
the Army-Navy store. As I hiked up and down hills, the rain pelted my
poncho and slowly seeped through. Before long I was soaked to the skin,
the cold sinking in. Ruefully I realized this was the difference between
water*proof* and "water-repellent." As the day wore on, the rain fell hard.

Pausing to rest, I began shivering. The only way to stop shaking was to keep on walking. Memory found the word for my condition: *hypothermia*.

Tramping on and on, afraid to stop for too long, by late afternoon I reached the last valley before the coast ridge, where my plan was to camp. In my pack was a tube tent, a cylinder of transparent plastic, and despite the damp sleeping bag, one blanket still mostly dry. I strung a cord through the tube and tied each end to a tree, then secured the bottom corners with stones. Wrapped naked in the blanket, still cold and damp, I fell asleep.

Once, hiking near the coast up in these mountains, early in the morning, I looked out over the ocean fog stretching soft as a comforter toward the horizon—and stepped right next to a rattlesnake coiled up on the edge of the trail, asleep. A moment of clarity: *just keep on walking*—until a few steps later, safely out of reach, looking back at the snake, a wave of fear flowed through me.

Now in my transparent tent I managed to stay warm enough to make it through the night, but the morning was still gray and rainy. Droplets rolled off new green leaves and dripped to the muddy ground. I had to go on.

Hiking uphill by switchbacks as the rain worked its way through the porous blue poncho, I reached a dirt road that went along the ridge. Once again, stopping meant shivering, and here the full blast of the storm came howling in from the dark, open ocean.

Perched amid brush off the trail was a small, weather-beaten outhouse, almost falling apart, no paint on the worn gray wood, just one stall—but it did have a crusty, dilapidated roof. Pulling open the creaking door, I went in. It was narrow and cramped, with an awful stench from years of untended use. I sat on the open seat and could imagine sitting there for hours, trapped in the fetid smell with no room to lie down. I began to get claustrophobic. Sitting in this decrepit outhouse with no toilet paper, how could I clean my karma? All my anger, all my mistakes and failures. The stink was so bad that I held my nose, and before long stepped back out into the storm. Amid wind and rain I stared at the surging squall raging in from the ocean. Was this my path of purification?

Somewhere down there was a paved road, Highway 1, winding along the coast from Big Sur. There was no trail—could I bushwhack down? It was not a sheer drop, but a steep one, with a jumble of exposed rocks and tangled growth—many places to slip or hit a dead end, and no place to hide. The wind, the blast of relentless wind, was whipping cold rain in my face.

Up here was the dirt road, also exposed, 15 miles along the ridge, then down to the highway. And back there, the ramshackle outhouse, where I could spend the night sitting upright in the stench of the past, hoping to wait out the storm.

Those were the choices: go over the side with a high risk of getting lost, spraining an ankle, or worse; stay up here stuck in the funky outhouse; or take the long muddy road that with endurance would get where I needed to go. I tried to think clearly, knowing that hypothermia might be clouding my judgement. The middle way, I decided, was to keep on walking, bracing myself against the onslaught of the storm roaring in from the ocean.

After a while one thing was clear—I couldn't take much more exposure. Then a trail appeared through some trees, leading back down to the shelter of the valley I'd come from. Turning there to get out of the wind, I stopped a few moments to rest, wondering what to do, as the shivering began again. Though reluctant to turn back, maybe I should take the trail down, camp for another night, and hike out through the valley to Big Sur tomorrow.

Just then came the sound of tires on rocks and gravel. Quickly I rushed back and stood in the middle of the road as a pickup truck rumbled into view. It stopped and a rain-streaked window rolled down, revealing two crew-cut men from the naval radar station. The driver said they couldn't let me ride in the cab (regulations) but gestured with a thumb toward the open back of the truck: "Only as far as the highway."

"No problem, I can hitchhike from there. Thanks!" I climbed in, still exposed to the rain and the wind, but knowing that now I could make it.

By the time we reached Highway 1 the storm had eased, and I hitched to Pacific Grove, where a friend who left Tassajara had rented a cottage. Reuven had a certain charisma; you might say he was a rain-maker. He once gave a farmer a loaf of Tassajara bread and talked him into giving us a truckload of surplus pears, if our crew would pick them. We dried the pears on the roof of our kitchen, where persistent raccoons found them hard to reach.

I thought Reuven had said his cottage was red, but at the address was a brown shingled house with a leafy yard. I knocked on the front door but no one seemed to be home. Where was Reuven? Tired of all this, I walked around the side of the house, saw the back door and went to look in. Then, with some hesitation, I tried the knob—and the door opened.

"Reuven?" I called, still cold and wet, then stepped in. A half-eaten chocolate cake sat on the counter. That didn't seem like him. But maybe he had given up on his radical grape-juice diet.

I had to get dry and warm. With a towel I dried off and exhausted lay down on the couch in the living room, happy at last to rest. Then I heard the back door open and close, and steps coming in. A strange man appeared, with short brown hair, in button-down plaid. He looked over at me with the air of the owner.

Suddenly, the phone rang beside me. Inspired by the chance, I picked it up quickly: "Hello?"

"Is Jim there?"

"Just a minute," I said, and looked toward the stranger: "Are you Jim?"

"Yes."

"It's for you." Handing him the phone, I sat there quietly until he finished, then explained I was looking for Reuven, who it turned out was not home, but had rented the bright red cottage behind some trees next door. Jim was his landlord.

Over in the cottage the refrigerator held nothing but a large bag of carrots. A heavyweight juicer sat on the counter. Ah, this must be the place!

The next day, as the fog began to lift, I walked down to the brisk breeze of the wide open ocean and stood on the algae-encrusted rocks, where I met a shaggy American yogi who showed me the authentic way of chanting OM to the wind:

"AhhOoooohMmm… AhhOoooohMmm… AhhOoooohMmm… "

The waves rolled in, one after the other, like mad taxis delivering foam from Japan.

*

Beyond the Last Canyon

Even wild boars
are blown together in
this typhoon!
—Basho

After looking up at high and smooth rock walls while walking through majestic Zion Canyon, there I was, standing for hours at a rural crossroads in the afternoon sun of southern Utah, holding my thumb out, hoping for a ride.

Then some young guy dropped off at the same spot started hitchhiking next to me. Traffic was sparse. I asked him to move down the road a bit to make it clear we were separate, since a driver might only want to pick up one person.

Hours passed—no luck. Sometimes we talked across the space between us. When at last the sun went down, I pitched my small tent in the pasture beside the road. The kid had no tent of his own, so he asked if he could sleep in mine too. It was a tube tent, very narrow. I did not want to be crammed in with a stranger, but the kid had nowhere to go.

Reluctantly, I gave in. He seemed innocent enough, like he just wanted company. We slept with sleeping bags squeezed in, our heads at opposite ends, like a big plastic Chinese finger puzzle. I had tried to push him away, and now this.

A loud MOOO woke me up the next morning with a large cow's white and brown face poking into the tent, her big bovine eyes staring right at me—as if to say, why are you here in this pasture?

The kid and I packed up our stuff. With different destinations, we stepped back on the road and hitchhiked together. Immediately a truck stopped and picked us up. That day the rides came one after another, all the way through Utah and Colorado.

*

Scattering Ashes

An old pond:
the sound when a frog
jumps in the water

—Basho

As my father grew older we became closer, and were able to reach each other more often in moments of understanding. Blind in one eye from glaucoma, he went for a walk every day until he wound up in a wheelchair at age 97, in an "extensive assisted living facility" near Virginia Beach, where we moved him to be near my sister Wendy. Some of his faculties began to slip. He could no longer decipher the time from the clock on the wall, and searched for the names of ordinary things:
"I was watching… what do you call it… that box you turn on with a button."
"The television?"
"Yes."

As the only Yankee onsite, he managed to get into a feud with a fellow wheelchair-using dementia patient, a Confederate rebel who insisted that he, not my father, was the oldest man in the house, and the more valiant soldier to boot. True, my dad had embellished his accounts of his service as an Army cargo officer on Liberty ships evading German U-boats at the straits of Gibraltar in World War II. In earlier days he told me his main job was to keep the sailors from stealing the officers' booze, but now he claimed he had pulled his gun on deck and shot an enemy torpedo as it approached the ship, which to me seemed unlikely.

The feud built up every day when the two men met on the way to the dining room, until his Confederate nemesis ambushed my father in the hallway and they fought a battle of crashing wheelchairs and a swinging crutch in the hands of the rebel officer. They had to be separated by nursing aides, and after extended negotiations by phone between families and staff, the Confederate was moved to another room, where he would not run into my Union father.

When later my dad was in hospice care, I flew out to visit and found him depressed, clenching his hands, slouched in his wheelchair. We had a heart-to-heart talk about death.

"Are you ready?" I asked.

With his face weighed down by sadness, he paused, then nodded and softly said, "Yes."

Back in California, when I got the message the end was near, I called my sister, who was in Dad's room with her husband. They sat watching a Patriots playoff game while my father lay on his bed. His breathing became heavy and labored, carrying the burden of all those years. How could he last much longer?

Wendy put her phone to his ear. I knew this was it. With quiet urgency, I spoke to him gently and calmly about how we all loved him, there was nothing to fear. "Move toward the light," I said, "Move toward the light." Though he could not respond, my sister said his breathing calmed down into a slow, gentle rhythm. Soon he was gone.

The memorial service was held at the Unitarian-Universalist fellowship my parents helped start in a small mountain town in New Hampshire, just over the border from Maine, where we had spent our summers at Lovewell Pond and they had eventually settled. I shared a rented cottage with Kyle, my photographer jazz-musician nephew.

That morning we were about to leave for the service when I saw a black and white Canada goose wading into the water, followed by a procession of her four little goslings. Guided by instinct they faithfully followed behind in a line, plopping in one after the other, from waddling on land to paddling smoothly through the new, sustaining, liquid medium where they would live and feel at home, and eventually leave their mother.

The next morning my nephew, my sister, and I launched a green wooden rowboat on Lovewell Pond, with Kyle at the oars, me at the bow, and Wendy in the stern, holding the cardboard box of my father's ashes. The wind came up, rippling the water, and the oars dipped and creaked as Kyle rowed the boat towards a spot offshore from the cottage we used to own.

"Let's do it here," I called out. When Wendy poured the ashes into the water, a small cloud of dust drifted up like a puff of smoke, and a sudden gust whipped the gray powder back in my face. Before I had time to stop breathing in, I felt the particles of bone-dust bite into my lungs.

No way to avoid it, I thought. My father and I are one. The sun caught the shifting gusts rippling across the water in fluttering patterns of tiny sparkling diamonds, like a swirling brilliant galaxy of stars.

Epilogue: Listening

Fifty-two years after I first went to Tassajara I came back to rediscover what I found there, and how it transformed my life. I enrolled in a workshop on The Poetry of Awakening, where we read poets like Cold Mountain and Kabir, who expressed a path beyond words—and did it with writing and singing to point the way.

Each evening in the wilderness canyon, walking back through the trees to my cabin beside the creek, I heard the sound of innumerable crickets, making together the infinite music of nature, reminding me that my deeper self is not just an image to identify with, but a continuous flow of vivid awareness beyond any attempt to label or grasp.

Music of the Night

Crickets, every evening
in this forest canyon,
invisible jazz musicians
listen to each other,
weaving dark reverberations
much bigger than we know—

I'm lost in a thicket of music,
a jungle of complex rhythms,
repeating yet not repeating,
filling space with oscillations
that can't be grasped.

Sisters and brothers,
listen to the crickets
jam their mysterious song
as down below the rushing creek
flows on through heavy stones.

The afternoon before leaving, I climbed up the hillside to Suzuki Roshi's rugged memorial stone, and bowed three times to the ultimate ground.

*

Year after year...
cherry trees nourished
by fallen blossoms

—Basho

Above the meadow
not attached to anything
a skylark sings

—Basho

*

May all beings be well, happy, and peaceful.

Acknowledgments

Many thanks to those who read or listened to and offered comments on this manuscript, especially Lynda Efros and Kerry Muir, who read or heard all or most of it, and those who responded to various parts: Allison Landa, Andy Touhy, Alison Luterman, Jenny Pritchett, Elaine Beale, Junse Kim, and Ben Jackson at the Writing Salon in Berkeley; Nishant Batsha at the Albany Library; Bill Hyman and Debra Ratner at the Albany Senior Center; Jessica Handler and Luke Whisnant at the Wildacres Writing Workshop in North Carolina; David Chadwick for his book *Crooked Cucumber*, website cuke.com, and comments on the chapters about Zen practice; Linda Hess and Kazuaki Tanahashi for the Poetry of Awakening workshop at Tassajara Zen Mountain Center; John Boe and Mike Irvine on jazz; Carol Teltschick; and students in these classes and workshops. Also thanks to those who offered encouragement, and let's not forget the people I wrote about. You have all been most helpful.

Printed in Great Britain
by Amazon